# able

# able

## DYLAN ALCOTT

### WITH GRANTLEE KIEZA

**ABC**
BOOKS

The ABC 'Wave' device is a trademark of the
Australian Broadcasting Corporation and is used
under licence by HarperCollins*Publishers* Australia.

First published in Australia in 2018
by HarperCollins*Publishers* Australia Pty Limited
ABN 36 009 913 517
harpercollins.com.au

**HarperCollins*Publishers***
Level 13, 201 Elizabeth Street, Sydney NSW 2000, Australia
Unit D1, 63 Apollo Drive, Rosedale, Auckland 0632, New Zealand
A 53, Sector 57, Noida, UP, India
1 London Bridge Street, London, SE1 9GF, United Kingdom
Bay Adelaide Centre, East Tower, 22 Adelaide Street West, 41st Floor, Toronto,
    Ontario, M5H 4E3, Canada
195 Broadway, New York, NY 10007, USA

A catalogue record for this book is available
from the National Library of Australia

ISBN: 978 0 7333 3987 5 (paperback)
ISBN: 978 1 4607 1111 8 (ebook)

Cover design by Joshua Beggs
Front cover photography and author photo by Kristoffer Paulsen
Back cover photo by Ray Rolla
All photographs courtesy of Dylan Alcott and his family, except as noted
Typeset in Sabon LT Std by Kirby Jones
Printed and bound in Australia by McPherson's Printing Group
The papers used by HarperCollins in the manufacture of this book are a natural,
recyclable product made from wood grown in sustainable plantation forests. The fibre
source and manufacturing processes meet recognised international environmental
standards, and carry certification.

*For my family and friends, who always supported me and pushed me to become the person that I am today.*

*And for anyone who isn't proud of who they are because of their difference, this book is for you.*

# contents

# *prologue*

THE EXPRESSION ON THE doctor's face as my brother Zack wheeled me back into hospital on Wednesday, 24 January 2018, said it all. I'd insisted on being released that morning, but I wasn't in much of a state.

It had all started on the previous Saturday. I should have been doing great. I'd spent that morning hanging out and having a laugh with one of Hollywood's biggest names. On top of that, I was the face of a national TV and print campaign that was raising my profile to new heights. And I was prepared and ready to attempt a historic Grand Slam first in my hometown. Why, then, did I feel so lousy?

My head was killing me, I felt constantly on the verge of throwing up and everything ached. I'm an elite athlete. I train for hours every day, pushing my body as far as it can go.

I know what hurting muscles feel like. This was something very different. Something bad.

I felt even worse on Sunday morning but tried hard to ignore it. No way could I possibly give in to whatever this was, not when I was due on court at Melbourne Park in a mere three days to compete in one of the greatest tennis tournaments on the planet, the Australian Open. Record numbers of people were expected. So many supported me, I couldn't let them down.

When I finally took myself to hospital on Monday morning, the doctor told me a tiny cut on my leg had opened the way for the dangerous bacterial infection cellulitis. I need antibiotics, and fast. I tried to explain that I needed to be well, I had somewhere to be very soon. But I couldn't quite get the words out and as the drip went into my arm, I gave up and sank back into an exhausted sleep.

Tuesday was a blur, broken by nurses changing the bag on my intravenous drip and taking my temperature. Waking on Wednesday morning, I had to fight the urge to fall straight back to sleep again. In all honesty, I didn't know how I was going to get to the end of the corridor, let alone get through a tennis match against one of the best players in the world. But I knew I had to try, and somehow I made it to the Open and got through the match.

Now, just a few hours later, I was back in hospital in a much worse state, feverish and vomiting. Once again I was admitted and once again I fell into a restless sleep.

The following morning the doctor walked in to check on me just as I was preparing to swing myself out of bed and into my wheelchair. 'What do you think you're doing?' he asked in alarm.

'I'm going back to the Open,' I said. 'Either you take this drip out or I pull it out. But either way I'm going now.'

Whatever it took, I was going to be there. I'd overcome the odd hurdle or two in my life already, so I wasn't going to give in now ...

# 1

# making an entrance

MY LIFE WAS SAVED by a woman who could have stepped straight out of a Roald Dahl story.

Until the moment I made my first appearance there was no indication that my life was in danger. Mum's pregnancy progressed normally, and everything seemed just as smooth and ordinary as it had been almost three years earlier with my older brother, Zack. Well, maybe there was a bit more discomfort below her ribs, but nothing to write home about. And the ultrasound done at nineteen weeks didn't show any abnormalities. My legs weren't moving around much, but no one worried too much about that.

In fact, even after I finally arrived, two weeks late and weighing a whopping 4.5 kilograms – I've always known how to make an entrance – I seemed like a healthy baby, except for the strange bulge the size of a man's fist on my back.

It looked like a lump of fat and the doctor who delivered me told my parents not to be too worried. He'd seen cases like it before and usually the lumps were harmless and simply fell away over time.

For a few brief hours on that morning of 4 December 1990, joy was the prevailing emotion. Relieved and happy, Mum and Dad were looking forward to taking me home. But soon everything changed, and they found themselves plunged into a nightmare all parents dread. A paediatrician broke the difficult news. This wasn't a simple cosmetic issue that would resolve itself. It was something much more sinister, something that would alter the course of all our lives.

*\*\*\**

Mum and Dad had met in Sydney seven years earlier. Mum was born in the Netherlands, where she gloried in the name Theresia Wilhelmina Franciscus Snepvangers. But she grew up in the little country town of Casino, New South Wales, where her name was unceremoniously shortened to Resie. In her teenage years she moved to Cronulla in the south of Sydney. She was running a successful hair salon when she met my dad, Martin, an up-and-coming sales and marketing executive. They were smitten and four years later they married.

My parents shared an optimistic and adventurous view of the world. As newlyweds starting their family, they moved from Sydney to Queensland and then on to Melbourne, where they made their home in a small cottage in Hampton, a quiet suburb beside Port Phillip Bay, about 14 kilometres southeast of the city. The plan was to stay for just two years and reassess, but Mum fell pregnant with me, and my birth changed everything.

If that fatty lump had been on my arm or leg it might well have been nothing to worry about. But its position indicated a very serious condition, the neural tube defect lipomeningocele. Neural tube defects happen when key parts of the nervous system, the brain and/or spinal cord, don't form properly in the womb. Spina bifida is the best known example.

With lipomeningocele, a tumour forms, either in the spinal canal or just outside it, and presses on the cord in a way that stops it growing as it's supposed to. The tumour, made of fat cells, is called a lipoma. You know how, if you put a heavy rock on a patch of grass, the grass dies off, even though the rest of the lawn around the rock is fine? Well, that was what the tumour had done to part of my spinal cord.

There had been no similar problems in my extended family, and no one could tell my parents why this had happened (even now, nearly three decades later, medical researchers still don't know). All they could say was that it was a very serious condition that affected fewer than one in 10,000 babies in Australia.

As my true condition became apparent, Mum and Dad would need to dig deep. They rang Dad's father, Kevin, a highly respected Sydney doctor, who confirmed that it was one of those things that can happen in foetal development, when cells are splitting at a fast rate in order to develop all those complex systems that make up the human body. One tiny glitch somewhere along the line can end up having far-reaching consequences, like one misplaced character in pages of computer code.

\*\*\*

The day after I was born, I was moved from Sandringham Hospital to the Monash Medical Centre a few suburbs away. There I was put under the care of the larger than life neurosurgeon Miss Elizabeth Lewis (it's a quirk of medical protocol that surgeons are known as 'Mr' and 'Miss' rather than 'Dr'), a formidable figure who could have stepped out of the pages of a story.

Australia's first female neurosurgeon and still working, Miss Lewis was old school even back then. She didn't mince words and she didn't suffer fools. Strong enough to undertake marathon surgeries, she had an imposing presence as she sailed into a ward, and an even more imposing reputation. Young nurses and doctors walked on eggshells, afraid of not meeting her standards.

Miss Lewis had nerves of steel, and while her bedside manner might have taken a back seat, her care and concern for patients was clear for all to see. (Her skill and the difference her care has made to countless lives is reflected in the accolades she has received, including being made a Member of the Order of Australia.) Although Mum and Dad were still desperately worried, they breathed a little easier knowing I was in such good hands.

For ten days, Miss Lewis conducted tests on me, assessing the extent of the damage and figuring out the best way to remove the tumour and mend what was left of my spine. She knew my condition was so serious that even if things went as well as possible, my treatment would be a long haul.

But I was still less than two weeks old and needed to get stronger before any surgery could take place. So she told my parents to take me home for Christmas. Officially, the idea was to get me as settled as possible and make sure I was feeding well. But even with a surgeon this good, there was no guarantee I'd survive the operation. The unspoken understanding was that if worst came to worst, at least my parents would have had one Christmas with me at home.

Because the tumour was tethered to my spine, every time I was moved I'd scream in agony. This made it very hard to determine if things were getting worse. All my parents could do was watch me continuously to try to establish a baseline of 'normal' agonised screaming versus a sign that something else was going on.

'Call me if his condition deteriorates or if you have any urgent questions,' Miss Lewis had told my parents before they took me home. Her offer had come with one condition – that if the date was 26 December, they would need to call the staff at Monash instead. This was because, as Dad discovered to his surprise, Miss Lewis was a hardcore cricket tragic. The start of the Boxing Day Test match was sacrosanct, and she was off-limits to everyone that day.

(Learning this, Dad got in touch with his brother Errol, my uncle, who was physiotherapist for the Australian Test cricket team. Dad knew just the thank-you present to give Miss Lewis after my operation. And he was right. She was absolutely delighted when, in due course, my parents presented her with a bat signed by all the Aussie players, as a token of their gratitude.)

Fortunately, there were no crises while I was home, and in January 1991, at five weeks old, I was judged strong enough to undergo my first operation, intensive surgery attempting to remove as much of the tumour as possible.

'He might die tonight. He might not. We'll see how he goes,' Miss Lewis told my parents in her typically blunt manner as they were wheeling me into theatre.

The operation took an incredible thirteen hours, during which this extraordinarily skilled surgeon painstakingly removed most of the lipoma. But, unfortunately, some was inside my spinal column and could not be touched. No one knew what the consequences of this would be. Would I have feeling in my legs? Be able to walk? Would I even survive long enough for that to matter?

Being so young, I was unaware of the ward I was taken to as I recovered from the surgery. Known as 42 North, it was a thirty-bed ward used for paediatric surgery, acute adolescent medicine, and renal and neurosurgical procedures. But over the years, I would come to know it all too well. A 'medical centre' sounds like somewhere you pop in for a quick visit, but this hospital would prove to be my de facto home for much of the first three years of my life, and I returned there for stays throughout my childhood. In fact, for the first part of my life I knew that ward better than I knew our family home.

I can't tell you how much I hate that hospital, even now. Don't get me wrong. The care and treatment I received from the doctors, nurses and other staff was excellent. They were fantastic and I'm so grateful for their kindness and skill. But I hated being there so much that, to this day, I can't drive past that place without feeling on edge.

Even some of my close friends don't really know about this period in my life. I usually gloss over it because I prefer to focus on the present and the future rather than the past. It's painful to revisit because it was so awful for everyone involved. My parents and wider family were put through the wringer, constantly taking me to hospital, fearing I might die on multiple occasions. And even a 'good patch' for me was difficult for them, because my condition brought about a total upheaval of family life for them and my brother Zack.

Mum and Dad were determined to do whatever it took to support me and made a commitment to never leave me in hospital by myself. Never. Think about the dedication that required. Dad was a sportswear marketing manager. Mum had given up paid work to raise children, but was hairdressing at home on the side, and toddler Zack was already keeping her pretty busy even before I came along. Sometimes Mum and Zack would sit with me all day while Dad was at work. When he arrived at the hospital, Mum would take Zack home. They'd swap their parking tickets when they switched to save money – the costs of parking alone really adds up when you're there all day and all night. Dad would then try to get some sleep in the armchair next to my cot until the next morning, when Mum would return with a fresh suit for him, and off to work he would go again.

The strain must have been enormous, and of course it affected Zack too. He'd gone from being an only child with as much attention as he needed to the eye of a crisis he couldn't possibly understand. Fortunately, we had incredibly kind neighbours, Paula and Chris Lane, who had five kids and yet were happy to make room for one more as often as needed. Some of Zack's earliest memories are of being under the doona on their couch worrying about how his little brother was getting on in hospital.

\*\*\*

All seemed to be going well in the period immediately after that first operation. But my parents soon found out how quickly things can change. Ten days after the surgery, Dad was with me one night when my breathing became shallow and strained and I began to swell up in the most alarming fashion, right before his eyes.

Dad was so alarmed he asked the nursing staff to phone Miss Lewis at home, who, on hearing my symptoms, rushed to my bedside, despite the late hour.

Once again Miss Lewis didn't offer a lot of comfort. But what she lacked in tenderness she made up for in expertise. 'We're going to give him what I hope is an *almost* lethal dose of steroids,' she announced. 'It will either stop the swelling and fix him, or it will kill him. If he's alive in the morning, then we've done the right thing.'

Dad stared at her dumbstruck. But when he'd gathered his senses, he rang Mum and asked her to take Zack over to the Lanes so she could come in to the hospital. It might be time to say their goodbyes to me.

While Dad waited for Mum, he took out the little camera he had with him and tried to focus through his tears. The photo he took shows me lying in the cot, a distorted figure, next to a blue teddy bear my parents had hoped would bring me luck. My eyes are squeezed tight with pain.

I can't even begin to imagine how Dad must have been feeling, thinking that this was perhaps the last photograph he would ever take of me. He was only twenty-seven years old at the time, the age I am as I currently write this, and I know I wouldn't be able to handle it.

Over the next few hours, my parents were in shock and despair. Telling me the story of this time, their memories are still painfully vivid, giving me some inkling of the torture they went through as they waited to see if I'd live through the night. For hour after terrible hour they stood beside my cot, waiting for the swelling to come down, willing me to breathe easier, longing for some good news in the long dark night.

The clock moved so slowly it seemed to have stopped. Finally dawn approached. Could it be that I looked just a little better, or was that just their own exhaustion and wishful thinking? At 8.30 am, the sound of Miss Lewis approaching briskly sent their heart rates skyrocketing.

My parents looked at the neurosurgeon's face, always so inscrutable. Was that the flicker of a smile beneath her stern expression?

Miss Lewis examined me, then studied my chart while my parents forgot to breathe.

Finally, she looked up.

'You don't have to worry about this one,' she said. 'He's a fighter. He'll be fine.' Mum and Dad's relief was indescribable.

Dad's parents arrived from Sydney to lend support. My grandfather read through my chart and talked to Miss Lewis for an hour, doctor to doctor. Then this famously stoic man stood next to my cot, looked at Dad, looked back at me, and burst into tears.

I certainly wasn't out of the woods yet.

\*\*\*

I spent the next three and a half months lying on my stomach. The constant threat of more infections and the delicate nature of the surgery on my spine meant that I could not be moved. Mum made me as comfortable as she could and fed me with a bottle. It was a very difficult thing to put a baby through when their instinct is to start to figure out their own bodies by moving their arms and legs around. It was even harder for my mother and father, who had to watch me suffer knowing it was for my own good.

As Miss Lewis and the rest of the medical team made clear, there were no guarantees. Still, everyone hoped that once this was over the worst would be behind me, even though I was likely to need more surgeries in childhood to keep up with the changes in my body as I grew.

Finally, in April 1991 at the age of five months, I was allowed home. It wasn't the straightforward start to life my parents had expected for me, but at last a more normal routine could begin, or so they thought. It proved to be a false hope. Just eight days after I'd been discharged, I was rushed back to hospital in the grip of another dangerous infection. With Miss Lewis away on holidays, I was placed under the care of her highly regarded colleague Mr Geoffrey Klug, at the Royal Melbourne Children's Hospital.

Before I'd been sent home, a kind of shield made of medical mesh had been placed around my spine as a temporary measure to protect the area where the bones hadn't fully formed. But my little body had rejected the foreign substance and the site had become infected. I was given an emergency course of antibiotics and had to go under the knife again to have the mesh removed. It was another very delicate and risky procedure and another gut-wrenching ordeal for my parents.

The surgery was successful, but it had to be followed by another ten weeks in hospital, when I was confined to lying on my stomach, crying in discomfort for hours at a time. I was approaching seven months old and I'd spent less than two weeks out of hospital and experienced not a single day free of pain or discomfort. Over the years, especially when I needed convincing that I could do something, Dad would say that he could tell even at that age I was tough and determined.

This time, when my parents finally got me out of hospital and back home, they knew I had a long and painful journey ahead of me. One of the hard parts for them was the fear of the unknown – there's no manual on how to raise and look after a child with a disability, and my parents didn't know anyone else who had one.

Mum and Dad had no close relatives living in Melbourne, but Dad's parents came down regularly from Sydney, and Mum's sister Anja and her mother, Anne, my 'Oma' (Dutch for 'grandmother'), were also frequent visitors. As well, they got great support from friends.

They needed all the help they could get, because it was far from easy looking after me. I was still in such a fragile state, Mum and Dad couldn't just put me in a baby seat and drive me around whenever they had to go somewhere. Most of the time I was immobile and had to have nurses coming to the house on a regular basis to check on my progress.

Then, when I was twelve months old, I suffered another medical crisis. This time it was renal failure. The nerve damage in my spine had caused problems with my bladder, triggering reflux to one of my kidneys, which stopped working properly. The result was a urinary tract infection that made me so sick I was admitted to hospital again. It would prove to be a major ongoing issue, and over the next few years I'd spend a lot of time in hospital on a drip, fighting infections, and kidney surgery would be among the thirteen major operations that lay ahead.

\*\*\*

At the age of three, I was allowed home from hospital for what would hopefully be a long stay. Mum often described me as her gorgeous little boy. But according to Zack, then five, I looked like a 'devil boy', and he may have had a point. I was still quite sick and unusually pale thanks to my long hospital stays. My kidney problems had left me with dark circles around my eyes like a panda's, and, as well as a shock of unruly blond hair, I had unusually sharp baby teeth that Dad privately thought looked like the spikes on a can opener.

Fortunately, I was too young to get overly self-conscious about any of this, especially when there was a whole new world at home to explore. I loved life 'on the outside' and hoped to never have to go back to hospital again.

All the early photos of Zack and me show us crawling around on the floor together, even when he'd reached school age. Our play was floor-based because I couldn't walk,

although I did have a pair of little crutches. With them under my armpits I could half-waddle, like a penguin. What I was actually doing was using the crutches to support my weight so I could stand tall enough to swing my legs through. I was able to build up a bit of momentum this way, but it wasn't really walking.

I had hours and hours of physiotherapy and would regularly go back to Monash where my walking progress (or lack of it) would be assessed. The physios kept encouraging me to keep on trying to put one foot in front of the other, and my family continued to hope that one day I might be able to walk unassisted. I remember Mum often standing me in a metal support frame beside a table on which there were toys, because the doctors had told her that the more time I spent upright the more chance I had of walking one day.

As much as I hated my trips to Monash, I also had to go back there to see my doctors every couple of months for check-ups and so they could schedule the operations needed on my feet and legs, to straighten the bones as I grew. As part of my disability and deformity, my ankles and feet grew crookedly, meaning that when my knees were straight my feet would stick out sideways, making an L shape. To straighten them up, I had tendon transplants in both legs.

But I also had increasingly long periods when I was well, and I made the most of them, soaking up all the new sights, sounds and experiences I could get.

Mum and Dad were absolutely fantastic. They were determined I would join in all family activities as a full and equal member, and they treated Zack and me the same.

Eventually our house would be rebuilt, complete with a three-person lift so I could have a bedroom in the newly created upstairs like the rest of the family. But back then the place was still a cosy two-bedroom cottage and Zack and I shared a room. My therapist at Monash had recommended a water bed as the best option for my damaged spine (how 1980s porn star of us!). Zack ensured the equality worked both ways and successfully argued that if I got a water bed, he should get one too. The sound of us both slopping around on our beds must have made Mum and Dad laugh.

Dad worked hard in his career and Mum worked hard at home. Looking after us two boys was definitely a full-time job for her, and she was always signing me up for activities that would allow me to fully participate in life, regardless of my physical challenges and limitations. Activities such as swimming lessons, for example. Can you imagine the poor swimming instructor when Mum turned up, threw her paraplegic son straight in the water and said: 'Go for it!'? They must have had a heart attack.

But I loved the freedom that being in the pool gave me, and I quickly became a good swimmer. Without even realising it at the time, swimming became my first sport. In fact, I used to try to swim underwater for so long that it made Mum nervous.

She also found an early intervention playgroup that catered for a mix of children, some with disabilities, others without. I had a fantastic time crawling around in the sandpit with the other kids – Mum was endlessly patient about the trails of sand I left throughout the house when I got home. I even had my first kiss in that sandpit when I was four – hey, Mia, if you're reading. The integration teacher who led the playgroup, Jackie Watt, was amazing at her job, helping me to get ready for a mainstream kindergarten and eventually mainstream primary school. I still have friends from those kindergarten days who I see pretty regularly.

All that crawling around in the sand and on the carpet gave me good dexterity and made my hands strong. It was a great help to me later on in my sporting career. Similarly, my upper body became strong because my arms and shoulders had to do all the work. These adjustments were my body's way of counterbalancing and compensating for the things I couldn't do. I strongly believe if you lose one thing – in my case the use of my legs – your body makes up for it with enhanced skills and abilities in other areas.

Because I really couldn't cover much distance using my crutches, Mum would use a stroller to take me to the shops. It's not uncommon for people to have three-year-olds in strollers, but I did attract some odd looks with my pasty face, pointy teeth and dark circles around my eyes. It didn't help that my speech hadn't developed, probably because I'd spent so long in hospital without constant interactions with other kids. In fact, even at three, I was still hard to understand. 'Zack' was one of the words most often on my lips but I didn't come close to saying it properly. Instead, it sometimes came out in a long, mournful crow-like 'Vaaaark', which sounded dangerously like the F word.

At the shops, five-year-old Zack would take every opportunity to run off, with poor Mum forever chasing behind him with me in the stroller. 'Come back, Zack, come back!' she'd call out. At this, I'd helpfully push forward, grabbing the front bar in order to lift myself upright. And with a face only a mother could love, I'd scream out apparent swear words at the top of my lungs: 'Vark! Vark!'

My diction might not have been up to much, but I could certainly project. 'VARK! VARK!' I'd continue as Mum, dodging filthy looks from everyone around her, would race full pelt around the aisles, chasing a mini blond Usain Bolt. I'm sure there are still people in our old neighbourhood who have that image burnt into their memories – a disabled kid in a pram yelling F*CK! as loud as he could.

Eventually, and to Mum's enormous relief, Zack taught me to call him 'Bruv' instead.

The older I got, though, the more socially awkward it became to use the stroller for me. By four, even I was starting to think something wasn't quite right, and a few months later it all came to a head. A little girl ran up to the stroller expecting to find a cute baby to coo over. I can still remember the shocked look on her face when she got a load of me instead. It was the first time in my life that I felt being different was a bad thing. I remember thinking that she and I were around the same age, and yet she was looking down on me.

That was the day I told Mum we had to lose the stroller. In its place, I received my first wheelchair.

# 2

# *wheels in motion*

GETTING MY FIRST SET of wheels at the age of four made me feel really free – after all, most kids have to wait until they're eighteen. For starters, the wheelchair was a great improvement on the stroller when we needed to go out somewhere. And Mum or Dad were happy to push it until I got the hang of it, which took a while. But in the same way the doctors thought that the more time I spent upright, the more chance I had of walking, they thought that my long-term mobility prospects were better if I used crutches or a walking frame instead of the chair, whenever possible. In any case, when it came to getting where I needed to go, particularly around the house, I preferred to crawl.

Zack, of course, had no mobility restrictions, giving him the advantage over me when it came to our frequent brotherly tussles. Or so you would have thought.

To the outside world, Zack was my defender and, if need be, protector. But when it was just the two of us, it was game on. I idolised him, but not in a way that made me want to let him run things. Even at the age of seven he was fiercely competitive, and the harder he pushed to come out on top, the harder I pushed back. Our endless fights for the TV remote was the perfect example of this.

When we were home, from the moment we opened our eyes to the time we reluctantly went off to bed, we wanted to watch TV, and because we each had our own favourite shows, control over the program choice was a perennial struggle. You post-millennials must be scratching your heads, wondering why we didn't just skip the fuss and each watch what we wanted on our phones. But this was the dark ages, not just before the existence of streaming services, but before the existence of smartphones. I know, shocking, right? I'm showing my age now.

As a consequence, if I wanted to sit glued to, say, *The Simpsons* or the wrestling, I had to defeat an equally determined Zack or I'd be left watching whatever he wanted. It was high-stakes stuff. Weekend mornings always started the same way. Whoever opened their eyes first was up and off down the hallway, closely pursued by the other. As running has never been my forte, this usually ended up in Zack getting to the TV before I did. But even if he did get there first, the fight was far from over.

The way Zack tells it, he'd be sitting on the couch watching his favourite show when I'd launch a surprise attack, crawling fast across the carpet in an attempt to snatch the remote. His solution was pretty simple: stand up to his full height and hold the remote tauntingly out of my reach. My response was just as basic: launch myself up and get hold of the outstretched arm and then just hang on, like a koala gripping a branch for dear life during a cyclone. Don't worry, my hand strength meant I could hang there for as long as it took.

If he showed no signs of giving up, I still had an ace up my sleeve. I'd call out to Mum in a distressed voice, then, Zack claims (though I'm pretty sure I was a little less violent than this!), I'd punch him in the nose and drop to the ground.

Mum would rush into the room to find a furious-looking Zack, with me sprawled on the floor at his feet. 'What have you done to your little brother?' she'd say angrily, dismissing Zack's protests and sending him to his room. Voila, now I had the TV all to myself.

That worked a few times but after a while Zack realised he'd have to take a more tactical approach if he was ever going to get the better of me. So instead of holding the remote up, he started putting it on the top of the fridge, far out of my reach. Then he'd go to the bathroom or do whatever he needed to do, grab the control on his return with a smile on his face and there was nothing I could really do about it.

You might think that his actions were underhanded, that he was taking advantage of his poor disabled brother. And you know what, at the time I thought it was a bit of a jerk move too! But in retrospect, I don't see it that way. Not at all. I reckon Zack was doing something great for me. He was treating me as a genuine equal. He was doing what any other normal big brother would do to get one up on me, just as he would have done if I'd been able to run and jump like he could. He wasn't making concessions or letting me off easy, he was challenging me to figure out my own solution.

I'll always be grateful that Zack played it straight instead of treating me differently or wrapping me in cotton wool because of my disability. Even now, with adult lives of our own, we're as close as two brothers can be. Zack's my best mate and one of only a few people I talk to daily. And yet, as brothers should do, we still gleefully take every opportunity we can to give the other heaps.

For example, back in 2015 I got him an absolute beauty, thanks to the story of our fight over the TV remote. I was asked to give a TEDx Talk to 5000 people at the Sydney Opera House. My topic: Mainstreaming Disability. I had plenty of observations and stories that I hoped would make people think and question their own assumptions, and our childhood tussles were a perfect inclusion. I'm a big believer in using humour to get my message across so I decided to tell our childhood story for laughs. I retold the story on stage, and showed a few photos of Zack and me before saying how glad I was that he went that route of treating me normally. Most of the audience totally got it, but there were a couple of ladies who were outraged on my behalf – they must have missed the part where I said I was happy about it. Afterwards, they spotted Zack and, realising who he was, they started booing him! Zack said he felt like public enemy number one. Luckily, now he sees the funny side of it ...

One thing we never disagreed about was Chad, the family cat, named after our favourite skateboarder at the time, Chad Muska. We both thought Chad was the coolest animal in the entire world. A black and white stray we adopted from a vet and who had come into our lives as a kitten one Mother's Day, he was affectionate and full of personality. Zack and I had originally wanted a dog but it wasn't possible because they tended to jump up on me in their enthusiasm, knocking me over, especially when I was in the walking frame. (To this day, dogs HATE my wheelchair. Every time I go by one they lose the plot and start barking. I feel like I have a dog curse.)

But Chad more than made up for us not having a pup. He was faithful like a dog, he'd playfully nip us like a dog, and when strangers came around he'd run up to them, wagging his tail. We even taught him to play fetch. Chad lived to an amazing eighteen and a half years. Best of all, he had enough love for the whole family to share.

Chad was good company for me when Zack was at school, but I was happy when it was finally my turn to put on the St Joan of Arc uniform and experience for myself the thrills and spills of the classroom and playground.

My parents knew from Zack's experience that St Joan's, which was less than five minutes' drive from our house, was a good school. But before deciding if it was right for me, Mum went to see the principal, who assured her that while there were no other kids with disabilities at the school at that point, they'd do everything possible to make me feel welcome and included. And that's exactly what happened. The upstairs classrooms were more or less inaccessible to me, but the teachers organised things so I never needed to use them. Everything else was easy, thanks to the aide provided to me for personal care and to help me carry things around.

Mum had lost a lot of sleep worrying about whether I'd fit in and make friends. She needn't have. Obviously, I couldn't run and jump or kick the footy around like the other kids, but by this point I was quite good at manoeuvring around in the chair, and I could keep up with them in the playground. They didn't treat me any differently to anyone else and I made heaps of new friends, some of whom I'm still very close to. (In fact, these days I share a house with Dan Noonan, my best mate from St Joan's, and the partner I introduced him to, Lucy Wilcox, a friend from high school.)

Two things that helped things go smoothly were having Zack there looking out for me and the fact I had no problem asking for help when I needed it. That's one message I'm always keen to get across to people with disabilities, especially kids: There's no shame in asking for help, even if it's just something small like requesting that someone hand you something from a high shop shelf because you can't reach it. A lot of people often try to be too independent. If asking for some help saves you time or makes things a bit easier, then don't be ashamed to ask for it. You'll enjoy life a lot better if you do.

Disability or not, it was only natural that I'd gravitate towards playing sport. My parents were both sporty in their day, with Dad playing rugby for the New South Wales Schoolboys team (he still has his blazer, and loves bringing it up in conversations!), and Mum played netball at a pretty high level. And then there was my unconscious desire to copy everything Zack did, from the way he dressed to the music he liked. Like many Victorians, AFL was a big part of our lives (I'm a big Carlton Blues fan) and we grew up with deadset stars of the game Greg 'Diesel' Williams and Glenn Coleman as friends of the family. I have great memories of being on summer holidays at Mt Hotham when I was about seven, sitting on the ground marking the pinpoint passes Diesel kicked to me from 30 metres away.

So naturally Zack played Aussie Rules, and he turned out to be quite good at it. I would absolutely have loved to have sped around the field and leapt for high marks just like he did. That wasn't to be, although I still got amongst it in the games in the playground. Unfortunately, I was more of a stepladder than a participant – jumping has never been one of my strengths. Clearly, I needed to find a sport of my own.

I took part in athletics events, with the school making adjustments so I could be included. In the school 50-metre running races, for instance, I'd start on the 25-metre line and use crutches. By then I had nifty aluminium ones, not the clunky wooden type, and Zack and my friends had helped me cover them in skate stickers so they looked cool. I liked tennis, too, and used to sit at the net in my chair hitting volleys as Dad drilled balls at me. But swimming was the sport that I first shone in.

In the pool I was free to move as I wished, and I represented my school in backstroke, butterfly and freestyle. I was competing against kids without disabilities and I won a lot of races because, while my legs were basically deadweight, my upper body was strong and growing stronger all the time. Proud of my sporting success, I became hungry for more.

Luckily, our neighbourhood provided good opportunities for me to test myself. Vista Road, the street I grew up on, was a dead end, home to four families who had kids our age. We were always out playing on the road – tennis, basketball, cricket, street hockey, skateboarding, water-bomb fights and whatever else we could dream up. All too often, I see parents of kids with disabilities who are so fearful they don't want their kids participating in any of that kind of stuff. They'd rather keep them wrapped in cotton wool at home because they're different, or because they're scared something might happen to them. I understand how hard it must be to let go, but I know from experience how great it is for kids whose parents can take a few steps back. The approach Mum and Dad took to let me experience life to the full in exactly the same way as Zack – or any kid my age – has allowed me to develop confidence and independence.

In fact, I was probably a bit too confident when it came to some things. Take cricket: it was one of my favourite sports back then and I loved playing it with the other kids. I wasn't much of a bowler (or fielder for that matter) but I loved batting. So when it was my turn to go in, I'd just park my wheelchair right in front of the stumps. It didn't matter how skilled the bowler was – there was no wicket to aim at. If I didn't hit the ball, it would hit the chair and the other team would appeal for LBW.

Me being me, I'd yell, 'It hit the wheel, dickheads!' and just sit there and keep batting. Although they'd be pissed off, they'd let me keep batting. I think they must have felt bad for me. I knew I was being annoying, but I sure did enjoy those long batting stints.

Zack played Aussie Rules with the East Brighton Vampires. When I was seven, Mum and Dad and the other parents running the team found a way of making me feel involved by appointing me team manager. My role was more or less limited to cutting up the half-time oranges and making sure my assistant manager (Dad) had brought the jelly snakes. But I decided to fully embrace it.

I really appreciated Mum, Dad and Zack pushing for me to be included in the team. Plenty of boys wouldn't have wanted their kid brother hanging around them in the first place, and I'm pretty sure there wouldn't be many who'd have been as tolerant as Zack was of me. It really meant a lot to me at the time. I looked forward to training and the Sunday games so much, it became my favourite time of the week.

Fortunately for everyone, I was about to get a glimpse of the way sport could help me carve my own way in the world. For the first time, I was about to really understand that my wheelchair didn't have to hold me back, that it could set me free.

I was too young to be aware of the 1992 Barcelona Paralympics, but one of the first Australian Paralympians to make the news was Louise Sauvage, who won three gold medals and one silver there in her chosen sport of wheelchair racing. Four years later, she again triumphed at the Atlanta Games, claiming four more gold medals. I remember seeing some highlights on the television, and it was my first real chance to watch people with a disability playing sport. Mum and Dad did some research and explained to me that she'd been born with myelomeningocele – not exactly the same as me, but very close. Like me, she'd been in a wheelchair her whole life, but she hadn't let it hold her back. I remember thinking how she'd been a kid just like me, and look at her now, an incredible champion, the best in the world. A spark was ignited somewhere deep inside me. I didn't know it yet, but my life's course had been set.

I thought about it a lot, and it was not long after that I told Mum and Dad I wanted to compete at the Paralympics when I was old enough. Just as they did in everything else, my parents provided the perfect mix of encouragement and realism, telling me that if that's what I really wanted to do I should go for it.

Swimming was still the focus of my sports ambitions at this point, and when I was churning up and down the pool at training three times a week, I would imagine what it would be like to swim for Australia at the Paralympics. When I heard about a triathlon for kids my age in Melbourne, it was my confidence in the water that made me determined to participate. It was something called the Weet-Bix Aussie Kids Triathlon, and it was huge. More than a thousand kids aged seven to thirteen came from all around Victoria to Port Melbourne Beach for an age-appropriate run, swim and cycle in February 2000.

A couple of my friends from school had signed up, and there was no way I was going to just sit back and watch. My event, the one for the seven- to ten-year age group, featured a 100-metre swim, a 3-kilometre cycle and a 500-metre run. I wanted to be in the middle of the action. But was that even possible?

'Of course it is,' Dad said. The next thing I knew he'd contacted the organisers to see if they'd allow him to swim alongside me and help me in the cycle part. They were happy to say yes: this wasn't the Hawaiian Ironman, after all. It was a fun event, designed to get kids moving. There were no winners or losers, no prizes for place getters, and kids of all fitness levels were welcome. It was a fantastic feeling to know I could take part, just like everyone else.

So, on the big day, off we went to Port Melbourne Beach. It was awesome – kids of all ages everywhere, everyone having a ball. Being for young kids, the swim leg was held in very shallow water, so Dad simply walked behind me as I swam, to make sure I was okay. I then used my crutches to get from the water to the tandem bike. Dad did the pedalling on the bike up front, while I sat on the back and pretended to peddle as best I could. In the lead-up to the triathlon, Dad and I had been on a few practice rides together to get the hang of it, and Dad had become pretty good at manoeuvring us both. On our training rides, everything had gone smoothly but on the day of the race, Dad took a corner too tightly and we fell off! Luckily, we weren't going too fast so no one was hurt. After the ride, it was the 500-metre 'run' home. I pushed my wheelchair as hard as I could go, with Dad jogging behind me, giving me the occasional push for good measure.

Approaching the finish line in last place, my arms felt like jelly and I was puffing fit to burst, but I was determined to make it. The ground announcer must have told the 3000-strong crowd my name because crossing the line, I could hear heaps of encouragement.

'Go Dylan! Go!' everyone was shouting.

I could hear Dad making choking sounds behind me and thought he'd run out of puff. In fact, it was sheer emotion, he told me later.

That was the first time I appeared in a newspaper. A photographer from Melbourne's *Sunday Herald Sun* captured the huge grin on my face and ran the picture big. 'When it comes to measuring effort, Dylan Alcott should be declared a champion "tryathlete",' the reporter wrote. I'm not going to lie – seeing myself in the paper was a pretty cool feeling for a nine-year-old. The combination of the achievement itself and the recognition I'd received for it fuelled me for a long time after that memorable day.

\*\*\*

My days weren't all about sport. I'd also started learning to play the saxophone, which eventually blossomed into a lifelong love of music. But sport occupied a large part of my time and energy. (The truth is, I was pretty shithouse at saxophone, and it was bloody hard to carry!) Towards the end of the year the next piece of the puzzle fell into place, when I had my first proper go at wheelchair tennis.

I went along to a 'come and try day' at the Kingsville Tennis Club in Footscray, organised by Wheelchair Sports Victoria. There I learnt that the only difference in wheelchair tennis is that the ball is allowed to bounce twice. Everything else is exactly the same.

One of the other kids there that day was a kid a bit older than me. His name was Heath Davidson, and he'd become a paraplegic after contracting the rare neurological condition viral transverse myelitis when he was a baby. I wasn't quite ten and Heath was already thirteen, but we really connected, and we both took to this new sport with a passion. We were also both driven to succeed.

Soon we were starting to show signs of talent, and were invited to join Kingsville's elite squad with another young wheelchair player named Jeremy Synot. Hours of hitting against the squad's other, able-bodied, players really sharpened our game. But no matter how hard I worked, I could never beat Heath. My time would come eventually, I told myself.

Footscray was a long way to travel for Heath and me – more than an hour each way – so both families were relieved when another local option popped up and we started training at the Moorabbin Indoor Sports complex, much closer to home. A young guy named Marco Persi was our first coach, and he did an incredible job (all these years later, Heath and I still do some work with Marco).

Although I was pretty active, I was also *very* overweight, and Heath was too. The first tournament I played in was the Thurgoona Open in Albury–Wodonga. It was played on synthetic grass and we were so heavy we had trouble pushing our chairs over the surface. But it didn't take long for our strength and stamina to improve along with our skills. We were on our way.

But just as my life began to take shape, I had another huge obstacle to overcome: yet more major surgery.

Cutting out the tumour from my back when I was a baby had left a deep crevice that acted as a reservoir where fluid built up, causing me some severe discomfort and recurring infections. The surgery, a nine-hour-long operation, was designed to fix this, and it did. Unfortunately, in the process, more damage was done. One of the surgeons made an error and damaged my bladder. The result was, I had to lie on my stomach in hospital for two months. This was followed by another four months at home with minimal movement. I wasn't even able to go to school. Spending that amount of time bedridden is bad enough when you're a baby but when you're an active ten-year-old kid, it's a killer. Also, because I wasn't able to move around, my leg muscles wasted away, and I completely lost the little bit of movement and strength that I had in my legs. I never got that back.

The confronting situations I faced in Monash Medical Centre's 42 North were also pretty hard to deal with. Some of the kids and teens in there were coping with relatively straightforward medical issues, but others like me had ongoing issues. I remember some of the kids in their early teens were gravely ill with anorexia, while others who'd taken too many drugs would have seizures and scream through the night. It wasn't a great place to be.

And if you were looking for distraction in the form of entertainment, you were out of luck. There was one Nintendo console to be shared amongst everyone in the ward. If you were very lucky, you might get an hour max on it before they wheeled it away. The days would drag on forever. There's only so much *Oprah* a ten-year-old can watch before he starts to go crazy. *Get me out of this place. I want to be back in school and living my life*, I thought every day.

The only consolation was meeting some like-minded kids with disabilities. Rosie Jenes and Patrick Jackson were the same age as me, and we became friends. Although hospital was where we met, we remained close on the outside as well, and so did our parents. I don't see much of them these days, but their friendship meant a lot, because we were all going through similar things.

The staff at Monash were great, always looking for ways to make things better. One of the best things they did was to nominate me for a wish from the Starlight Foundation, a charity set up to brighten the lives of sick kids. And when I was well enough, six months after I'd fully recovered, Starlight sent Mum, Dad, Zack and me on an all-expenses-paid, two-week holiday to Queensland's Gold Coast. At the time, it was a real lifeline for us. When I was sick it took a toll not only on myself but the whole family. I'll forever be indebted to the Starlight team, and I'm super proud to be a Starlight ambassador to give back in any small way I can to help kids who are currently facing similar situations to those I faced.

On the trip, I did what any ten-year-old would do. I met Batman at Movie World and got to swim briefly with the dolphins at Sea World. It was exactly what my family and I needed.

Back at home and fully recovered, sport became my focal point. It was something I could focus on and it motivated me to build my strength up so I could once again take to the court. I worked hard and got back into shape in time to be chosen to represent Victoria at the 2001 Junior National Disabled Games in both tennis and swimming in the under-14s category. The Games ran from 28 September to 7 October and both Mum and Zack flew up to Brisbane to support me.

Although Dad had to work, he entrusted Zack with a video camera to document everything that went down. Zack carried the camera everywhere with him and did a ripping job. 'Give us a wave! Give us a wave!' he'd yell to people as he passed, pointing the camera towards them. But he stopped yelling after he realised that one kid he'd shouted out to had no arms! Smooth.

It was a massive buzz for me to be able to compete against kids from all over Australia, and even cooler to meet other kids with disabilities who were similar to me. Even though I was up against kids older than me, I won a bronze in the doubles tennis, silver in the 50-metre freestyle and 50-metre backstroke, and gold in the 50-metre butterfly, where my time was good enough to break the Wheelchair Sports Australia record. I still hold that record to this day.

\*\*\*

A few months later, in February 2002, I realised another dream when I got into the finals of the under-18 boys' wheelchair singles at the Australian Wheelchair Open (it used to be separate from the able-bodied Australian Open) and Heath and I won the doubles. It was a really cool experience. And at the Open, I met someone who became a really important mentor to me – the world number one women's wheelchair player at the time, Danni Di Toro.

A Victorian like me, Danni was paralysed at the age of thirteen when a perfectly normal school swimming carnival went terribly wrong. Along with her classmates, she was sitting in front of a wall, cheering on those in the pool, when the wall collapsed on top of them. It left her a paraplegic.

Danni's enthusiasm was infectious. She always spoke about her life in such a positive way. She could easily have been killed in the accident, but she survived and her view was that every single thing she went through enriched her in some way, even the really tough stuff. She was one of the most inspiring people I'd ever met – she still is.

The personal coaching Danni gave me was gold, but just being around her was even more important. She made me believe that I, too, could do anything, and she was happy to share that view with the world when we were interviewed together by the well-known sports journalist Neil Kearney. 'Dylan's opponents are older, bigger, faster and better hitters,' he wrote, 'and he's struggling with the basics of a sport where he wheels himself madly into position, only to see his opponent hit to the part of the court where he's just been.' He was right. As Danni noted, I was 'a little guy against seventeen-year-olds, and there are a million reasons for him not to stick at it'. But, Danni being Danni, she added: 'If wheelchair tennis teaches him to go past the million reasons not to do something, then that's wicked. He'll kick arse.'

Although I wouldn't be kicking any arse literally, I was going to give it my best crack.

# 3

# *just jump the fence*

THROUGH A STROKE OF incredible good fortune and remarkable generosity, I spent my final year of primary school and my high school years at Brighton Grammar, a private school in Melbourne's southeast. The school would be incredible for me, although I'd have to go through some dark times first.

Even though it was nice and handy to our family home, just one suburb over, Mum and Dad had never even considered Brighton as an option because of the cost. Instead, I'd been all set to join Zack at the nearby Catholic high school St Bede's. That all changed when out of the blue I was offered a full scholarship to Brighton (worth about $150,000) to cover seven years of education.

The scholarship was set up by local couple Paul and Christine Comport, whose son Mark had attended there a few years earlier. Mark had been born with a disability and had, tragically, passed away when he was in Year 6. In his memory, the Comports wanted to help another boy with a disability who couldn't otherwise have afforded to go to Grammar.

I was the inaugural recipient of this incredibly generous gift, even though I had no idea it existed. The school had advertised it in various publications and apparently loads of people around the bayside suburbs rang the school to nominate me. We'd never expected this to happen, especially because I'd previously sat the test for a scholarship there but don't think I even came close. There were some incredibly smart boys there.

It was a pretty cool moment for our family when the school got in touch to invite us to come and discuss the possibilities. I must have said something right at that meeting, because they let me in.

Heading off for my first day in the very formal uniform of grey dress pants, blue blazer and tie, I was nervous and proud in equal measure. I didn't know what to expect – safe to say it was *very* different to my primary school at St Joan of Arc. The biggest difference was the sheer size of Brighton. It had three campuses, which made it a fair challenge to get around.

It took a little while for me – and the school – to adjust. While the place wasn't initially well set up for disabilities, ramps were soon installed everywhere, so I and another boy in my year, Julian Marks, who had muscular dystrophy, could get around. (Very sadly, Julian died of his illness while we were still at school.)

But it didn't take long for me to feel right at home at Brighton, where students were encouraged to get involved in as many different activities as possible, and given amazing opportunities to pursue a wide range of interests – academic, sporting and cultural. Playing music was compulsory, and, as usual, I wanted to push myself to do something most people would think I couldn't. So I decided to learn to play the drums.

I was lucky to have drum lessons from the John Butler Trio's Michael Barker, who was a teacher at the school. The fact that I couldn't use the foot pedal on the kick drum was a bit of a problem, but Michael wanted to help, so he tuned a tom-tom to sound like a kick drum for me. Problem solved. Still, safe to say I was pretty crap. I also sang in the school choir – until my voice broke, when my singing days were numbered.

There was a lot of emphasis on public speaking and debating, and the training and experience we received were so good I have no problem speaking to anyone in any context, from an audience of thousands to leaders and royalty. I can't help thinking that public speaking turned out to be one of the most useful things I ever learnt at school because it gave me the ability to speak up about my disability. I did quite a bit of competitive public speaking with my best mate from school Tim Biggin, and he was there the day I made a speech in which I said how lucky I was to be in a wheelchair because of the different perspective on life it gave me. Afterwards, Tim told me how surprised he was that I was confident enough to say that, especially to a group of able-bodied kids from privileged backgrounds. Biggsy and I came to be really good friends, and he grew very close to Zack too. In fact, Zack and I thought of him as another brother.

I loved getting involved in anything I could, especially sport. At Brighton, one of the cool things we did was house sports competitions – swimming, athletics, football, cricket and more. I was still a keen cricket player, along with most of the school. These days, I played by the rules, with no parking in front of the wicket. I really appreciated being treated as an equal, even if that meant missing out on the glory moments.

In my very first game, I set myself two goals: 1. Take a catch in slips; and 2. Score a run.

We bowled first and I was fielding in the slips, in my wheelchair of course, waiting for the chance to snare a catch the way Ricky Ponting did. Finally on the last wicket the batsman edged one straight to me. *This is my moment!* I thought. It was almost in my lap … until it wasn't. One of my other close mates, Jimmy Davis, the wicketkeeper, had leapt in front of me and taken a one-handed screamer. It was the best catch I'd ever seen – and I was so filthy! Jimmy let me know about it too, and he still reminds me of it to this day.

When it was my turn to bat, I came out with the full pads on, ready to slap a few runs. Scott, another good mate, was the bowler and he sent down an absolute sitter. But instead of connecting I managed an air swing for a first-ball dismissal, clean bowled.

'Not out,' called the umpire (who was our English teacher), clearly thinking I should have a second chance. I'm sure he meant well but he wouldn't have done it for anyone else. I didn't want to be treated with kid gloves, so I told him I was out fair and square. That day ended my cricket career and to this day remains one of the worst sporting performances of my life.

\*\*\*

Unfortunately, my time at Brighton wasn't always so much fun. There were a few people at school who gave me a hard time. It seems they wanted to make sure it didn't slip my mind that I was in a wheelchair. They did this by loudly calling me 'the cripple' and 'spastic' whenever I entered a room or went out on the weekend.

As with most bullying, it started small and then grew until it really affected me. I still don't know what triggered it. My first couple of years there were great, with no problems at all. But then, as kids sometimes do, they started calling me names more and more, and unfortunately I started to believe them.

I've thought about it a lot and the only explanation I can come up with for their behaviour was that they were trying to impress the other kids. It became so frequent it was hard to get away from at times.

Now I regret that I didn't tell anyone about how it was affecting me. In public, I tried to laugh it off and pretend I was fine. But, looking back, those words really did hurt. I was already pretty self-conscious about my disability and being different, and the bullying only compounded that for me.

Their words cut deep, no matter how many times I told myself these kids were just saying anything they could to hurt me and the best thing I could do was ignore them.

It made me feel really isolated, and one of the toughest things was that I didn't know too many people with disabilities to ask how they handled their insecurities – what they did to become comfortable with who they were.

In addition, it didn't help that whenever I turned on the TV or the radio or flicked through a newspaper, I never saw anybody like me, so I had few people to look up to. I'd never seen a politician or a CEO in a wheelchair. I didn't know of any lawyers or doctors or even musicians who'd overcome the challenges I faced.

When there were people in wheelchairs or with other disabilities in TV shows and movies, they always seemed to be presented in a terribly depressing light. None of these onscreen characters just happened to be in a wheelchair like they happened to have blue eyes. Disability was either used to signal a scary, bad villain, like *Peter Pan*'s Captain Hook with his metal hand, or the storyline was about how, once someone had a disability, their life was basically over.

Take *Million Dollar Baby*, for example. This movie came out when I was fourteen, and I took myself off to see it along with lots of other people, drawn by the rave reviews and Oscar wins. It's a really well-made movie, no doubt about it, but (spoiler alert) Hilary Swank's character breaks her neck and ends up as a quadriplegic. The rest of the movie is about the fact that she wants to die. The big dilemma is not about whether there's another way she might be able to see the world, it's about whether anyone will help her get her wish to end her life. Extra spoiler alert: there's no surprise happy ending.

The audience walks out of that movie having absorbed the message that life with paralysis is not worth living, and that wanting to die is a perfectly reasonable response to having a disability. Even at the time I thought to myself, *I know a broken neck sucks, but that's bullshit*. And yet the more the movie went on, the more self-conscious I became. I felt sure the other people in the cinema were glancing over at me, conspicuous in my chair, thinking: 'Check out that kid. Wonder if he wants to kill himself too?'

I couldn't totally blame them – after all, they got the exact same message from the road safety messages that featured on every second billboard and ran frequently on TV. The ads showed someone speeding or drink driving, having an accident, then ending up in a wheelchair and despairing because their life was now over. I get it that the idea was to get through to people what was at stake when they drove carelessly or dangerously, but with no positive, ordinary images of people in wheelchairs to balance things out, the takeaway message was that a life with a disability was a life that might not be worth living. Which couldn't be further from the truth.

So it's fair to say that, growing up, I experienced some challenging moments in terms of my own self-perception. The days back in primary school when I could easily keep up with my friends in primary school games were long gone – which was fair enough because my mates were growing up and getting fitter and stronger. Now often on the sidelines, watching them run and jump without a second thought, I wished I could experience such freedom. And sometimes I got a bit sad thinking that I'd never be able to kick a footy to my own kids or stroll along the beach hand in hand with a girl.

On the whole, I knew my life had value. And yet, I couldn't quite be comfortable with who I was. The bullies' words were designed to wound, and they did. Adolescence is a tricky time for self-esteem, no matter who you are. All teenagers feel like they're out there alone at some point. But when you really are different from everyone around you and you don't have any role models whose path you can follow, well, you can't hold out against bullying forever.

I started to feel pretty flat. Previously, I couldn't wait to get to school each day. Now I started to dread it. And as I sank into a depressed state I began to seriously wonder if life was worth living.

In retrospect, I can see that I should have told the people around me what was going on right from the start. Instead of sinking further into myself, avoiding going out if I didn't have to and trying to comfort myself with endless junk food, I should have reached out. Help was there, but I just couldn't see it.

If you ever find yourself in a similar situation, remember you don't have to deal with it alone. Talk to people who you know care – it will save you so much pain. I only wish I'd known that back then. I'm sure I said some dumb things to kids at school too, and it's something I really regret. At the time we probably think it's just harmless banter, but in my case the 'harmless banter' that was directed at me did hurt. And I'm sure the people who gave me a hard time probably regret it. We all make mistakes, and I definitely don't hold any grudges. But we can all learn from our mistakes as well.

Luckily, I had two lifelines that saved me – sport and music. I don't know how I'd have got through that time without them. My music of choice was hip hop and it came to me via Zack. Left to my own devices in my younger teen years, my taste in music was pretty questionable (plenty of Jack Johnson – 'Banana Pancakes'!). But when I was thirteen, Zack introduced me to hip hop. He knew plenty of underground rappers, like Atmosphere, Aesop Rock, MF Doom to name a few, as well as old-school nineties acts such as Nas and A Tribe Called Quest. I was instantly hooked.

At the time, Dad was working for a skate company called Airwalk, and was making regular business trips to America. He'd often come home with presents, and one trip he came home with a MiniDisc each for Zack and me, on which we could record as well as play music. These things were *very* cool at the time, replacing the now-extinct Walkman. I still remember the first song I ever put on mine – Bomfunk MC's 'Freestyler'.

That track was great, and the heavy-rotation video that went with it was just as good. It features a young guy with dreadlocks who gets hold of a controller that he uses to make people do his will. Among the many cool things about this guy is the fact that he's carrying a MiniDisc, so when Dad handed over our gifts I was ecstatic.

Sport was also a powerful tool for me, a space where I could focus on something other than school and compete with other people with disabilities. Sticking with it was the best decision I ever made.

By this stage I was unfit and overweight. But I was still winning competitive tennis matches and in January 2004, at the age of thirteen, I made it all the way through to qualify for the national junior team in wheelchair tennis's answer to the Davis Cup, the World Team Cup.

That year, the tournament was held in New Zealand, at Wilding Park in Christchurch, the tennis stadium known to Kiwis as 'Davis Cup City'. There I was, ready to represent my country on the international sporting stage for the first time, with Mum there to cheer me on. I thought how cool it was to be wearing the green and gold just like my tennis hero, Pat Rafter. I never missed watching him and Australia's other players as they competed against the world's best for the

Davis Cup and now here I was, an Australian national tennis player too. It was a big thing in anyone's language, and in that moment I really understood what a special opportunity I'd been given. It felt like the beginning of something huge.

As it turned out, we were pipped by the Netherlands, who also took out the men's and women's titles. But our junior side was honoured with the Team of the Year Award, judged on performance, sportsmanship and team spirit.

Playing in the World Team Cup changed everything for me, giving me back a sense of purpose and value, something I had previously lacked.

It was also pretty cool to be able to do something that really made my friends and family proud. As I mentioned earlier, my family are pretty sporty, but the most recognised family member was definitely my uncle Errol Alcott, the national cricket team's physio. He did that job for nearly thirty years, working with some of the best players in the game, including Steve Waugh, Alan Border, Ricky Ponting, Justin Langer, Matt Hayden, Michael Clarke, Shane Warne, Glenn McGrath and of course the big-hitting keeper Adam 'Gilly' Gilchrist. The Australian cricket team during those years was one of the most skilled and inspirational sporting sides I've ever seen.

Being the nephews of Errol gave Zack and me privileges that other kids could only dream about. Every Christmas we'd have lunch with Errol and the Australian cricket team and their families as they geared up for the start of the Boxing Day Test at the Melbourne Cricket Ground the following day.

These guys were mobbed wherever they went, but most of them remained grounded, none more so than Gilly, as I had discovered the first time I met him when I was just nine.

I was shocked when this all-time great came up to me, put his hand out and said, 'Hi, I'm Adam.'

*I know who you are. The whole country knows who you are!* I thought to myself. *Why are you telling me your name?*

But it was a real lesson in staying true to yourself, no matter what. Regardless of the fame and all his achievements, Gilly was the same friendly, genuine guy he'd always been. I thought right then that if I ever made it big, I wanted to act like that too.

Occasionally, Zack and I were allowed into the dressing room (as long as the team had okayed visitors – sometimes, when they'd lost, they just wanted to be alone – fair enough too). We recognised what a privilege it was, but we were no longer nervous being around legends. In 2004, Dad took us to the Australia–Pakistan Boxing Day Test at the MCG. On the fourth day, the match was all but done, so Zack passed on the opportunity to join us. It looked like he'd made the right call too – as it turned out, Australia won easily, only losing one wicket before wrapping up the Test. But then Uncle Errol ushered Dad and me into the Australian dressing room.

It was always a treat, if a bit surreal, being among the best-known sportsmen in Australia as they sat around cracking jokes and yarning about the day's play. A lot of them remembered me from our previous meetings and it was easy to talk to them. On this particular day, I challenged Darren Lehmann, who happened to be wearing only a towel, to a game of table tennis. The big-hitting batsman didn't bother to get dressed – maybe he should have, because I thrashed him. I suspect that, at the start, he went a bit easy on me, but by the end we were playing full boar. He'd just helped his team romp to a win on the pitch, but that was no reason for me to go easy on him, and I sent one rocket after another his way.

'So where's your brother?' Adam Gilchrist asked me, once I was done with Darren.

'He decided to stay home,' I said. Then Dad and I had an idea, and we asked Gilly if he'd give Zack a call to let him know what a great time he was missing.

He was happy to oblige. 'Hey Zack,' he said. 'It's Adam Gilchrist here, mate. I'm with Dylan in the Australian dressing room. Where are you?'

'Piss off,' Zack said before hanging up. The look on his face when we got home and told him that it really was Gilly was priceless. Pretty sure he even smashed a skateboard on the fence of the house. Zack is still dirty about it to this day.

\*\*\*

By the time I was almost fourteen, things had really turned around for me. In fact, it was hard to remember how miserable I had been the previous year. I had a newfound confidence that spurred me to stretch my wings, gain some independence and make some changes.

The first step was telling Mum I didn't want her picking me up from school anymore. Instead, I wanted to push my wheelchair the 3 kilometres from Brighton Grammar back to Vista Road.

Mum's first response was 100 per cent no: 'You're *not* doing it. It's too dangerous. Cars can barely see you when you cross the road!'

But I was persistent. Finally Mum and Dad let me have a go at making the journey by myself.

I'd been so intent on getting Mum to agree, I hadn't thought about what it would be like to actually do it. It was a long way, especially with a heavy school bag full of books on my back. Mum was also shitting herself, and I half-suspected she was trailing me in the car to keep an eye on me. But of course, in the way of these things, as soon as I'd done it once I was absolutely fine, and from then on it was part of my daily ritual to wheel myself and my bag full of books home from school.

The next thing to change was my fitness – I was really self-conscious about being so overweight. I also legit had no eyebrows until I was seventeen – not sure why, they just never grew – so let's say I was an extremely weird-looking unit until I was fifteen. Unfortunately, I couldn't control my lack of eyebrows, but the excess weight was something I could control. So I decided to cut out the junk and eat only nutritious food. I was very disciplined and I eventually lost about 20 kilos. Now I felt healthy and confident.

Around this age I also wanted to start seeing my friends out of school more. But while I had a great group of friends and we had lots of fun together at school, I began to realise I was being excluded socially. Kids had started having parties but I would only hear about them after the fact, on Monday mornings when everyone was talking about what a great time they'd had together over the weekend.

At the time, I couldn't understand it. My mates seemed to like me just fine, but they ignored me when it came time to hang out in groups. In the past, I'd withdraw into myself and not do much about it, but now I decided on a different approach, and it's one of the best decisions I ever made.

The turning point came when one of my friends organised a party. A big one. And, as usual, I wasn't invited. That really stung. I thought we were good mates, so why the cold shoulder? So I decided to invite myself.

I wasn't really sure how to go about it, so I asked Zack what he and his mates did when they weren't invited somewhere.

'Easy,' he said. 'We just jump the fence.' Good advice.

I laughed. If only I had that luxury. But without some kind of crane to lift me over, it's safe to say I wasn't jumping any fences anytime soon. Instead, I'd just have to roll up to the party and see what happened.

Nervous as I was about what might happen, I finally decided to tackle it head on. So I asked Mum to drive me to my mate's house, where the party would already be in full swing.

'Are you invited?' she asked.

'Yeah, course,' I said confidently.

Satisfied, Mum dropped me outside the house (with four UDLs – she wouldn't let me take the full six-pack). As soon as Mum's car was out of sight, I took a couple of deep breaths and headed to the door.

I knocked and tried to look casual, although I was feeling like a bit of an idiot. Finally, my friend opened the door. When he saw me, he looked surprised. For a few seconds neither of us said anything. He clearly didn't know what to do and neither did I.

*Dylan, you idiot, why did you come? He just doesn't want you here*, I thought to myself.

But then my friend blurted out: 'Mate, I'm sorry we didn't invite you, but there are a few stairs in my house and I didn't know how you'd go handling them.'

I couldn't believe it. After so much self-doubt and insecurity, it turned out that it wasn't something I was doing wrong or something about my personality. Instead, it was more about the fact that my friends were too embarrassed to talk about my disability with me. They didn't know if I needed a carer, they didn't know if I could stay at their place, or even if I could handle some stairs myself. And they were too embarrassed to ask. Even more importantly, I realised I'd been too embarrassed to talk about my disability with them! I never told them what I could and couldn't do because I was too scared to open up with them.

My mate welcomed me inside and I had a great time that night – the first of many, many good times to come, because I was never excluded again. Going to that party changed my life, because, from that day on, I decided to never let my disability get in the way of anything I wanted to achieve ever again.

I couldn't believe how much time I'd wasted by never having had this conversation. I realised that I'd probably laid the groundwork for this awkwardness myself by shying away from ever talking about my disability. It was a real epiphany: instead of ignoring it, I needed to embrace it and be open with everyone, answering any questions they might have and being clear about what I could and couldn't do. Talking about disability normalises it. It doesn't make things awkward. Just the opposite, it makes people more comfortable. It breaks down barriers.

Coming to understand all this changed everything for me, and started me on a path towards life as I know it now.

# 4

# *ball games*

AFTER MY DARK AND rocky time in early adolescence, things started to fall into place for me on every front, and my newfound confidence helped me make the most of all sorts of social and sporting opportunities.

For most of my youth I'd focused on wheelchair tennis. But when I was fourteen, all of that changed when I met a guy called Shaun Groenewegen at a Wheelchair Sports Victoria open day, where there were multiple sports on offer to try (for the record, I kicked Shaun's arse at tennis that day). Shaun was a wheelchair basketballer who had played for the Australian national team, the Rollers, at the Sydney 2000 Paralympics (they had placed fifth). It had always been in the back of my mind that I'd like to give wheelchair basketball a go.

I'd loved playing basketball since right back in the days of the Vista Road neighbourhood pick-up games. Shaun was playing in a local competition at Knox Basketball Stadium in Boronia, where anybody, no matter their level, could give wheelchair basketball a try – even an able-bodied player could jump into a wheelchair and give wheelchair basketball a crack. Shaun told me I should come along myself. I did, and I immediately loved it.

After a few weeks of competing, Shaun and some of the other players mentioned an upcoming junior training session, something they regularly organised, where you could come along and further develop your skills. Tennis was great, but I knew that basketball would give me the chance to be part of a team. It would also open up a whole other network of people with disabilities, and I was ready for that.

The session was held at a rehabilitation centre in the Melbourne suburb of Kew, just half an hour's drive from home. There I met the coach of the Dandenong Rangers national wheelchair basketball team, Greg Warnecke, someone who has made a huge impact on my life. One of the things that makes Greg so good at his job is that he understands that elite achievement in any sport is only possible if the grassroots level is well tended. The fun come-and-try wheelchair basketball sessions for young and upcoming athletes were part of this.

Wheelchair basketball is pretty much the same as able-bodied basketball. It's played over four ten-minute quarters on the same court. It has the same scoring and follows most of the same rules – for instance, having five players on court at one time, the same charging and blocking rules, etc. The basketball court is the same size and the hoop is at the same height. There are a few modifications to make it work for wheelchairs, for example, a 'travel' in able-bodied basketball is no more than two steps per bounce, while in wheelchair basketball it's two touches of the wheels. It's a very physical sport and the frequent collisions cause some seriously massive falls!

I loved it immediately, both the sport itself and the social aspect of being part of a team. Luckily, I had pretty decent wheelchair skills due to my tennis training, but my biggest asset on the court was my ability to shoot the ball. Due to my big hands and really long arms (I have an arm span of almost 2 metres!), I had pretty good range for someone sitting down, and could shoot the ball from the 3-point line with relative ease.

When I told Greg I wanted one day to be a Paralympian like Shaun, he invited me along to start training with the Dandenong Rangers in the national wheelchair basketball league.

I absolutely loved training with the men. They were big-bodied and took no prisoners so I had to learn a lot fast. But I didn't want to drop tennis, so, four nights a week, I was somewhere across Melbourne either training or competing in one sport or the other. People often forget just how much time and effort parents put in driving their kids to and from sport events and practice. At the time, I'm not sure I fully grasped how much Mum and Dad gave up so I could chase my dreams. I'll be forever indebted to them for that.

Between the encouragement and development I was getting and my own determination, it seemed like no time at all before I made the official Dandenong Rangers squad and had been chosen to play in the Victorian state junior team.

I was still loving my tennis, too, and in the middle of 2005, when I was fourteen, I was chosen for my second

World Team Tennis Cup. The event was being hosted that year by defending champions the Netherlands, in Groningen, about 200 kilometres northeast of Amsterdam. It was a great chance to reconnect with Mum's heritage. She and Oma made the trip over with me and it was a very special feeling to know that my sporting achievement had been the catalyst for our visit. Not speaking Dutch myself, I was a bit like a rabbit in the headlights at the special barbecue our relatives organised in Mum's hometown, Geleen. I swear there were a hundred cousins there, and barely any of them spoke English. All I could say in Dutch was 'sex in the kitchen'. Not very helpful. Playing tennis was a breeze by comparison!

In the tournament itself, we made it all the way through to the final, but lost to the Netherlands. My family were thrilled that I'd come so close to a world title, which made the surprise all the greater when I told them I wanted to significantly scale back the energy I put into tennis and channel it into basketball instead.

It was a pragmatic decision: Greg Warnecke had pointed out that basketball offered me a much better chance of realising my dream of becoming a Paralympian than tennis did. The reason was that my men's tennis open ranking wasn't high, and at the time I played in the open wheelchair tennis classification, which meant that a single amputee who had all three other limbs functioning had a significant advantage over someone like me who had no strength at all in their legs. If you think leg power doesn't make much difference when someone's in a wheelchair, think again.

Serious wheelchair basketball competitions use a point system under which each player has a classification and the score for all five players on the court at a given time cannot exceed fourteen points. The classification starts at one and goes up to four and a half; a low number equals low function. My official assessed classification was one: I was a low-point player because my abs and legs don't work the same way as those of a below-knee amputee, who can call on these muscles to generate power. I do, however, have an unusually long reach. That allowed me to stretch the defence a lot more and set up high-point players in scoring positions close to the basket. As I was quickly learning, a 'one-pointer' who can shoot is extremely valuable and at that time was quite rare. A one-pointer who can shoot is a very handy person to have on the team.

My parents were not convinced by my rationale, and I'd have to say they were a little frosty towards Greg for a while. They loved tennis and they wanted me to stick with that. But I wasn't to be dissuaded, because, on top of all its other attractions, I was really enjoying the team aspect of basketball. It was great travelling with the guys for interstate games, learning from them not only on the court but off it as well. But, as a result, I probably grew up a little too fast.

One of my very first away trips was to Wollongong, a double header where we played Friday and Saturday nights, flying home Sunday. After the game, a whole heap of us, including Shaun and Greg, went out to a notorious nightclub called the Glasshouse to celebrate. It turns out that sneaking into bars is a lot easier when you're underage if you're in a wheelchair. For one thing, there's no height discrepancy to give you away. And I guess bouncers don't want to be seen to be picking on the disabled guys. Anyway, the players formed a sort of human shield around me and in we went. I was only fourteen and *very* happy with myself.

After just two drinks I was wasted and in fine form. Shaun and one of my other good friends on the team, Tom Fraser, decided it was their mission to get me a kiss. They picked one of the best-looking girls at the bar – a tall, beautiful blonde. I still remember it to this day. The boys had chatted her up and somehow she was keen. She was maybe eighteen or nineteen and I certainly wasn't about to let on I was in Year 9. The next thing I knew, she started kissing me. It was the first time I'd kissed anyone properly.

Turned out Shaun had asked the girl's friend to ask the girl to kiss me. I didn't care at all if that's how it went down. A kiss is a kiss, and at that stage I'd take anything! Anyway, she hadn't exactly run off screaming. In fact, she seemed to be enjoying herself. In retrospect, I do feel a touch bad – she didn't know she was kissing a fourteen-year-old who was still carrying a couple of kilos and had no eyebrows (well, I guess she knew about the kilos and the lack of eyebrows). But knowing what was possible did put some pep in my step when it came to future endeavours with girls.

\*\*\*

Even though I had cut back on the number of tennis tournaments I was playing in, I was named in the junior wheelchair team for the 2006 World Team Cup. It was to be played on clay in the Brazilian capital, Brasilia, where this time Belgium would win.

We prepared for the event at a training camp in the Argentinian capital of Buenos Aires. We were staying in a really nice, modern hotel, and it was here that I had one of the stranger meetings of my life. We'd stayed there for a week but the training camp was over and it was time to check out. I came down in the elevator to find an area of the lobby had been cordoned off with a rope. I really didn't want to wheel the long way around and it didn't look like anything much was going on in the cordoned-off area, so I thought I'd just quickly nip across.

I got under the rope okay and had my head down, making good ground, when I ran smack bang into an obstacle. I looked up to find the obstacle was a bald man wearing glasses and a robe. He had a look of amusement on his face – a very, very familiar face. Turns out, I'd almost bowled over the Dalai Lama. I stammered an apology as I manoeuvred backwards, but he just continued to gaze at me with his serene smile and twinkling eyes. There was no mistaking his spiritual charisma. I'm not a particularly religious person, and I really only go to church for Christmas and weddings, but I remember thinking to myself, *Dylan, you're a dickhead. Surely that'll bring you bad luck somehow!'*

\*\*\*

Back in Australia I continued to juggle my school commitments with sport. It was sometimes a delicate balance, but all the practice was definitely paying off and my progress in wheelchair basketball was rapid. Greg Warnecke paid me a huge compliment years later when, looking back on those days, he told a reporter that I was 'a remarkable character, with an incredible drive and competitive streak'. Very touchingly, he added that coaching me had been one of the highlights of his career, which included coaching some of Australia's top able-bodied basketballers, including Aron

Baynes. I feel incredibly lucky and grateful to have met him when I did.

Greg was the team manager when, nearing the end of 2006, I was given the chance to make my debut in the Australian national men's wheelchair basketball team. The event was the Far East and South Pacific Games for the Disabled, held in Malaysia. The second-largest sporting event for people with disabilities after the Paralympics, it featured more than 4000 athletes from sixty-three countries taking part in nineteen sports.

It felt very special to be chosen to represent Australia in a second sport. I was acutely aware that I'd been handed an amazing opportunity. But even so, being in the Rollers as a fifteen-year-old was a bit intimidating. Most of my teammates were grown men and when I first started playing with them, the blokey mentality really threw me. They trained hard, played hard and didn't hold back in letting me know if I stuffed up on court. It took a lot of getting used to.

Fortunately, by the time we got to Malaysia, I was playing well enough to get many opportunities on the court. The games took place at the 13,000-seat Malawati Stadium in Shah Alam and I was absolutely shitting myself the first time we played. The stadiums weren't full, maybe only a thousand fans tops, but it was still the biggest crowd I'd ever played in front of. The Rollers were hot. After six matches we were undefeated, having beaten Chinese Taipei, India, Hong Kong, Malaysia, China and South Korea – in a couple of cases with what looked like cricket scores. We beat India 97–11, for instance, and Hong Kong 106–16. Unfortunately, we fell at the final hurdle in the final, losing to a very strong

Iran squad. The coaching team said I'd provided 'valuable support' in the match, and that praise plus a silver medal felt like a pretty decent result for my first time in international basketball.

Young as I was, I was already dreaming of the 2008 Beijing Paralympics. For the Rangers, I had gone from being a back-up player to being in the starting five. I had also led the Victorian junior team at two National Junior Championships finals, where I'd been awarded Most Valuable Player and a spot in the All Star Five. Still, it was a long way from those teams to the Rollers. But then coach Ben Ettridge took me aside and said I had a real shot at being part of the team that would go after that ultimate prize. It was a new goal to aim for, and I grabbed it with both hands.

Only a few years earlier I'd wanted to stay home from school every day, embarrassed about who I was. Now, at just sixteen, an Australian national coach was telling me I had a real shot at achieving my dreams of competing at the Paralympic games. Not bad.

I decided I was going to do whatever it took to make that dream a reality. I trained like never before: hill sprints and gym sessions, roaring around witches' hats to improve my agility, and practising as often as I could on court. Every athlete needs to do strength training, but it's absolutely vital for athletes with disabilities. If an able-bodied person damages a shoulder, it's not always a big deal. They can still get around and live. If an athlete in a wheelchair injures their shoulder, they're in big trouble. They can't transfer in and out of their wheelchairs, move around, or have a shower. So injury prevention is key and I did everything I could to not only make sure I was in peak condition to compete, but also to make sure I looked after myself to prevent injuries derailing my career and my life.

It was around this time that I was also feeling pretty good about something else – my first serious relationship. Easily the biggest insecurities I've faced in my life are in regard to dating. Asking out someone you think is really special is nerve-racking for anyone. But being sixteen and unmistakably disabled, well, all these feelings were magnified a hundred-fold. The fear of the unknown and how other people would react to my disability were pretty scary. Plus there's also the misconception that people in wheelchairs don't date, a misconception I also believed when I was younger.

But that all changed when I met Chelsy, a boarder at Brighton Grammar's sister school, Firbank. We met at a party in Year 11 and I was immediately drawn to her. She was beautiful and funny, and from the moment I met her I knew I wanted to take things further with her. But I'd never had a girlfriend before, and I was absolutely shitting myself. Around Valentine's Day, I asked her on a date at a school function. I gave her a rose and she baked me some very burnt (almost inedible) cookies, which I pretended were delicious. We started going out from that day.

It was another huge, life-changing moment for me. I'd spent so many sleepless nights wondering if I'd ever meet someone who would love me for me and look past my disability, and not care about some of the differences and challenges it might involve.

It really was pretty progressive of a sixteen-year-old girl to say, 'Yes, I'm going to go out with a guy in a wheelchair.' I'm sure her girlfriends quizzed her about the physical side of our relationship – it's a question that seems to preoccupy a lot of people when one half of a couple is in a wheelchair. It's still the number one question I get asked to this day. 'Can you have sex?' And the answer is yes.

But I still had to prove that to myself too. I remember the first time we made love she remarked afterwards that she'd been amazed how confident I was. Confident! I thought I was going to have a heart attack.

I appreciate that for some people with a disability and their partners, sex is a scary prospect, the main misconception being that people with disabilities can't do it. But, really, all people can have sex in some way or another, and that connection you have with people is a really important part of life. It really devastates me when I see so many people with disabilities getting left out of the dating pool, and I know it's something able-bodied people often take for granted. But I was one of the lucky ones who got to meet someone and have that connection at a young age.

Chels was and still is an incredibly amazing person. Although she doesn't think as much of it, I am forever indebted to her for taking a risk on me and giving us a shot. It meant so much to me back then and now, and we remain close friends today. She's someone I love heaps.

Unfortunately, while my relationship with Chelsy grew stronger by the day, my parents' marriage was going in the opposite direction. Things came to a head at the end of 2006. Mum and Dad had been together for more than twenty years. They'd been a wonderfully supportive team as Zack and I grew up and they faced challenges that would have broken many couples years earlier.

But now it wasn't working out between them, and it was one of the hardest things that Zack and I had ever gone through. It's really tough when your parents split, especially when you're at an age where you understand what's going on. We didn't want to pick sides, but Zack and I always felt like we were in the middle of the arguments.

The only silver lining at the time was how close it brought Zack and me together. That period of our lives solidified our close bond. We only had each other to lean on, and I'm not sure I would've got through it without him.

These days, Mum and Dad are much happier than they were back then, so I can see now it was for the best. I also have an awesome step-mum Dana, who Zack and I love.

Luckily for us, Mum and Dad's split didn't diminish the love and support they showed for us boys, and they continued to encourage Zack at school and me in my sport. By this time, I'd made it into the Rollers squad to compete at the 2007 World Cup event in Manchester. It would be one of my last chances to impress, to keep my dream alive of competing in the Paralympic Games in Beijing in September 2008.

One of the coolest things about being in the Rollers was playing alongside my teammates. These guys had been through a lot in their lives, the majority having acquired their disabilities through accidents. First there was Brad Ness, our captain, a Western Australian. Then thirty-two, Brad had spent the past fourteen years with his disability after a freak accident brought an end to his previous sporting career.

Brad had been a deckhand on the high-speed ferry carrying holidaymakers between Perth and Rottnest Island. He was also a promising Aussie Rules player who had realistic hopes of being drafted into the AFL.

One night the ferry crew was preparing to leave the island and the skipper thought he heard Brad give the All

Clear signal. But Brad was still readying for departure and happened to be standing in a loop of rope whose other end was still tied to the dock. When the ferry began to move off, the rope tightened and sliced off Brad's right foot, in his words, 'as neatly as a chef chopping through a carrot'. The pain was immense and Brad would likely have bled to death if a paramedic who happened to be on board hadn't sealed off his artery.

Brad's leg was so mangled that when he finally got to hospital, the surgeon amputated below the knee. But, like all the guys on the team, Brad just got on with his life, disability and all. Then he caught a wheelchair basketball match on TV and was hooked. Brad thought it was one of the most exciting spectator sports he'd seen and, coming from an Aussie Rules background, he loved the sheer physicality of it. Of course, he was an absolute natural and was *absolutely huge*. The first time he ever laid a hit on me in a scrimmage, I thought I'd been struck by a freight train.

Another of the team's key players was Shaun Norris, who was also from Western Australia. While riding his bike at age four, Shaun had been hit by a car and paralysed. He'd taken up wheelchair basketball at the age of ten. Both Brad and Shaun were crucial members of our team, alongside two other players from Perth, Justin Eveson and Michael Hartnett. Together, those guys made up four of our starting five players.

At Manchester, we had some early victories against Britain, as well as the defending champions Canada and the Netherlands, with Brad top-scoring for Australia in each match.

Canada fought their way back to become the team we would face in the final. Under the guidance of their coach

Mike Frogley, they had beaten the Rollers often enough to have become Australia's nemesis. We went in determined to win and were the best side for most of the match – at the end of the third quarter we were ahead 37–29. But the Canucks put on a burst of quick points to draw level and right on the buzzer they snatched victory from us, 49–47. It was a painful loss and we itched for the chance to get even.

Now we were even more focused on the Paralympics but first I had one more tennis commitment to fulfil. So from Manchester I travelled on to Stockholm to play in the 2007 World Team Cup, where Great Britain claimed their first junior title. It would be my last serious tennis tournament for many years – at the time, I thought it would be my last competitive match ever. From here on out, I thought, it would be basketball all the way.

***

The day before my seventeenth birthday I was named in the Australian men's team for the 2008 Wheelchair Basketball International Invitational Tournament in Beijing. I was the youngest member of the team by six years. To be run in January, the tournament was a test event for the Paralympics and the first major international contest for the Rollers in the lead-up to the Games. We had a tough draw, pitting us against China, world number one Canada, and the Netherlands. But our coach, Ben Ettridge, boasted an impressive record in international competition and reckoned the team he had assembled could improve on that.

Beijing was the most incredible, chaotic, crazy place I'd ever seen. The Chinese were in a mad rush to get the city

ready for the Olympics and Paralympics, and even though it was mid-winter and freezing cold, there were teams of workers going nonstop, twenty-four hours a day, finishing off stadiums, hotels, trains – everything.

I roomed with Troy Sachs, who was thirty-two at the time. He comes from Wollongong and had a leg amputated when he was two and a half after being born with a deformed foot and no tibia.

Troy was one of the best players to have ever worn the Rollers' uniform. Sometimes he could come across as harsh, but he also gave me a lot of encouragement. He had a huge amount of valuable knowledge of the game to pass on, having made his own Paralympic debut in Barcelona at just sixteen. He'd won gold four years later in Atlanta, scoring a world record 42 points, had competed at Sydney in 2000, and four years later had been denied the gold medal in Athens by our biggest competitors, Canada. Troy urged me not to worry about my lack of years but to focus on my abundance of possibilities. It was strong advice from a great mentor.

The Beijing event had been dubbed the 'Good Luck' tournament, and fortune certainly favoured us early on. We trounced China before their home fans in our opening game, before going up against Canada. For the first time in my career, I was in the starting side for the Rollers rather than coming in off the bench as a substitute.

Ben waited to tell me until just before the game began. It was a smart move. I was so focused on the task at hand that it wasn't until after the game that it hit me how big an honour it was, so I didn't get overwhelmed. Instead, I got straight to work and scored 6 points, including the first basket. Excited is an understatement. The whole game was a thriller. Canada fought hard and we were trailing them at three-quarter time but we dug deep to surge home and finish all over them in the final term, eventually winning 57–46. Ben had ensured each player spent at least ten minutes but no more than twenty-five minutes on court, and the tactic kept us all fresh and firing, working wonders for our upset victory. Energised, we battered the Netherlands 66–32 in the final match of the opening round and thrashed China in the semi-final. But again, Canada did nothing to change our feelings about them by beating us 55–49 when it really mattered.

We were gutted. But we knew that the gold we were after was in September, and in June, three months out from the Paralympics, we got the chance to show Canada who was boss at the Four Nations tournament in Germany. Unfortunately, we went down to them again. From there we went on to the North America Cup in Alabama, and had to settle for the bronze medal behind, you guessed it, Canada and the United States.

After that tournament I stayed on for a week longer in America to attend an elite training camp at the University of Illinois under the guidance of the Canadian coach Mike Frogley. That might seem like a strange choice, given that we detested his team so strongly. But he liked the way I played and had invited me to spend a week there so he could assess whether I had the goods to earn a college scholarship once I finished high school. There was no way I'd pass up an invitation like that.

I was thrilled when Mike got in touch to tell me the scholarship was mine so long as I passed my Year 12 exams.

First, though, I had to get through my final year at Brighton Grammar. The school was remarkably proud and supportive of my sporting career so when I had to put my studies on hold in July, they completely understood. After all, I had a pretty good reason: I'd been officially named in the Australian team for the 2008 Beijing Paralympics. My dream was about to become a reality.

# 5

# *going for gold: beijing 2008*

FOR MANY PEOPLE OUTSIDE the movement, the Paralympics represents a space for people who have overcome adversity to live out some inspirational narrative. I guess there is a bit of that, but for me, the Paralympics is the mecca for elite performance – the highest level of competition I could ever reach.

Ever since I found out about Louise Sauvage's success at the Paralympics, I had it in my head I wanted to go to the Paralympics too. I remember, when I was about seven years old, I was playing totem tennis with Dad and Zack (you know, that silly game with a tennis ball attached to a pole by a string that goes round and round and round with no end), and I told them I wanted to go to the Paralympic Games.

Back then I didn't really have any idea what the word 'Paralympic' actually meant and a lot of people still don't understand it. The common misconception is that the 'para' in Paralympic means paraplegic or paralysed. If you thought that, well, don't feel bad because I did too! But it's obvious as soon as you look at the range of Paralympic competitors that paraplegia is just one of many types of disability involved, along with amputees, cerebral palsy, congenital short stature, visual impairment and more. In fact, the word 'Paralympic' comes from combining the Greek 'para', meaning beside or parallel, with 'Olympic' – the Paralympics run alongside the Olympics, parallel to them. They're held around the same time, featuring the same sports, competing for the same gold medals. The only difference is that at the Paralympics everyone has a disability (and is heaps better looking and more marketable to sponsors – call me biased).

The event has grown from a small competition for British World War II veterans in 1948 to become one of the biggest of all the international sporting gatherings. In all, there were 3951 athletes from 146 countries in Beijing for the 2008 Paralympics. I was so excited to be one of them, representing my country and going up against the world's best while I should have been at high school. I often felt a bit sorry for my mates back at school trying to stay awake through accountancy lessons. It was surreal.

I'd been overseas many times before, representing Australia at tennis and basketball in New Zealand, the Netherlands, Argentina, Brazil, England, Malaysia and many other places. But not even my experience of being in China earlier in the year fully prepared me for being there as a Paralympian.

There were no jackhammers this time around. Somehow everything had been completed and they were read to go. The Chinese government took no chances in its efforts to impress the billions watching the Olympics and Paralympics from around the globe, and everything was gleaming. At the time, Beijing's population was nearly 20 million and its smog was notorious. Not during the Games, though. The government closed factories, called a complete halt to the city's construction projects and drastically cut the number of vehicles on the streets at any one time. It worked. I have a touch of asthma but I had no trouble at all with the air on that visit.

They also went all out to impress the athletes. When I first arrived, the coaching staff told us to do a complete lap of the athletes' village and take the time to get a good look at the amazing facilities. But the place was huge, so I asked my friend Kelly Cartwright, a gold-medal-winning Paralympic runner, to do a lap with me. Kel is an above-knee amputee, meaning she uses a prosthetic to walk and ride a bike – kind of – so the plan was for me to follow behind in my wheelchair, holding on to the back of her bike.

We set off together, taking in the sites, the apartments, the man-made beach, the gym. The atmosphere was electric – a combination of nervous excitement and unstinting determination. I was enjoying the tour when disaster struck – Kel's prosthetic leg fell off, causing us to take a fair tumble. The sight of a guy in a wheelchair and a girl with one leg stacking it on a bike would be pretty strange and hilarious anywhere in the world. But in the Paralympic village, it seemed surprisingly normal.

One of the coolest things about the games was the ridiculously large food hall. It was sensational, a place of endless pleasure with hundreds of delicacies. There was 24-hour breakfast, pizza, pasta, steaks, chicken, a Peking duck stand – even a kebab stand! (What Olympian smashes kebabs I am yet to find out!) Whatever you wanted was there and everything was free. It was like paradise.

Even more impressive were the other athletes. In fact, I witnessed some of the most astonishing sights I've ever come across in that food hall. A Chinese swimmer named He Junquan particularly captivated me. Both his arms had been amputated at the shoulder after he accidentally touched a live electricity cable at the age of three. Most people who are missing arms or legs will use prosthetics and then are pretty much normal contributing members of society. But this guy had nothing! Beijing was his third Paralympics and he was looking to add to his haul of seven medals, five of them gold. It was impressive enough seeing him carry his food tray in his mouth, but how was he going to actually eat? Would he need a carer? Would he face-plant in his food? I honestly had no idea, so I followed him to find out.

I needn't have worried. After all, despite his complete lack of upper limbs, his favourite event was the backstroke. Clearly he was a master of adapting to his circumstances. I watched carefully as he put his tray down and took off his shoes before walking over to where the cutlery was located. There he picked up some bamboo chopsticks with his toes, carried them back to his seat, took the chopsticks out of their wrapper using his toes, inserted them between the toes of his right foot and started feeding himself rice with his feet. I find it hard enough using chopsticks with my hands. I couldn't imagine using my feet! It was truly incredible. Dana, my Dad's new partner and my soon-to-be step-mum, was in tears watching. But He Junquan was so dextrous he didn't drop a single grain of rice.

I sat there thinking about what that bloke had to overcome in life. Other people might look at him and feel sorry for him, thinking his disability stopped him doing ordinary things like brushing his teeth or hugging his child. But all the while he was just getting on with it, smashing out 100 metres of backstroke in around a minute and ten seconds (What?!), making the most of every day and living life to the full. It was impressive to see and has stuck with me to this day.

\*\*\*

Even though we were ranked number three in the world heading into the tournament, the Rollers were considered outsiders to make the final, given the track record of the USA at number two and the Canadians, who had been riding high in top spot for a long time. But we didn't care what anyone else thought, we were going to show the world what we could do. We weren't there just to make up the numbers – we had set a gold-medal standard for ourselves, very aware that if we didn't win the gold medal we would have to stew on it for four long, long years until we got another chance.

We were confident in each other and in Ben, our coach. Even though it was his first time coaching at Paralympic level, he was continuing a family legacy that had begun with his father, Len, three decades earlier.

Len had competed in the Commonwealth Games as a track and field athlete before becoming a paraplegic at nineteen after a freak accident on a farm north of Perth, where he was working as a shearer alongside his brother. The two of them and a couple of mates had gone out kangaroo shooting one night, with Len driving one of the utes. A loaded shotgun lying behind him accidentally discharged and fired through his seat, hitting him in the lower back and shattering his spinal cord. He was very lucky to survive. In fact, his medical report noted that his heart stopped twice on the three-hour drive to the hospital.

After his recovery, Len began playing wheelchair basketball and was in the Rollers team for the 1980 Moscow Paralympics. It might have been the national team, but Len had to train himself, pushing himself along the Western Australian bush roads and up gravel tracks as young Ben shouted encouragement.

Ben grew up playing Aussie Rules but switched to able-bodied basketball in the mid-1990s, and later became the coach of the Perth Wheelcats in the National Wheelchair Basketball League. He understood the game extremely well, was a huge supporter of my game, and was great at getting us to come together as a team. Before matches he'd remind us that our drive to succeed came from within ourselves and from playing for each other. We'd all had to deal with many struggles in day-to-day life long before we got to the sporting arena, and we'd overcome a lot to represent our country.

I was the youngest on the team, and easily the biggest smartarse. The next youngest on the team, Shaun Norris, was nearly six years older than me. Despite my age, I was lucky to be totally accepted by the other guys, who gave me plenty of opportunities to do well. Along with Shaun, Troy Sachs and Brad Ness, other team members included Adrian King from Tamworth, who once told me that he'd lived two lives that were each longer than my one life – eighteen years walking and eighteen years as a paraplegic. Brendan Dowler, from Wollongong, was another veteran more than twice my age. Brendan, too, had become a paraplegic as a result of a spinal tumour. Tristan Knowles from Wodonga had lost a leg to cancer aged nine and then a lung at eleven, but had won silver with the Rollers at the 2004 Athens Games and was itching to go one better in Beijing. Tristan and I roomed together at the Games, and watching him hop to the bathroom completely naked every morning, his bits flopping around, will forever be etched in my memory!

Michael Hartnett from Perth became a paraplegic after a car accident, as did Grant Mizens, whose accident happened when he was in his final year of school in Sydney. Tige Simmons from Brisbane, a one-pointer like me, punched well above his weight as a player. He had become a paraplegic the day his motorbike was hit by a truck as he was on his way to work and he 'didn't bounce too well', as he said. Brett Stibners from Wollongong had also had a road accident, in his case a smash between his car and a truck.

Justin Eveson from Perth had lost a leg after coming off second best to a lawn aerating machine when he was twelve. He, too, had won silver in basketball in Athens, having already taken silver and bronze in swimming events at the Sydney Paralympics four years earlier. Justin was an absolute powerhouse, intimidating to the opposition and even sometimes to his teammates. He wanted to win more than anyone, and I reckon he was the best player I ever played with.

The team got great support from Ben's assistant coach Craig Friday (the current coach of the Rollers), physio Ian Lowther and manager Kelvin Browner. Our team was sixteen deep – twelve players and four staff – and everyone contributed equally.

As we got ourselves pumped for our first game I felt bad that Mum wasn't in Beijing to see my Paralympic debut. She'd been there for so many of my important moments, but money was a bit too tight at the time to allow her to come to China. Instead, she told me, she'd watch every minute of my games on TV. I still look back and wish I'd been a bit older and able to fly her over. Unfortunately my pocket money as a school student didn't cut it.

I also had great courtside support from Zack, Dad and Dana, as well as my Dandenong Rangers coach Greg Warnecke, who was determined to witness the kid he'd developed from scratch go for gold. I'd luckily come a long way as a player since Greg first encouraged me to come to the muck-around sessions. When I started, much as I loved it, the only prize I qualified for was the Glen 20 award for stinking up the court.

Thanks to hard work and good coaching, I'd developed into a pretty good shooter – good enough to be here in the national team. But Ben Ettridge was quick to remind me there was still something missing from my game: defence. In fact, he used to call me 'Ylan without the D'. It stuck, and even some of the opposition started calling me that. F*cking hilarious.

Before the action began in our opening match on 7 September 2008, ABC-TV interviewed me. I was lucky enough to get some coverage due to being so young and thanks to my sheer love of talking. I wasn't backwards in coming forward. 'I don't think the doctors who worked on me as a kid ever thought I'd be playing basketball at the

Paralympics,' I said. 'I think they thought I'd be a bit of a vegetable, but you just have to go out there and live with what you've got and love life.' It had always been what I lived by, and it felt great that it was starting to pay off. As you can see, not much has changed in ten years.

\*\*\*

The venue for the first game was the fan-shaped National Indoor Stadium and it was packed. I went through my own superstitious ritual of touching the baseline three times before the match began and then we formed a circle and embraced in a team huddle, gave each other one last slap on the back and then went out to face Brazil, a team known for their flair and fighting qualities.

A good day-to-day wheelchair costs about $8000, but a competition chair, made of titanium with angled carbon wheels and a protective bar for collisions, can cost in excess of $10,000. That's what we were all using – we were lucky to come from an affluent country, and our equipment was top of the line. The Brazilians, however, were using big, lumbering chairs like something you might find in an old hospital. It was a bit like we were in brand new Ferraris and they were in 1972 Daewoos. We weren't quietly confident, we were just confident. But, boy, could those guys play basketball. I thought I'd played at the top level, but the pressure of that opening match was tougher than anything I'd ever encountered in a sporting arena.

Given my age and relative lack of experience, I started on the bench wearing number 13. I was willing my teammates to find their rhythm, but two of the opposition, in particular

Erick Silva and Irio Nunes, couldn't seem to miss. By the end of the first ten-minute quarter we were down 24–12, with Nunes landing a 3-pointer right on the buzzer. I started to wonder if Michael Jordan had fathered a Brazilian love child who'd had some sort of workplace accident, lost his leg and was now playing wheelchair basketball. These guys were on fire! Not to be left out of things, Silva sank one right on the half-time buzzer. Now we were down 45–28. This was not how I'd pictured it going down.

At the half-time break we were pretty sombre, but Ben told us to stick to our process and the result would come. After the break, Justin Eveson and Brett Stibners got us going, hitting a few baskets in a row, and when I was finally sent into action five minutes and fifty-five seconds into the third quarter (not that I was counting), the gap had narrowed to 47–40. It was like an out-of-body experience – I was so nervous and yet fired up at the same time. This was the moment I'd dreamt of, and now it was actually happening, I had goosebumps.

The ABC was covering the game and renowned commentator Peter Walsh commented that I looked about twelve years old. His co-commentator, Nick Morris, who'd won gold with the Rollers in Atlanta a dozen years before, told him looks could be deceptive. 'He's a baby face,' Nick said, 'but, boy, he can play.' That was nice, even if he did refer to me as 'Little Dylan Alcott'.

(Nick and I would eventually become great friends and business partners at Get Skilled Access. He's one of Australia's leading accessibility consultants, helping to identify problems and find solutions for planners, developers, architects and building consultants around the world. Previously he worked

on the Sydney Olympic and Paralympic venues, Rod Laver Arena and Melbourne's Royal Children's Hospital and had been consulted during the construction of the very stadium we were playing in now, along with the other venues as well as the athletes' village in Beijing.)

I wasn't on for long – but when I was, I scored 5 points, and my first basket was incredibly exhilarating. The tactics were working – holes were opening up in Brazil's defence, and by the end of the third quarter we'd shaved a bit more off Brazil's lead. Now they were only ahead by 5 points.

With only four minutes left in the match, I was back on the court. The scoreline read 65–59 in Brazil's favour. Two minutes later we were breathing down their necks 67–65. My heart was beating faster than it ever had before, and the atmosphere in the stadium was tremendous as our supporters in the stands waved stuffed kangaroos and Aussie flags like their lives depended on it.

With just one minute and twenty-seven seconds left, Brazil was ahead 70–67 and things were looking dire for us. With his eye on the clock, Brazilian star Nunes missed an easy shot. Then Brad Ness rocketed back and passed to Justin Eveson to shoot, only for Justin to be tipped out of his chair in a collision.

There were fifty-eight seconds of play remaining and Brazil were still in front by 3 points. Eveson scored again, taking him to 39 points in the game so far. With forty-seven seconds left in the match, scores were finally level at 70 each. Ten seconds later, with the score still even, our hearts were in our mouths as Silva was awarded three shots for a foul.

It was 70–70 and Brazil were in the box seat.

Silva's first shot went in. 71–70.

Ouch.

The second one missed.

Thank god.

The third went in. 72–70.

Ouch again.

Brazil called a timeout.

Basketball is not for the faint-hearted – we absolutely had to make sure scores were level when the buzzer went. Otherwise our Paralympic dreams would be in tatters after only one game. With twenty seconds left, Brad Ness got it to 72–71. Five seconds later, Brazil's Nilton Pessoa hurtled down court for the match-winner, lined it up ... and missed. If we could score on the rebound the game was ours.

We charged up court. Justin Eveson passed to Shaun Norris, back to Eveson and then to Brad Ness, who from the right side of the basket took a shot.

To this day I swear it was the ugliest shot I've ever seen.

The ball seemed to hover for a moment, then hit the rim and did what in Australia is called a dunny roll. It went around the ring once, twice, wobbled agonisingly, and at long last fell down through the basket.

We'd done it! We were ahead 73–72!

But there was still a sliver of game time left. We couldn't let Brazil score again. They made one last desperate drive but we held them off. The siren sounded and it was all over.

The crowd, many of them decked out in Aussie shirts and hats, went nuts. I was so happy I raced down the middle of the court, throwing my arms around like I was Mike Tyson going for a knockout.

Peter Walsh didn't mince words. 'The Australian Rollers, in an absolute ball tearer, have beaten Brazil,' he told the viewers back home. He and Nick Morris concurred that Brazil was the better team for most for the way. If we'd played them one hundred times over from the position we were in, they would have won ninety-nine of them. But not this one.

There was no stopping us now.

A lot of sport stories focus on hard work and resilience, and there's no doubt those things are very important. But one of the most important life lessons I ever learnt came from my time in Beijing, and it started with that unlikely win. The lesson was about the importance of buying into team culture. We weren't the best team in the competition in terms of skills, we didn't have the most funding or the best record. But what we did have was the best culture. Each of us was equally important to the team as a whole, whether they scored 40 points or didn't score at all, whether they played forty minutes or forty seconds. We believed in each other and had each other's backs. It was a case of shared responsibility and shared glory.

After the match the feeling among us was electric and it took a long time to come down from the high of our dramatic victory. But we knew it was just one step on what was going to be a long road to reach our ultimate goal.

\*\*\*

Our next test was going up against Great Britain. They were no slouches either, having won the bronze medal at the Athens Paralympics four years earlier, and former Rollers coach Murray Treseder was their coach. Murray had a great pedigree, having steered the Aussies to silver at the

Athens Paralympics in 2004 and bronze at the 2006 World Championships. He also coached the Rollers through an awesome 2004 victory, when they'd become the first team from any nation to beat Canada in six years.

Many of our best players had benefited from Murray's advice and they respected him a great deal. But this was a take-no-prisoners competition, and we were out to show him he was on the wrong side this time.

Unlike our able-bodied basketball counterparts, we didn't make any money from playing, but in every other respect the Rollers were a professional side. We trained hard and smart, worked on skills, kept our bodies in the best possible shape and intensively analysed our opponents' strengths and weaknesses. We were very serious in our approach and determined to prove we were the best team in the world.

Up against the Brits, our skipper Brad Ness was on fire. Having scored the winner in our first match, he continued to lead by example, delivering 16 points and nine rebounds as we cruised home 67–48. A day later, Brad turned it up another notch, scoring 31 points as we rolled over China 79–44. But the following day, our fourth match delivered a reality check, and we had to fight hard for a last-gasp 66–59 victory over Israel.

Having scored four wins within a week and already qualified for the quarter-finals, we had the feeling we were on the path to glory.

But Israel had reminded us that we had to be at our very best every single time, and the next day the Americans demonstrated that even more forcefully when we lost 61–68. The result left us gobsmacked but Ben told us not to panic, assuring us we were still in the box seat for a semi-final place.

I was playing about fifteen minutes per match and was scoring in most matches so I was pretty happy with how I was going on the court. I was determined to maintain my concentration and not let the occasion get to me, especially as we headed to the knockout quarter-final stage. I also had faith in the team that we'd be able to turn it on when we needed it most. Sure enough, we shook off the loss and resumed our winning streak, beating Japan, then Great Britain in the semi-final to earn a shot at gold.

We were in the dressing room after the semi-final when I had an encounter with a politician that I've never really topped. Bill Shorten was then a rising star in the Labor Party who had been in Federal Parliament for just a year as part of the Rudd government, in which he'd been appointed Parliamentary Secretary for Disabilities and Children's Services. Attending the Paralympics in that role, he was visiting all the Australian competitors. He'd been pushing hard for a National Disability Insurance Scheme (NDIS), so there were lots of conversations to be had.

When he made his impromptu visit to the athletes' village we happened to be in the ice baths. (We were having ice baths after every game to recover and maintain peak performance.) Now, if you've never had an ice bath, half your luck. They're very effective but, holy shit, they're like torture at the time.

Bill looked at me shivering in the freezing water. 'Is it cold in there?' he said with a big smile.

'Why don't you get in and find out for yourself?' I said, like the smartarse I am.

'All right, I will,' he said. And still dressed in his shirt and pants, the Hon. Bill Shorten climbed into that bath while all the players applauded.

An ice bath is a pretty cramped space for one body, let alone two, and it was pretty cosy in there, but as the cold water slopped out onto the floor Bill asked me questions about our chances for gold.

Eventually he got out, dried himself off, had a chat to the other guys in the team then went on his way. Bill and I have stayed in touch ever since, and he's remained a strong advocate for people with disabilities The NDIS soon became a key Labor government initiative. Let's hope both sides of politics continue to fund it and see it through.

\*\*\*

There was now just one match to go, and everything was riding on it. We'd be taking on Canada – our bogey team for so long – after they'd mown down everyone in their path. Germany, South Africa, Sweden, Japan, Iran, Israel and the United States had all gone up against them and come off second best. The reigning World and Paralympic Champions were the hot favourites as they aimed for three Paralympic gold medals on the trot.

Patrick Anderson was their big gun. He was twenty-nine years old and had been playing wheelchair basketball for the best part of two decades, after losing both his legs below the knee courtesy of a drunk driver. Patrick had scored 32 points in Canada's win over the United States. Then there was their coach, Mike Frogley, the most impressive mind in wheelchair basketball I'd ever encountered, with decades of knowledge and experience and a coaching track record second to none.

Brad Ness, Troy Sachs and the team's other elder statesmen had experienced the sting of losing to Canada when the Rollers had been trounced in the Athens final four years earlier. They didn't want to experience that pain again, and I was determined not to let any of them down. We'd come so far, there was no turning back now.

The National Indoor Stadium had been hosting capacity crowds of 12,000 almost every night since the tournament began and there was not an empty seat for the final on the evening of 16 September 2008.

I watched the start of the match from the sidelines, chewing gum nonstop and constantly looking over at Ben, hoping he'd throw me on as soon as possible. We scored first, thanks to Shaun Norris, but Canada edged ahead late in the first quarter and led 17–16 at the break. I came on midway through the second quarter, with Canada ahead 25–22, and I was into the action straight away, passing to Shaun to score. The first shot I took I missed by *heaps*! It was almost an airball! Not exactly the way you want to start.

Canada had increased their lead to 4 as the first half ended. We were pretty nervous, and so were our families, friends and fans, if the looks on their faces were anything to go by. As usual when I compete, my family was more nervous than I was. It must be tough watching someone you love compete at the highest level, having absolutely no control while you sit in the stands and watch on.

We kept fighting and had crept ahead early in the final quarter but we were keenly aware that the Canadians only needed a sniff of the basket to hit the front.

With seventy-three seconds left in the match, the Canadians were just two good shots away from levelling the score. Our defence had to be tight, and it was. We held firm. Then Troy Sachs landed two final buckets to seal the deal

72–60, raising his long, powerful arms in triumph at the buzzer.

After a long and gruelling journey, the Rollers had come out on top. The gold medal was ours!

It's really hard to describe exactly what it felt like. All around me, big, tough men, guys who had been through hell and back to get there, burst into tears and embraced each other. We'd all given up so much to be there. We were unpaid, we'd left our families, skipped work or school, sacrificed so much to win that gold medal, and we'd done it.

We draped ourselves in Australian flags as our friends and families cheered almost loudly enough to bring the roof down.

A reporter put a microphone in front of my face. 'This is awesome!' I enthused. 'To be seventeen and a Paralympic gold medallist – it doesn't get any better than this. We knew we'd been playing well all week, but I think we were at the very top of our game tonight.' I still believe that, and I'm lucky to remain the youngest ever male wheelchair basketball gold medallist to this day.

Every one of us had ridden the emotional rollercoaster that comes with having a disability. All of us had to overcome major obstacles to reach this moment. Many of us probably thought the day might never come. I know I did. If you'd asked thirteen-year-old Dylan, who was embarrassed about who he was, he would've said his life probably wouldn't amount to anything. These challenges and, in some cases, terrible tragedies had been the fuel to propel every single one of us. And now we were the best team in the world.

Brad called the team together. We sat in a circle, dripping with sweat. 'It's a great moment for everyone,' he said. 'Enjoy this wonderful feeling, guys. There've been a lot of fine Aussie teams over the years, and now the Rollers are one of them.'

My family had been cheering themselves hoarse in the stands and now they ran down. Dad hugged me so tightly, my god, he nearly choked me to death! I actually couldn't breathe, and could feel through every part of my body just how proud he was of me. Zack, too, was overcome, tears running down his face. It was only the second time in my life I'd seen my big brother cry. The first was when I was six and I'd hit him in the head with a spanner (trust me, he deserved it). The second time was when I won a gold medal. Seeing how much it meant to them made it an incredibly special moment for all of us.

\*\*\*

Being up on the dais with my eleven teammates as gold medals were placed around our necks was one of the best moments of my life. I'd imagined plenty of times how it would feel to be there as the Australian flag was raised and the national anthem rose up out of the stadium speakers, but nothing matched the head-spinning reality.

The moment the anthem started to play I lost it. I'm not much of a crier (unless I'm watching *The Green Mile* – damn, it always gets me when John Coffey is put to rest), but the emotion of the moment took hold of me and I was crying like a little toddler. I was proud of myself, but more proud of the guys sitting next to me. I was relatively new to the team, but these guys had given their whole lives to be there, some almost two decades of service. To share it with them was very special.

After the ceremony, with the great weight of competition off our shoulders, it was time to celebrate like never before. With beers flowing, we rewatched the game in one of our apartments in the village. It was a tradition that the boys smoked cigars when celebrating a big win. It was the first time I'd smoked anything and, not knowing what to do (and trying to impress the others), I took a huge drag and inhaled. Big mistake. I vomited everywhere, still wearing my gold medal around my neck. Smooth.

The next day, feeling a touch under the weather, we decided to toast the victory with a beer or two and gold medals on the Great Wall of China. Perfect, yeah?

Every team at the Paralympics had a translator assigned to them. We had a guy whose Western name was Lance. So we explained to Lance what we wanted to do and he set about organising it. Eight of us ended up going – the others had celebrated a bit hard the night before. First stop was a tiny convenience store, where Brad picked up some supplies for our trip. Then, with our gold medals around our necks, we set off on the hour-long drive to the Wall.

Four of the party could walk, using prosthetic legs, but the other four, including me, were in wheelchairs. So it was a shock to arrive at the Great Wall and realise that Lance had taken us not to the part where an elevator is provided for disabled access, but to a seemingly uninhabited area where the only way up was at least 300 really steep stairs that looked as though they'd been untouched since the 1200s.

We stared at the stairs, which seemed to go on forever, then stared at Lance. 'Mate, what's goin' on?' someone asked. 'How the hell is this going to work?'

People with disabilities are often good at problem solving. So, in the end, we decided to make the best of it. We couldn't magic up an elevator but we found an alternative solution: paying four Chinese guys $100 each to carry us and our chairs to the top, one by one.

Nothing about the experience was what we had expected, but it turned out far better than if we'd gone to the section with the elevator, a spot where thousands of tourists gather. Here we were virtually by ourselves, just eight mates drinking our beers and brandishing our gold medals on the Great Wall of China. On top of the world. It was a moment I'll cherish forever.

That night, back in Beijing, the party continued. There was a Western bar in the city called China Doll and my mate Tristan Knowles and I went there in a cab with Cobi Crispin and Clare Burzynski from the Australian women's basketball team, the Gliders.

Later, Clare bundled me into a taxi for the ride back to the hotel, but too much wine and bouncing along Chinese roads at 90 kilometres an hour was a bad combination. Before I knew it I was vomiting out the open door of the moving taxi, my gold medal dangling just above the bitumen. Luckily my friends dragged me back to safety inside the car. What an idiot!

I woke up the next morning with no idea how I'd gotten home and, more importantly, *without* my gold medal. I couldn't believe it – gold medals are *never* replaced. I found out later Clare had taken it for safe-keeping.

The whole team was still floating on clouds when we arrived back in Australia. Mum was ecstatic about our success, and so was Chelsy and all of my mates. Mum had followed our games closely, cheering at home in front of the television. One of my best mates, James Carlile, hosted a viewing party for the final, so all my friends and family back home could watch it together. I made sure Mum knew how much I appreciated all the time and effort she'd put in to help me get there.

Brighton Grammar had a big banner out the front of the school celebrating the win. So did a nearby pub, the New Bay in Brighton, where we had a bit of a party. The place was heaving – there must have been 500 people there. I brought my gold medal with me – that thing had not left my sight for more than a week. Everyone was amazed how heavy it was. They also wanted to know what the braille writing on the medal said. In fact, it's the number one question I'm asked about the medal to this day.

My response is always the same. 'I don't know! I'm not f*cking blind!'

People assume that when you have one disability you can do all the disabilities. No – I read with my eyes. And to this day, I have no idea what the braille says.

\*\*\*

My Year 12 exams were due to start just a few weeks after I returned from Beijing. So much of my year had been taken up with training camps and overseas competitions that I'd lost sixty-nine days, equivalent to nearly a term and a half, of face-to-face teaching time. I needed to put in a massive effort to catch up and prepare for my VCE end-of-school exams. Plenty of mates had offered to help me with study notes for the classes I'd missed (Thanks boys! You saved my arse!) and, in the end, I did really well. My parents were super proud of the gold medal, but I think they were also very relieved that it hadn't come at the expense of a leaving mark that would get me into university in Australia.

My school had played a huge part in helping me become the person I am today. So I was extremely honoured when in 2012 I was inducted into the school's Hall of Fame at the age of twenty-one. I'd never forgotten that my experience at Brighton was made possible by the incredible generosity of Paul and Christine Comport. We hadn't met while I was at school at their request, but we were lucky to catch up a few years down the track. They're very modest people, but without them, who knows, maybe I wouldn't be doing the things I'm doing today.

Thanks to the Comports, I'd been able to aim high and achieve my dreams. And as far as I was concerned, this was just the beginning ...

# 6

# *taking it to the next level*

I SUSPECT A LOT of people underestimate just how much work goes into competing at the highest level. I know I did. The early mornings, the gruelling hours of training every day, the isolation of practising by yourself in empty stadiums, the immense body soreness. Don't get me wrong, it's all worth it, but after a while it gets tiresome.

So, the afterglow of the Paralympics – on top of finishing school forever – felt incredible. I'd worked my arse off academically and on the sporting field for so long, it was nice to finally let my hair down.

It was the perfect time too. Summer had arrived, and I finally got to experience a bunch of firsts I thought may never happen. Disabilities can prevent people attending all kinds of events. Establishments and organisations can forget (sometimes they deliberately turn a blind eye) to make their premises accessible to everyone, which means a lot of people miss out. Growing up, I was one of those people. Some things are just really tough, and often can't be changed too much. Going to the beach is one of them. It sucks when you're in a wheelchair. You can't move, you get bogged, and you find sand in places you shouldn't for weeks to come.

But with a bit of smart thinking and hard work a lot of events and places can be made accessible. Ever since I was about thirteen and discovered my love for music, I'd always dreamt of attending music festivals. On paper, they always looked like a challenge that might be too tough to overcome, but I never really gave up on the idea. For one thing, when I'm told I might not be able to do something, I want to do it even more. Also, there's something special about the vibe at huge events, whether they're sport, music or whatever. They're places where people leave behind their normal, everyday lives – and often their biases and inhibitions as well – and come together to enjoy a shared passion, sometimes with up to 100,000 people.

So when the basketball year was done, and school had finished in December 2008, I thought I'd give a music festival a crack. My first ever festival was relatively small (about 10,000 people). It was called NeverEverLand and was staged at Melbourne's Myer Music Bowl. It had rained for three days straight beforehand, which made getting around on wheels even more of a challenge (I watch the weather forecast like a hawk before a festival, because rain equals mud and mud *sucks* when you're in a chair). As usual, though, I was surrounded by an incredible group of friends who had my back. Some of the names on the bill were The Presets, Tame Impala and Cut Copy and I loved every minute. It was hard to see much of what was happening on stage, though, because I sit so low, and the venue hadn't provided higher viewing areas.

Still, NeverEverLand whet my appetite for more, and two weeks later I went with a big group of friends down the Great Ocean Road to the town of Lorne, home to the legendary three-day Falls Music Festival.

Where the Myer Music Bowl has concrete paths and disabled-access toilets, Falls is a true outdoor festival. It's held in a forest, festival goers have to camp out in tents and the facilities are what you'd call rustic, but that's half the fun. I knew the hilly terrain would be tough to negotiate in a wheelchair, and I'd never even been inside a tent before. (I'd always skipped school camps because they usually involved hiking or other outdoor activities and so were never very accessible. Still, when report time came I always strangely got an A – I think the poor guy didn't know what else to write!) But I wanted to prove to myself I could do it. I'm so glad I did. I loved it.

At times, it was pretty gnarly to get around, especially given the place was all hills and grass, coupled with the fact we had a few beers or ten every day, but it was incredible. There was also this vibe where everyone wanted to make sure the people around them were having a good time. The sloping ground made it a bit easier to get a good view from my chair and I felt totally included, on an equal basis with everyone else. It was Falls that really ignited my love of music festivals, which has since played a huge part in my life (and about which you'll hear more later on).

\*\*\*

The New Year kicked off with the thrilling and unexpected news that, along with my Roller teammates, I was to receive an Order of Australia Medal in the 2009 Australia Day Awards. Having just turned eighteen, it was extremely humbling to be given an OAM alongside leading humanitarians, scientists, military officers, philanthropists and captains of industry. I had to google what the hell it meant, though – I was so young, I don't remember ever meeting anyone with an OAM before!

I was able to take Mum and Zack with me to Government House to receive this huge honour, which was only fitting because I'd never have qualified for it without their unstinting support.

There were so many incredible Australians there, I felt overwhelmed and I wondered whether I deserved it. One woman (whose name I later found out was Barbara Roberts) received an OAM for saving the eyesight of countless people in New Guinea and Southeast Asia. It seemed far more important than shooting a basketball into a hoop.

My citation said, 'Mr Alcott won a Gold Medal at the Beijing 2008 Paralympic Games in the Men's Wheelchair Basketball. He represented Australia in an exemplary manner and brought great credit to himself, the Australian team and the nation.'

Receiving an Order of Australia medal remains one of my proudest moments. I've always been super proud of being Australian, so to be part of such a select group of amazing Australians was humbling. It still means a lot to me to this day.

\*\*\*

After a well-earned break, basketball was back on the agenda. The Rollers were officially the best side in the world and we wanted to stay number one. A lot of national sports work on a four-year cycle, built around the Olympics or Paralympics. But basketball operates on a two-year cycle, with the World Wheelchair Basketball Championships falling between the Paralympics. So we worked hard on our game in the lead-up to the Visa Paralympic World Cup (an invitational tournament held every year), which would be held in Manchester that May.

There were a few changes to the team. Troy Sachs had retired and so had Brendan Dowler, one of our low-point players and an all-time great. Brendan retiring was a big loss to the team – his experience and caring nature had brought a lot to the number 14 jersey. Then, seemingly out of nowhere, a fantastic guy named Jeremy Doyle came along, a guy I grew pretty close to.

JD and I had first met at a tennis tournament back when I was sixteen. He lived in New South Wales and was a bit older than me, but we got on well from the moment we met. Safe to say, while he always had a crack, tennis wasn't his strong suit. But when it came to basketball, he shone.

A real workhorse and fighter, JD was exactly what we needed. Like me, he was classified a one-point player, having been paraplegic since the age of four, when he was the victim of a hit and run. He was small in stature and by his own admission had been overweight when he first took up basketball just a couple of years earlier. But he turned himself into a top athlete through sheer grit and determination – qualities that characterised his life and his game.

JD had built a big set of shoulders and arms and could push hard on the court for a full forty minutes if he had to. He was so talented that he'd only spent one year playing in the national league before he was picked to attend a training camp and chosen to play for his country.

He made his debut for Australia in that series and quickly became a valuable member of the team. He was very smart: he soon picked up the nuances of low-point play and working with our big guys. His role on the court was to do the dirty work, all the tough defending and blocking, and he gave it everything he had, never backing down, no matter how large or intimidating the opposition was. He was also a legend to have around – one of those people who, no matter what life throws at them, always seemed to be smiling.

The new team line-up gelled really well and we beat Germany, Great Britain and the USA to take out the title.

Back home in Australia, our status as Beijing gold medallists gave us the leverage to shine a light on our sport. Interest in Paralympic sport seemed to be growing generally, and we noticed more media coverage and larger national league crowds. So the Rollers hadn't played in a major event domestically in almost a decade, since the 2000 Sydney Paralympics. But with the support of ABC-TV, Australia hosted the Rollers' World Challenge in Sydney that July. It was a great showcase for wheelchair basketball, letting sports fans see up close what an exciting game it is. The success of the tournament itself was capped off by Australia winning the final in front of a packed home crowd, defeating Canada in a reprise of the

Beijing duel. I had to miss it, however, because I'd injured my shoulder and needed to be fit for the Under-23 World Championships in Paris.

Playing in a junior team is always fun. Everyone's a similar age, so when I was asked to caption the Under-23s, I was ecstatic. It was a great team, and I made some really good friends on that trip, including one of my best mates to this day, Jannik Blair. Jannik, or 'the Bizzness' as he likes to call himself (deadset, he made up that nickname himself and somehow it stuck), and I started our playing career together in the Victorian junior wheelchair basketball team.

How the Bizz ended up in a chair is one of the more crazy stories. He's from a place called Horsham, in country Victoria, and is extremely proud of it. Jannik was a normal kid who loved the farm and playing footy, but that all changed when he was twelve. Jannik was racing his grandfather's ute in a dirt paddock on the family property when the ute flipped and rolled. He wasn't wearing a seatbelt and was thrown out of the window, breaking his back and wrist and suffering a collapsed lung.

A week-long induced coma was followed by three months of rehabilitation, but due to the damage to his spine, he was now a paraplegic. Jannik was lucky to have an incredible family just like mine, who were able to support him during that tough time and help him become the legendary bloke he is today.

When I reflect on what happened to Jannik, I always wonder what would be 'easier': being born with a disability or having an accident and ending up with one. It's a question I'm asked often, and it's a hard one to answer. Would you rather know what it's like to feel the grass between your toes then lose it, or never know? What I do know is, going through that trauma at the age of twelve would've been extremely tough, but the Bizz came out stronger than ever.

As happened to me, a rehab worker and family friend told Jannik how life-changing wheelchair sport could be, and he threw himself into it, participating in para-triathlons, wheelchair basketball, para-table tennis and wheelchair tennis (kind of – I used to carry him when we played doubles together).

I was only a year and a bit older than Jannik, and we bonded straight away. Though he denies it, I like to think I took him under my wing, and just like I used to copy Zack, Jannik liked to do what I did. If I started wearing a headband, he started wearing a headband; and if I started wearing skinny black jeans on the weekend, so did Jannik.

Anyway, Jannik and I became the best of mates. Our first overseas trip together was to England for some practice games against the UK's under-23 team. Results went our way, and we moved on to Paris for the Under-23 World Championships.

Heading into the championships, we were third favourites. We started out well, beating Brazil, Malaysia, South Africa and Turkey before losing to the eventual winners, the USA. In the play-off for bronze, we were knocked over by Sweden with a half-court shot on the buzzer. I felt pretty flat about falling short of a medal – I was the captain and I wanted to do everyone proud. But there would be plenty of opportunities to make amends down the track.

After the games, I headed back to Australia for arthroscopic shoulder surgery to clear up a niggle I sustained while training for the World Junior Championships (or lifting my chair out of the car – to this day I'm still not sure). The two-month recovery absolutely and utterly sucked. There I was, a guy in a wheelchair who couldn't use his legs and who relies fully on his upper body, and I'd temporarily lost the use of one of my arms. I was *screwed*. I couldn't do anything, and I had no independence. It was a tough time, but my family and Chelsy did an amazing job looking after me. (Even if Chelsy did borrow my car for the duration and ended up crashing it into the back of a BMW. Smooth, Chels.) I was trying to recover as quickly as I could, not only so I could get my life back but also to prepare for my move to America. I had been awarded a scholarship at the University of Illinois. Luckily I did recover pretty fast, and in September 2009 I made the move to America.

Situated in Champaign-Urbana, about 200 kilometres south of Chicago, the University of Illinois was the first university in the United States to establish a wheelchair basketball team way back in 1948. Canadian national coach Mike Frogley had coached there for more than a decade.

It offered its 45,000 students a smorgasbord of subjects. I was lucky enough to be offered a near-full wheelchair basketball scholarship, with my tuition and board covered, but I still had to study and maintain good grades. I chose Commerce, one of the more serious courses on offer in a selection that included weightlifting. Another subject I signed up for was 'food critiquing' – a subject where they gave you fifty bucks to eat lunch at a restaurant and then write a review. Not bad.

I'd been completely sold on the idea of going to Illinois from the moment the possibility was raised when I attended the Illinois training camp in 2007, but my parents had been worried. I was an adult now, but it was a long way away and there was the freezing Chicago winters to deal with, so I could understand their concerns. I was heading off to the other side of the world where I had no family or friends. What if I needed help? But in the end Mum and Dad could see it was way too good an opportunity to pass up.

When I headed off in September, Dad flew over with me to help me get settled in. I know he found it very hard to say goodbye when it was time to go. 'Don't get into trouble, be safe and call me if you run out of money,' was all he could get out as we hugged. Dad knew I'd be fine and would definitely be keen on a little trouble, especially with Zack's 21-year-old ID in my pocket. It was one of the very handy things about looking like Zack's twin, and his IDs had worked a treat ever since I was sixteen. (Naughty, I know.)

When I walked onto the campus for the first time, I just couldn't believe the size of it. It was *huge*, like a city, with dorms, apartments, bars, restaurants, nightclubs, parks and recreation areas, huge fraternities and sororities – even its very own strip club (huh?!). The thing that stood out most to me, though, was the size of the sports stadiums. Just across from my dorm room was the football stadium, and, no joke, with a capacity of 70,000 people it wasn't much smaller than the Melbourne Cricket Ground! *Surely they won't fill that*, I thought when I first saw it, but, boy, was I wrong – it sold out every week.

Just a few months into my stay, an early autumn cold snap came slamming into campus like a wall of ice. Basketball practice started at 6 am, but as I was the rookie of the team, my job was to get there early and unpack all the wheelchairs before training began. Sometimes I'd wake at 5 am to find a foot of snow outside my dorm room. At first I thought it was pretty cool to see so much snow, but after about a week I was over it. Even rugged up in layers of clothing, it was often so cold I genuinely thought I might freeze to death. I don't know how people ever get used to the winters where minus 20°C is standard and it hits minus 30°C if you factor in wind chill.

One morning my hatred for the snow came to a head. There I was, rolling along to practice when my chair started to feel wonky. Suddenly one of the wheels fell off, depositing me in deep snow in below-freezing temperatures. I found out later that they put salt on the roads to stop water freezing – not a common practice down in St Kilda. Over time, the salt had rusted through one of my front caster wheels. I was in deep trouble, and had to do a wheelie on my back wheels all the way to my dorm – about a kilometre. (Once, in Year 8, I did a wheelie during an entire religious education class – sixty minutes without dropping it!) At the dorm door, I needed help to get in. Luckily, I had my phone on me and help arrived quickly, or I'd never have made my nineteenth birthday.

Being based in the US gave me lots of opportunities to travel for pleasure, and I took every chance I could. In November 2009 I popped over to London for a week with another Australian who was studying at Illinois, Shelley Chaplin, who'd won a silver medal in Beijing with Australia's female wheelchair basketball team, the Gliders. Then I headed over to Paris with some school mates who happened to be in the UK. I also escaped the cold during spring break with a quick trip down to Cancun, Mexico, with a couple of other mates from school for spring break. It was great to have the time to really look around, which you never get to do when you're in a new city to compete.

One of the few downsides of being based in the US was being so far from family and friends. Chelsy and I had hoped our relationship would continue while I was away, but distance made it tough. She was killing it volunteering throughout South America while I was doing my thing at college but distance made it hard, and eventually we conceded it was time to move on. But, even though our relationship didn't work out long-term, I am forever thankful that Chels came into my life, and to this day we remain incredibly close friends and I'm proud of everything she does.

\*\*\*

On the court at college, our team was something special. We went the whole season undefeated, and in March 2010 we were crowned the Intercollegiate National Wheelchair Basketball Champions.

Then, the following month, Zack came to visit, and after eight months away from home I sure was happy to see him. He'd recently completed his marketing degree at RMIT University in Melbourne and, having just come out of a long-term relationship, he was ready to enjoy a three-month boys' own adventure around the country with a group of seven mates. Zack had never really been overseas before, apart from on family trips, and we were pumped to be doing some travelling together. He spent a week sleeping on the floor of my dorm and, with basketball finished, we got fairly loose. In fact, one night Zack had a few too many wines at a party and ended up in the *very* sketchy side of town, and not knowing where he was. Luckily I heard his phone calls or he might still be there.

After our week together in Illinois, Zack and I decided to head to California to tackle one of the most renowned festivals on earth – Coachella. Coachella takes place in the desert in Palm Springs, about 200 kilometres southeast of Los Angeles, and it's justly regarded as a must-do for any music festival fan. Crowds of more than 90,000 people partied and soaked up the good times as 120 bands, DJs and artists played on five stages.

Zack and I were there with a group of mates and we loved the music and the whole vibe. The sheer size of Coachella was impressive – it was like an Australian music festival on steroids. But the crowds were so dense, it was always tough to get to a position near the front where I could see – I've never been one to sit at the back of the crowd and not get involved.

I always felt bad when my friends would say, 'It's all right, Dyl, we can wait at the back', as if they felt obliged. I didn't want to take away from their festival experience, so I'd always surge through the masses to a spot where they could see. Meanwhile, all I was looking at was a sea of arses.

Midway through the festival, I'd had enough of missing out on all the action, and my friends wanted to get me involved too. So, on a whim during the set of one of my favourite rappers – Jay-Z – Zack and my good friends Charlie Cotton and Rory Hancock decided to pick me up and crowd-surf me in my wheelchair. I'd never done it before and I was shitting myself! But, my god, the view up there was indescribable. Everyone started screaming and cheering, and the adrenaline really started pumping. It was legitimately the best seat in the house.

Then Jay-Z spotted me and stopped his song. 'Hey, give it up for that guy!' he shouted, pointing. Life made.

From that day on, for me, wheelchair crowd-surfing was born. A few photos from the event went viral online and after that I started seeing a lot more people giving it at crack. Sure, it's pretty dangerous (I've only been dropped once – stop what you're doing and search Wheelchair Crowdsurf Fail on YouTube. Yes, that's me and no, I didn't end up any more disabled than I already am). But, hey, you gotta live your best life, don't you?

\*\*\*

My short break with Zack over, and it was back to training as I got ready to join the Rollers to vie for the World Championship in Birmingham in July 2010. We had form, having claimed gold in Beijing, won the Paralympic World Cup a year later and come out on top in seventeen of our previous nineteen matches.

The core of the team that had been at the Paralympics was boosted by the welcome addition of Jeremy 'JD' Doyle, Bill Latham and John McPhail.

The fact that JD was there was remarkable. He'd been diagnosed with bladder cancer earlier in the year and after undergoing surgery and treatment, had fought his way back into the Australian team. He set the benchmark for courage. To this day I still can't believe he made it there, and still can't believe how well he played.

Bill Latham, whose grandfather Tedda Courtney played rugby league for Australia, was another whose determination to achieve was absolutely inspiring. He was five when he was run over by a tractor and slasher on his family's property near Coffs Harbour. He suffered a fractured skull and severe damage to both legs, requiring four months of acute hospital care in Sydney. His recovery was long and slow and the damage done was so great that he finally had to have his left leg amputated at age thirteen. Resilient and determined, he was in Birmingham ready to help the Rollers make sporting history by claiming Australia's first World Championship in the sport.

Seven of the twelve players in our squad, including me, were playing professionally overseas at the time: Justin Eveson was with Galatasaray, Turkey; Bill Latham with Once Andalusia in Spain; Shaun Norris with Fundosa Grupo in Italy; Brad Ness and Michael Hartnett with Lottomatica Elecom Rome; and Tristan Knowles with Valladolid in Spain. Back home in Australia, Grant Mizens and JD were with the Wenty League Wheelkings in Sydney; Brett Stibners was with the Wollongong Rollerhawks; John McPhail was with the West Sydney Razorbacks; and Tige Simmons was with the Brisbane Spinning Bullets. Unfortunately, Jannik Blair just missed out, but he'd make up for it in years to come.

It did make our preparation disjointed but it was great to hear the stories everyone brought back, as they made a life for themselves playing professional wheelchair basketball.

In July 2010 we hit Birmingham for our assault on the World Championships. The preliminary rounds went as expected. We beat France, but it was a tough grind against a well-drilled and disciplined team. Still, everyone played their part and it was the type of game we needed to kick us off. Next up was Turkey, then Algeria and Mexico, all of which we despatched pretty easily.

Then, five days into the competition, we faced reigning world champions Canada. They opened the game with a blistering 6–0 run, but were missing Patrick Anderson, their star player from their 2008 Beijing Paralympic silver medal team, and we ended up taking the match 67–49. It was only a pool game, but it was still a real thrill to get one over our greatest rivals. For me it was especially thrilling, as it was the first time in a major championship that I'd started for Australia. A dream come true.

In the quarter-finals we pushed hard against Poland, forcing them into errors and dominating on offense. The final score was 68–34 but the lopsided nature of that game was a false indication of what we would need to do to triumph overall.

Any thoughts that we were untouchable were banished in our semi-final against the undefeated Americans. It turned out to be a cliff-hanger, the most exciting and toughest game of the championship, and one of the best games I'd ever played in my life.

After leading at the first break, we had to play catch-up for most of the remainder of the match. With two minutes left in the second term, the USA had bounced away to a 9-point lead. We fought back to be within 2 points in the third quarter but by the final break we were down by 8 and, as always when the Americans were winning, they were enjoying themselves, chanting, yelling and talking shit. But a scoring burst by our own Tristan Knowles cut their lead to 4 points, leading to an incredibly tense final seven minutes as we cut their lead down to 2 points. But soon they were back with a 4-point margin. We managed to shave that back to a margin of 2, then just 1. With about a minute and a half to go, the game was tied and it could have gone either way. With the shot clock winding down, I made a deep, ill-advised, very low percentage 3-point attempt. *What are you doing!* I remember thinking to myself as I took the shot. *The boys will kill you!* But hey, as Michael Jordan said, 'You miss 100 per cent of the shots you don't take.' So I shot it, and SWISH! It was perfect. Nothing but net. I don't think anyone in the stadium could believe it, me included. One-pointers never take shots like that. It was one of the stupidest yet proudest moments of my career.

We were now up by 3 and we never looked back, going on to win with a score of 68–58.

Our massive effort in the final quarter of that game made us confident we could handle France in the gold medal tussle on 17 July, despite the tough battle they'd given us in the tournament opener. A one–two play between Shaun Norris and Brad Ness saw us up 6–0 and before long 10–0. The French finally got on the board and worked to close the gap but we led 20–15 at the first break and 45–29 at half-time. By the time the clock showed just forty-nine seconds remaining, we were ahead 76–69.

In desperation, France tried their chances from long range, but with our fans chanting wildly, we pulled it off, taking Australia's first ever World Championship title in wheelchair basketball!

Later, along with Justin Eveson and Shaun Norris, I was named in the Championship All Star Five as the best player in my position at the tournament. Any one of the Rollers could have been up there and, given the standard of the players from all the teams, it was a tremendous accolade, one I wouldn't have come close to winning without the help of my teammates. I'd joined the Rollers as a boy, so petrified and in awe of them that all I wanted to do was not let them down. Now I'd been voted in the top five in the world. It had been an incredible journey and I felt there was plenty more to come.

# 7

# *birds of a feather flock together*

IT WAS TO BE a four-week jaunt through Southeast Asia. Fifteen of us were going, all old school mates, and we were ready to let loose and have fun.

I was often a little worried about accessibility when I made travel plans – bathrooms are key to living an independent life and some of the bathrooms around that neck of the woods are questionable, to stay the least! So to start with I hadn't even been sure I'd go. I wanted to, but I didn't want to be a burden on my mates and I didn't want to slow them down.

But, as always, my friends came to the rescue. My great mate Tim Biggin, plus Scott, Antoine, Ryan, Max, Ed and the rest assured me we'd be able to handle it, that we'd figure it out and be fine. So I decided to lock it in.

We kicked off in Thailand in January 2011. I'd been there before with Chelsy to meet her dad, who was living in Thailand at the time, but this trip was shaping up to be a little different. This time my mates and I would be staying in hostels, doing it on the cheap, partying on beaches – everything I'd assumed I wouldn't be able to do.

Our first stop was the full moon party in Koh Phangan, a destination very popular for young Australians. The party takes place on a long white beach with bars all the way down. I was *extremely* nervous about the sand, because, as I said, sand and wheelchairs are not the best of mates. If it was soft, I was screwed. I'll never forget getting to that beach and touching the sand. 'It's hard! It's hard!" I screamed. I can't tell you how relieved I was, because it meant I'd be able to join in and be independent. Five nights of partying in nothing but body paint and fluorescent board shorts followed, some of them all-nighters. That party was loose – if you haven't been, I recommend it!

Within the larger group, Tim and I and another of our great friends, Ryan Burge, made a three-man bet that whatever one person in our trio did, the other two had to do too, no matter what. It stemmed from one of our favourite sayings, 'Birds of a feather flock together.' So after I'd said no piercings, naturally, twenty minutes later, Tim and Ryan went and got their noses pierced, meaning I had to follow suit. Let's just say we all looked like idiots.

The fifteen of us travelled everywhere together doing all sorts of adventurous things: kayaking and cruising around islands, touring through isolated villages, drinking and enjoying being together.

People were amazed when they saw Tim, Ryan or one of the other boys carry me down a little plank to a small boat, say, while someone else carried my wheelchair. But it worked. The ability to do all sorts of adventure activities together trumped any inconvenience, and I'm so grateful to those guys for making it such a great trip.

In the Phi Phi Islands off Phuket the three of us got matching ankle tattoos of three little 'seagulls', a symbol of birds of a feather flocking together (much to the dismay of Tim, especially since they looked like they'd been drawn by a four-year-old, or like the M from the McDonald's symbol).

After Thailand, we headed to Vientiane in Laos and the banks of the Mekong River, a 4300-kilometre long brown ribbon of silt that cuts through Tibet, China, Myanmar, Laos, Thailand, Cambodia and Vietnam.

The river was one big playground for travellers. Young guys and girls were swinging from Tarzan ropes into the water, or setting off on tubing pub crawls, where you lie on inflatable tubes as the current carries you down the river and guys with ropes haul you in to the different bars along the way.

Tubing really had death written all over it, but I decided to give it a crack. So Tim and Ryan put me into one tube and my wheelchair in another. I don't know what I would have done if the chair had sunk or floated off into the distance. It was an incredibly stupid move, but, whatever, it was worth the risk. Facilities for the disabled aren't exactly first rate in Laos, and even with my mates to help me, I reckon it would have been a pretty uncomfortable ride home to Australia without my chair. As it turned out, I had a sensational time.

As I said, I am forever grateful to all of my friends on the trip who made it possible, because it showed me that 'backpacking' around pretty inaccessible countries was possible. When we'd researched this trip, there was absolutely no information available in terms of tips or tricks on backpacking in a wheelchair. Nothing. But what I found was that, with a little bit of planning, a positive attitude and resilience in the hard times, anything was really possible. Travelling is one of the greatest gifts you can give yourself, and everyone should experience it no matter who you are, what your abilities are or what your situation is.

Back home in Melbourne, I kept the party going at another music festival – Soundwave at the Showgrounds. Late in the afternoon American rockers Queens of the Stone Age were on. They were kicking arse and, once again, I was wheelchair crowd-surfing. Crowd-surfing had become a real buzz for me. No one ever seemed to mind lifting me up – it was all just part of the we're-all-in-this-together vibe. It's a wild ride up there and the rewards outweigh the risks many times over.

Anyway, there I was in the best seat in the house when Josh Homme, the band's lead singer, spotted me above the 15,000-strong crowd. 'We're not playing until he's on stage with us!' he yelled. Next thing I knew I'd been passed 100 metres along and two massive security guards were lifting me in my chair up onto the stage next to Josh.

As the band played 'No One Knows', I played air guitar, as you do. 'You're one bad-ass motherf*cker,' Josh said, which, trust me, is the highest form of praise from him. It was an absolute buzz.

After the set, I went backstage and the band invited me to see their show in Adelaide. Sadly, I had to decline. I was needed back on the basketball court.

\*\*\*

I spent a lot of the next eighteen months on planes, catching glimpses of cities as we went between hotels and stadiums. First stop, in April 2011, was a Rollers training camp at Varese in northern Italy, not far from Cantù, where we'd beaten the local team a year earlier. Many of our best players stayed in Australia in order to give the opportunity to some younger guys and see if they were ready to go to the next level. But even though our first match was against the Italian national team, which was virtually at full strength, we won the contest in a hit-out that was invaluable for the squad. The Italians fought back, though, and we lost two subsequent games.

Still, we came out of the warm-up tournament with a lot of positives, and the belief that, at full strength, we were a good chance to win gold at the London 2012 Paralympics. Back home, we reconvened and trained together at the Australian Institute of Sport in Canberra and in June had a clean-sweep there in a Tri-series against South Africa and the Netherlands, winning all six of our games. Then, in November, we played in the Asia Oceania Zone Championship in South Korea, which was a qualifying tournament for the Paralympics. This was a big one – if we didn't perform here, we could miss out on qualifying for the Paralympics altogether.

Luckily, we were a tight group, with everyone playing an important part, and we hit the ground running. In pretty impressive fashion we beat China, Chinese Taipei, New Zealand, Iraq and South Korea, then to cap it off we rolled Japan, giving us a perfect, unbeaten tournament. We were in!

Much of our success was due to the intensive training we'd put in over the previous six months at the Australian Institute of Sport. We knew how important it was for us to raise the bar even higher for London. After all, we were no longer the hunter but the hunted, and everyone was chasing after us. The best thing we could do was focus on our game.

Our other secret weapon was our fighting qualities – on the court as a team and off the court as individuals. But in the middle of 2011 we'd received news that rocked us all and made us question whether those qualities would be enough to get us through.

We'd all endured large doses of hardship during our lives, but maybe none more than the ever-smiling Jeremy Doyle. He'd fought back from the childhood hit and run that put him in a wheelchair to become one of the best at his chosen sport in the country. He'd then come through cancer surgery and treatment to win a World Championship with us in 2010.

Then, in July 2011, JD had learnt that his cancer was back and worse than before. This time it was in his pelvis and liver.

JD had to immediately withdraw from the Rollers' lead-up events, including our trip to Korea. Ben Ettridge kept a positive spin on it, and told JD that his place on the Australian team for London would be waiting for him when he was right again. Through it all, JD kept smiling, making everybody feel at ease with his situation. He never complained and always put other people first. I really hoped that I'd be able to share the court with him again.

All through chemotherapy treatment, which the doctors hoped would shrink the cancer, JD talked about playing again, and he seemed more concerned about preparing for London than the painful, uncomfortable treatment that he was going through. But in October, JD told us that the cancer 'had him beat'. He'd fought with everything he had, but late in November he caught an infection which turned septic and he passed away in the arms of his wife, Melanie, on 18 December 2011. He was twenty-eight years old.

'When you were around him you couldn't help but be happy,' Melanie later told a journalist. Ben Ettridge summed up the mood of our whole devastated team. 'As a person, JD was first class,' Ben said. 'For someone who'd had so much adversity throughout his life, for him to be as successful as he was, he was an amazing guy and an inspiration to everyone that he came in touch with ... As a teammate, there was no one better. He was first to ask how you were doing on any given day, was the first guy to send you a text or a phone call if something was going wrong or if something was going right, he was never far away from anyone ... Even when we saw him last week, he was still like "When is the next camp? Which of the boys need to do more work? Who do I need to send an email to, to fire them up?" He was more worried about everyone else than his own situation. He was a rare human being to be like that.'

As I write these words, seven years have passed since we last saw JD's smiling face. I hope he's resting well.

\*\*\*

Losing JD devastated us all, but as the 2012 new year began, we knew we had to stay focused on getting ready for the London Paralympic Games. It's what JD would have wanted.

Jannik Blair and I had moved into an apartment in St Kilda in order to train together every day. I'd also transferred to a commerce degree at Melbourne University, which I was on track to complete.

But not long after, in March 2012, my career, and nearly my life, was derailed thanks to a freak accident. It was one unfortunate moment of craziness that changed my life drastically forever. It happened while I was with Zack at one of his work functions. Somebody I knew came over to say hello, and, safe to say, he'd had a few drinks under his belt. He came up behind my wheelchair, grabbed the back of it and tried to pick it up with me in it. As he did so, he accidentally pulled the chair from under me, and I tumbled onto the floor. Unfortunately, the floor was covered in smashed glass, and I cut my right hand to pieces.

Immediately, blood gushed everywhere, and as I looked at my hand, blood spurted into my eye. It fast looked like a crime scene.

Security staff ran from everywhere. Grabbing towels and gaffer tape, they wrapped up my hand in an attempt to stop the bleeding, while Zack put pressure on from the outside. I was lucky they acted so quickly to slow the blood loss before the ambulance arrived – I'd severed an artery and could have died.

On the way to the hospital, I was super stressed – I knew, deep down, this was serious. Later, in the hospital, the surgeon asked me to move my fingers. Nothing. He asked me to make a fist. Nothing.

I panicked. Was this the end of my basketball career? Would I even be able to push my wheelchair?

After a series of scans, I was told I'd severed my ulnar nerve, tendon and artery on my right hand. Immediate surgery was needed to save the use of my hand.

The surgery was extensive and had to be followed by months of rehab. London was just six months away, and I had no way of knowing whether I'd be able to regain enough movement to compete.

At the time, I was really angry at the guy who did it. It was a silly thing to do, but I was more mad about how much it ruined my life for that period. In retrospect, I know he didn't mean it, and these days I've fully accepted his apology. Life goes on.

But the three months of rehab that followed were extremely tough. I was completely out of action. I couldn't put any weight on my wrist or hand, which, as you could imagine for a dude without the use of his legs, meant I was barely able to do anything. I couldn't get dressed, couldn't get out of bed – nothing.

Even though Jannik was in a wheelchair, he basically had to act as my carer for months, and my god he did a good job of it. I was so fortunate to be sharing a house with such a patient friend – he shopped, cleaned, cooked, did everything, while I sat there on the couch doing my hand rehab pretty much twenty-four hours a day.

It was very tough having to be on the sidelines for so long. And I was still out injured when the Rollers headed to Belgium for the ninth Easter Wheelchair Basketball Tournament, a lead-up to the Paralympics. I sat at home and worried about whether I'd recover in time for London, or if someone else was performing well in the Rollers and would take my spot. Would I even regain the use of my hand at all?

Those three months went past so slowly but, day by day, my hand got a little bit better. It never fully recovered, and to this day I have significant nerve damage in my hand. But when, in July, the twelve-player Paralympic Rollers and Gliders squads were announced and my name was on the list, it was the greatest feeling of relief. Apparently, even though I hadn't been playing, I'd still been on the selectors' minds.

I was very happy for my mate Bridie Kean, who was named captain of the Gliders. Bridie lost her feet to meningococcal disease when she was a baby. She was a super close friend of mine who also studied with me at the University of Illinois (we actually had a radio show while we were there called 'Dylan and the Bird' – my god, we were crap!). Brad Ness was again Rollers captain, for what would be his fourth consecutive Games, and I was super proud that Jannik was poised to make his Paralympic Games debut.

We faced a tough assignment in London, drawing the USA, South Africa, Turkey, Spain and Italy in our pool. But Ben Ettridge told us that we were ready and reminded us that during the past four years we'd been preparing for this very moment. We were ready to defend our Paralympic title.

The Australian Paralympic Committee CEO and 2012 Chef de Mission Jason Hellwig was also confident that we were strong contenders for a gold medal in London. 'Australia has a proud history in wheelchair basketball,' he told the media, 'having competed in the sport since the first Paralympic Games in 1960. More recently, it is a sport that has brought Australia a lot of success. It is wonderful for every Roller and Glider heading to the 2012 Games to know that they are part of a sport with such a rich Paralympic history of which Australia plays a significant role.'

The Rollers were certainly a big deal: gold medallists and world champions in a sport with an enormous worldwide profile. Australia was punching well above its weight and had become recognised as an international basketball powerhouse. It was frustrating that we didn't get the air time, sponsorships or the massive paydays of some of the able-bodied players, but we were immensely proud of the fact that we led the way in international success for Australia.

Given we were heading to London as gold medal favourites, we needed the strongest possible competition to prepare. When I first joined the Rollers, we'd adopted the mentality of hunting down the top teams. Now that we were the number one side in the world, the other teams would be hunting us. Our toughest prospective opponents for London 2012, Canada and the USA, were technically strong and fast with great chair skills and basketball skills. We had plenty of skill too, but our biggest asset by far was the way we functioned as a cohesive unit.

In the lead-up to the Games, I was making my living as a motivational speaker, often in schools, on behalf of the Victorian Institute of Sport. I loved telling kids about my Paralympic experiences and sharing the thrill of winning a gold medal. It was tremendously satisfying to know that I might inspire someone to reach great heights of their own, and I hoped that I'd have even more inspiring stories when I got back from London.

Jannik had taken my place as the baby of the team, but it was awesome having him there with me. He and I were the only Victorians on the team, and we'd worked together so hard every day, often in cold, isolated basketball stadiums and gyms. I told him that being seventeen and a gold medal winner was the best feeling I'd ever had, that I wanted to experience victory again in London, and that I wanted to share it with him. So that's what we headed off to London to do.

This time, I had a much bigger support crew with me. Mum would be there to see me play in a Paralympics for the first time, which was really exciting. Zack, Dad and my step-mum Dana would be there, too, as well as about twenty mates – Carlile, Gus, Jimmy, Jibba (who won best on ground for loosest on tour), Spencer and Morgan, just to name a few.

The athletes' village accommodated around 7000 athletes and officials from 166 countries. The village was purpose-built to accommodate the 1800 wheelchair users among the competitors, with wide corridors and accessible bathrooms for all.

I'd thought the athletes' food hall at Beijing was as good as it gets, but London's was even better, being as big as several footy fields placed end to end. Every type of food you could imagine was on offer, all of it free. There was even what we took to calling 'decision pizza', a slice of pizza you ate while checking out the options and deciding what you really wanted.

Strangely, McDonald's was incredibly popular, with long queues throughout the whole Games. I never really understood why, but someone told me people feared they'd get food poisoning from the other options, so chose Maccas because they trusted it. Chinese, Indian, Japanese, French, Italian, Greek, Middle Eastern, English roasts, trout with almonds, mac and cheese – whatever you wanted was on offer. A foodie's heaven.

People often ask me whether the rumour about the number of condoms used at the Olympics and Paralympics is true. And yep – it is. They're everywhere. Huge bowls filled with them were everywhere, free for the taking, with an estimated 150,000 (!) 'used' at the London Games. To be honest, though, I don't think they were all used for their chief purpose. I remember Jannik and I grabbing bunches of them and throwing them to our mates in the crowd. Still, 150,000 is an impressive number!

Although there was fun to be had, the competition was very serious. I think for a lot of people who don't fully understand the Paralympics, they often see it as a 'feel-good event', where everyone is inspirational and competitors sit around singing 'Kumbaya' and are just happy to be there. It couldn't be further from the truth.

As time passed, the wider public were beginning to understand that the 4300 Paralympians who came from all around the world had trained their arses off to put on a show.

We looked good, we created some great sporting moments, we drew big crowds and we gave a great return to sponsors and spectators alike.

The Rollers opened their London campaign against South Africa on the night of 30 August 2012. Each match required total focus. As always, our team's motto was simple. 'To stick to the process and to FLF (fight like f*ck).'

We got away to a fast start and were already leading 27–16 when we really hit the accelerator. We were up by 27 at halftime and the final lopsided score, 93–39, justified our status as the team to beat.

Our next opponents, Turkey, had emerged as the giant killers of the competition, thanks to an upset 59–50 win over the USA in their opening game. They turned on the fireworks against us too. With just four minutes and forty-four seconds remaining in the match, they were leading by 1 point, but Justin Eveson was unstoppable and we held them off, winning 71–64.

Next we accounted for Spain 75–59 and then, in another polished performance, put away the Americans 65–49. We wrapped up our preliminary fixtures with a comfortable 68–48 win over Italy, before turning our attention to the quarter-finals.

Although I was still having some issues with my hand, I was happy with how I was performing. Unfortunately, though, I wasn't the player I once was, and wasn't playing as much as I had been in previous years.

During the game against Italy, Zack and Tim Biggin, who had also come to London to support me, were randomly picked out of the crowd for the half-time entertainment. As their big heads filled the giant screen, I had a feeling it would end in tears. They had to come onto the court to play two-on-two basketball and were roundly beaten by a pair of young women, with Tim reckoning Zack cost them the game. Fortunately, the Rollers were in much better form.

In our quarter-final against Poland, we raced out of the blocks to lead 26–11 at the end of the first quarter. The Poles never got close, with the final score of 76–53 a demolition, ensuring we would at the very least be bringing a bronze medal home to Australia.

But the whole team had set a gold medal standard for ourselves – we had an appetite for victory that only gold could satisfy. First, though, we had to beat the USA in the semi-final. The Americans had not won gold in Paralympics wheelchair basketball since 1988 and hadn't won a medal of any colour since 2000, so our confidence was sky high in the lead-up to the game.

The Americans were extremely skillful, and provided a fun match-up with our physicality and aggression. With just over a minute remaining in the semi-final, they roared to within 3 points of us. We needed steady nerves to handle the pressure. Jannik might have been the baby of the team but he showed real maturity when it mattered most, nailing a turnaround lay-up to improve our lead to 5 points and kill off the American momentum (he still claims it was the greatest shot in wheelchair basketball history).

And so, for the third consecutive Games, Australia was into the wheelchair basketball gold medal match – and for the third consecutive Games, Canada was the team we'd go up against for Paralympic gold.

We were confident we had Canada's measure, having outplayed them several times in the years since Beijing. Now, four years of hard training were about to come down to forty minutes of intense drama.

It was 9.15 pm on 8 September 2012. The 20,000-seat venue, normally known as The O2 Arena, was packed. The two teams lined up for the playing of the national anthems, Canada in red and the Rollers in white singlets with green and gold trim. My nerves were intense. The Olympics and Paralympics are these beautiful things that only come around every four years. It means losing isn't an option, because you have to wait nearly 1500 days to get another chance. Losing means four more years of hardship and sacrifice before you get a chance to make amends.

The Canadians were now being coached by Jerry Tonello, who had been assistant coach of Canada's gold-medal-winning team at the Sydney 2000 Paralympic Games and Mike Frogley's understudy in Beijing in 2008. The team themselves were veterans who knew how to hang on in a tight game.

We didn't want to give them even a sniff of victory, so we started fast, and at the first change we held a 15–14 lead. First blood to us. We pushed the lead out to 5 points early in the second quarter, but our opponents were not going down without a fight. The straight-shooting Anderson went on a scoring run and Canada clawed their way back to trail by just 1 point, 27–26, at half-time.

We just had to stay in front for twenty more minutes. But sixty seconds into the third quarter, Anderson charged up court to put the Canadians in front. Their supporters, decked out in red wigs and waving maple-leaf banners, urged him to increase the margin, while our fans, just as spirited in their green and gold outfits, screamed at us to hang on.

The atmosphere was crazy. On the court I could feel the floor vibrate beneath me with the sheer intensity of the screams of the fans.

By the end of the third quarter, Canada was up 46–42. Four points is a lot to make up in a quarter against a polished team: but we knew we had it in us. Sure enough, it didn't take us long to level the scores – Justin Eveson went on a charge and passed to Jannik to score. Bingo.

It was now 48–48, and we felt more than up to the challenge of regaining the lead and holding it for six minutes until the buzzer. However, Anderson saw a window of opportunity to score. This guy was a freak. Suddenly the Canucks led 50–48. Our hearts raced as we desperately tried to steal back the lead. We threw everything we had at it, but time was on their side.

I was dripping with sweat when, with twenty-five seconds left in the match, the basket beckoned. I desperately fired off a shot, hoping for a 3-pointer. It had the height and the distance, and my eyes followed the ball as it glided towards the rim, seemingly in slow motion. My heart hit the floor as the ball sailed just over the ring. When the buzzer sounded twenty-five seconds later, Canada had rolled to a 64–58 victory.

We were devastated. Gutted. In a two-horse race, you don't win a silver medal, you lose a gold medal. Images of our sad, flushed faces were beamed all around the world. We'd gone in as favourites and the loss was tough to accept. It was bad enough for those who had already won gold in Beijing, but I really felt sorry for the new guys like Jannik, who had worked so hard and come *so* close to the ultimate victory, only to have it snatched away.

We sat together in a huddle after the game, our arms on each other's shoulders, sharing the pain. Everyone did their best to bolster the team's collective spirit, but we were all as disappointed as the next person. But we accepted we were beaten by a better team on the day.

Justin Eveson was almost overcome with emotion. 'It makes me proud to be next to you guys,' he said. 'We had each other's backs out there. It makes me proud to call myself a Roller. Win or lose, I'm proud to be among you boys. Thank you so much for the last four years. Beautiful.'

Brad Ness, now thirty-seven, was raising questions about his future in the game. 'I'm keen to keep going but we'll look at that,' he told a reporter soon after the loss. 'For the good of the Rollers, if me stepping aside means someone else is going to get a step up and a look in and we'll be better off in Rio in 2016, then I'm happy to hand over my jersey and maybe go out to pasture. I'll go kicking and screaming, of course, but if that's the decision, that's the decision.'

I was only twenty-one and could easily have worked towards the next Games, but as much as I loved the sport and the team, I was already wavering about whether I wanted to continue.

At the medal ceremony I cried like a little kid. Onlookers probably thought that the tears rolling down my face were an indication of how moved I was, having been part of the event, in the Paralympic spirit of idealism, where the important thing was to do your best, regardless of the outcome. But my tears were about something else. The London Games *were* a great event and I *was* grateful to have had a part in it. But I really, really, really wanted to win. Coming second hurt like you wouldn't believe. I'm not going to sugarcoat it.

I'd given basketball everything I had. I'd trained for countless hours late into the night, gone without money and put my relationships on hold because winning gold was my sole focus. To have that medal ripped away by 6 points in the last few moments was tough.

Things changed for me after that loss. I firmly believe if you're passionate about something you'll be good at it, and if you're good at it you'll be successful. But after that, basketball became a bit of a job. I'd lost the passion, and if you aren't doing something you enjoy, then I firmly believe you're wasting your life.

I knew at the end of the London Paralympics that it was time for me to bow out of the Rollers. I would always feel a special connection to the team, and I'm endlessly grateful for the opportunities that being a Roller gave me.

But I had other things on the horizon.

# 8

# *like an episode of wheelchair survivor*

A LOT OF PEOPLE imagine that when you play sport internationally you spend a lot of your time being a tourist. But when I was representing Australia, my time away was made up of travelling, training, competing, recovering, room service. Repeat. People would ask me what I thought of all the exotic destinations I visited and I'd have to answer that the competition venue was fine and my hotel was nice, but beyond that I didn't really know.

I'd always had the itch to do some *proper* travelling, where I could skip the basketball stadiums and gyms to experience different cultures. So, after the London Paralympics, I decided I'd allow myself some time to discover as much of the world as I could. I wanted to throw myself into it and do what millions of people had done before me – go backpacking all around the world. The only difference for me was that I'd be doing it in a wheelchair. I'd have a little help from mates for some of it, but a lot of the time I planned to travel alone, seeing everything the world had to offer, from historical spots to the inside of dingy nightclubs, from award-winning restaurants to amazing music festivals, meeting up with the many old friends I knew scattered around the globe and making plenty of new ones.

I also wanted to prove to myself that I could do it. My trip to Southeast Asia had been a great stepping stone, but it was only for a month. This trip was going to be seven months, and the fear of the unknown, of wondering whether I'd be able to survive, was always in the back of my mind. I was also super worried about how I'd carry all my luggage. In the end I had a big duffle bag made that fitted on the back of my chair. It was the perfect size to carry all my gear without dragging on the ground. So, having assessed all the risks, I thought, *Stuff it, I'm doing it.* Then I saved up and leapt in head first.

My first stop was California, where I went north of Los Angeles to the college town of Santa Barbara to see two mates, Charlie Cotton and Rory Hancock. I'd met both boys in Cancun, Mexico, a couple of years earlier during a US spring break. From there, we returned south together to go to Coachella. I'd have to say I was pretty excited because we'd get the chance to see my favourite band in the whole world, hip hop group the Wu-Tang Clan.

It was the twentieth anniversary of Wu-Tang Clan's iconic album (and my favourite of all time) *Enter the Wu-Tang (36 Chambers)*, and it was the first time in years that

**Above** Mum, Resie, and Dad, Martin, in Sydney in 1986, a year after their wedding. Both their haircuts doing plenty.

**Right** Getting bathed by Mum a couple days after being born. You can see the tumour on my back before it was cut out.

**Below** The picture my dad took in hospital after surgeons told him that I might not wake up in the morning. He said he couldn't focus the camera through his tears.

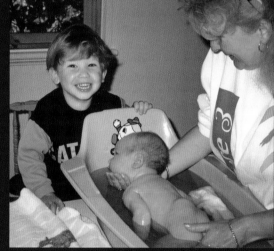

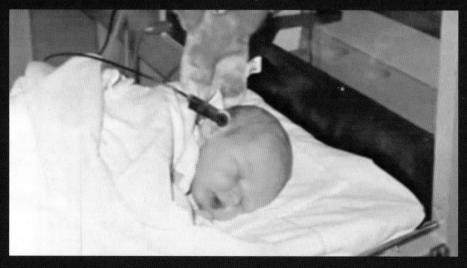

**Above** In my standing frame, playing with Zack, when I was one. Zack has never left me out of anything, even when he was four.

**Right** Who says white kids in wheelchairs can't jump? Dad rolling some impressively fast sunnies at the time.

**Below** Our skateboard crew used to play on the street every night. Mum was forever petrified I would get run over by a car. I made it out alive.

**Top Left** The first sporting event I competed in, the 'Weet-Bix Tryathlon', 2000. Safe to say, I was eating way too many Weet-Bix (and Doritos) at the time.

**Top Right** My favourite pic of all time – my Year 7 school photo, 2003. I know what you're thinking, where the hell are his eyebrows?

**Left** Zack's under-11s football team – the East Brighton Vampires – that I managed at age 9, and Dad 'assistant managed'.

**Below** The Davis Cup and me, in 2001. Clearly, I tried to eat it afterwards.

**Above** My brothers from the Rollers when we became Paralympic Champions at the 2008 Beijing Games. It was an honour to play with every single one of them.

**Right** The very moment my dream became a reality – Paralympic gold medalist at the age of 17. Here, hugging teammate Shaun Norris.
Frederic J. Brown/AFP/Getty Images

**Below** Celebrating Paralympic gold with Dad and Zack. Following tradition to cut the net down after a championship win, it's proudly hanging around my neck.

**Above** Celebrating with Mum and Zack after being presented with an Order Medal at the age of 18. An incredible honour.

**Below Left** Partying on a beach in Thailand in 2011, with two mates – Tim Big Ryan Burge.

**Below Right** The Thailand trip was a milestone for me, proving that I could t even the most inaccessible parts, and survive, with help from great friends.

**Above** The last time I would play competitive wheelchair basketball – winning silver at the 2012 Paralympic Games. Back when topknots were cool (were they ever?).
Brendon Thorne/Getty Images

MELBOURNE

**Above** My first time winning the greatest Grand Slam of them all – the Australian Open, in 2015.
Robert Prezioso/Getty Images

**Left** Lucky to always have someone there to give me a helping hand. With my friend Guy Walker and Zack at the Laneway Festival in 2014.

**Above** The best seat in the house – wheelchair crowdsurfing at Coachella in 2013.

**Above** Wu-Tang is for the children. Me and RZA, the leader of the Wu-Tang Clan, in Melbourne, 2014.

**Right** Graduation day at the University of Melbourne, 2015, with a Bachelor of Commerce in the bag.

*Above* One of the most nerve-racking moments of my life – delivering my TEDx Talk 'Mainstreaming Disability' in front of thousands of people at the Sydney Opera House, in 2015.
JJ Halans | TEDxSydney 2015

*Left* Winning Grand Slam number 2 – the 2015 US Open champion.
Mike Stobe/Getty Images for the USTA

**Right** Two in a row at the Australian Open – lifting the 2016 title. The trophy is deadset almost bigger than me.
Darrian Traynor/
Getty Images

**Left** I've had a photo of Pat Rafter, my tennis idol, on my wall since I was eight years old. Now, I get to call him a friend. At the 2016 Australian Open.
Vince Caligiuri/Getty Images

*Above* Heath and me on court the night we became gold medalists in doubles at the 2016 Rio Paralympic Games.

*Left* With step-mum Dana, after winning the singles gold in Rio, getting photobombed by my drunken cheer squad.

**Above** Being presented with the 2016 John Newcombe Medal – the highest award in Australian Tennis – by the man himself and his delicious mo. A big moment for me.
Quinn Rooney/Getty Images

**Below** 'Oi, Novak! Do you need a push, brother?' Giving Novak Djokovic a tip or two on how to wheelchair tennis, at the 2017 Aus Open. Michael Dodge/Getty Images

**Above** Embracing with Andy Lapthorne after winning the 2017 Australian Open at Rod Laver Arena – the first wheelchair tennis final played on centre court at a Grand Slam. Historic.
Robert Prezioso/Getty Images

**Below** Hosting freaking *PLAY SCHOOL*! What up, LITTLE TED! Jemima, where you at?
ABC © Andy Baker

**Left** Portrait painted by friend Hugo Gruzman (of Flight Facilities fame) for the 2018 Archibald Prize. I think we were an extremely close second.

**Below** Selfie during my first shift on radio – hosting weekend arvo on triple j.

**Below Left** Hosting *The Project* in 2017. Realising my dream of contributing to inclusion for people with disability in mainstream media.

*Above* Celebrating Heath and my first-ever doubles Grand Slam win, surrounded by friends, family and fans, at the 2018 Australian Open.
Pat Scala/Getty Images

*Right* Sharing a moment after my fourth-straight Australian Open win, with the greatest of all time – Roger Federer.

*Below* When Arnold Schwarzenegger asks for a selfie and you give him nothing: 'Dylan! You son of a bitch!'

*Above* One of my favourite photos from one of the best days of my life – punters loving the inaugural Ability Fest in 2018. Kate Shanasy

*Below* Backstage at Ability Fest 2018 with the first grant recipient from the Dylan Alcott Foundation, eight-year-old tennis-playing legend Jin.

**Above** History made after a lot of hard work. Pulling on the whites for the first time at the All England Club, Wimbledon 2018.
Henry Browne/Getty Images for Tennis Foundation

**Above** Dylan and the Duchesses. Got a nice ring to it. Wimbledon 2018
Get Skilled Access

**Right** My sixth Grand Slam and (hopefully) counting – the 2018 US Open

the whole group would come together to perform the album in full.

I'd waited a decade for the chance to see them live and my expectations were sky-high. I wasn't disappointed. They started with 'Protect Ya Neck', and thousands of fans rapped the verses with them. I knew every word, and loved joining in with the masses. I was so excited I nearly got up out of my chair and started walking. Then they dropped all their hits: 'Bring Da Ruckus', 'C.R.E.A.M.', 'Gravel Pit', everything.

It was the highlight of Coachella, which was awesome. Afterwards I headed back to my old home of Chicago, Illinois. There, however, I ran into a little trouble.

My idea had been to savour every morsel of US life – the grit as well as the glamour. I've always been pretty loose about trusting people; after all, as I assured my mum, who'd steal off a guy in a wheelchair?

One night I was using the bathroom at the back of a bar (due to the toilet inside being inaccessible – I got pretty good at peeing on dumpsters), when I noticed some shady units walk past. I didn't think too much of it, but afterwards realised my wallet had been pinched off the back of my chair. It contained a couple of hundred dollars cash and all my credit cards.

I had a pretty good idea who'd nicked it, and being a few beers deep I was determined to get it back. I thought the direct approach was best and decided to appeal to their better natures. So I wheeled myself over to them. 'Look guys,' I said, 'I know you took my wallet. You can keep the cash but please give back my cards. I really need them because I haven't got long to live and I'll need them for the hospital.' Smooth.

Who wouldn't be moved? Them, apparently. They just looked at me, looked at each other and walked off, wallet and all.

At the time, I was very flat. What a way to kick off a trip! But, hey, I am all for inclusion. So good on them for treating me like anyone else, I guess?

After a quick transfer of emergency funds, which is a nightmare without any ID or cards except your passport, I headed to the University of Illinois to catch up with my old college friends. The place held a special spot in my heart and it was so great to see what my mates were up to three years on from my departure.

My next stop was the University of Alabama, where Jannik was on a wheelchair basketball scholarship. Even though I'd spent more than a year in the United States studying, being down south was a rude awakening, with a regressive mentality all too obvious in many places. Confederate Rebel flags are still flown, there was even a restaurant called 'County Country Cooking' – but all the first letters were spelt with Ks. Crazy to think that places like that still exist!

After a week on campus, Jannik and I departed for New Orleans, a place I'd strongly encourage anyone to check out. It's almost too cool to be in the United States, with amazing music and chilled vibes throughout the whole city. We then travelled throughout Texas, before I left Jannik and headed up to New York City solo. It would be the last stop of my American journey.

From New York I flew to London and then on to Paris. Europe is a funny place in terms of accessibility. It is so old in some places and pretty modern in others. But every day I felt like I was playing a game of *Wheelchair Survivor*. For one thing, I can't begin to tell you how many goddamn stairs there are! Travel websites and hostel booking sites would state that a certain place was wheelchair accessible but I'd arrive only to find it looked more like the Great Wall, with steps for days.

This applied to hotels, shops, museums, railway stations, you name it. If one of these places happened to be on a section of the trip where I was with some of my amazing friends, they'd carry me and the chair up the stairs. If I was travelling alone I'd just ask for assistance as best I could. I reckon out of every hundred people I asked for assistance, ninety-nine said yes. Most people were amazing and always willing to help, even if I'd never met them before or even spoke their language. I learnt a very valuable life lesson – if ever you need help in life all you have to do is ask for it and most people will be happy to.

Some of my mates, including Tim and Antoine, to name a few, were joining me in Croatia, where, through an organisation called Sail Croatia, we'd arranged to take a boat trip from Split to Dubrovnik. It was supposed to be a week-long party and I'd been looking forward to it as one of the highlights of my time away. A couple of weeks before we were to set sail we thought we'd better check what sort of disabled access they had. The answer was none. In fact, in response to our query, the company told us they wouldn't allow me on the boat because their insurance wouldn't cover it.

Tim and Antoine found breaking the news to me really difficult. I found hearing it very difficult too. In fact, even though I put on a brave face, I was devastated. All my mates were going and I wasn't. I appreciate that it might have been hard with the wheelchair on the boat but I know we could have got it done.

This wasn't like rocking up to a museum and finding out it didn't have a ramp. It was a real kick in the guts, knowing there was nothing we could really do. I suspect the guys thought about pulling out of the trip in a show of solidarity, but there was no way I was going to let them do that. I, in turn, thought about meeting them in Dubrovnik, but the transport arrangements were just too difficult. There was nothing for it but to wish them well and go our separate ways.

In the end, I decided that it wasn't going to stop me having a good time. I hung out in Croatia by myself for a while before some other mates arrived and we went to a festival in northern Croatia called Hideout. Ten thousand people came from around the world for a series of boat and pool parties, held over three days and nights on Zrce Beach on the Croatian island of Pag. Most of the crowd were sunburnt and hungover after the first day, but that didn't stop the fun. I went with three friends – Anna Howkins, Dom O'Keefe and Guy Walker – and we partied till sunrise every day. I felt happy and free, doing exactly what I wanted to do. Then I headed over to Portugal for more sun.

I arrived in Lisbon to find that most of the streets were cobblestone, a product that I believe to this day is the worst invention in the whole world for people in wheelchairs to get around. Also, they don't even look that cool. The steep hills made it even worse. I went out on the first night and my front caster wheels constantly fell between the huge gaps in the cobblestone, sending me flying out the front of my chair. Legit, I fell out of my wheelchair about ten times. It was such a pain in the arse, I only stayed one day before heading south to spend some time in the beautiful city of Lagos on the Algarve holiday coast.

From there I flew on to Prague with my mate Guy. All in all I probably visited about twenty mates in different places. All of them gave me so much support throughout the trip, I'm not sure I would've been able to do it without them.

My last stop was Berlin, one of my favourite cities in the world. The German capital is the ultimate party city and it's

been at the forefront of techno music, a genre I've always loved. In our first week I headed to the huge open-air Melt! Festival, which well and truly lived up to its reputation. The event space was massive and the venues fascinating, including the Ferropolis open-air museum, the famous 'city of iron' full of massive cranes and other decaying machinery.

Melt! had ended and so had my cash. It was time to head home. Then Zack came to my rescue, lending me $1000 to prolong my trip by two weeks. They turned out to be two of the best weeks of the trip. There's something about Berlin's history, combined with a freedom to be whoever you want to be, that drew me to the city. A highlight was a visit to one of the world's most notorious nightclubs, the

Berghain. A disused concrete powerhouse surrounded by drab architecture from the Communist era, it looks like a run-down old industrial building on a weekday. But on the weekend it becomes the ultimate party warehouse. With one of the most powerful sound systems in the world, Berghain stays open from Friday night right through to Monday afternoon. It's a club where anything goes, to the beat of the loudest techno you've ever heard.

Trouble is, it's one of the hardest places in the world to get in. The lines of hopefuls stretch for hundreds of metres and you can queue for hours just hoping to be considered for entry. The bouncers are all-powerful and are prepared to turn anyone away, no matter how rich, famous or beautiful you are. I loved that about that club. Most tall, blond, blue-eyed people get into venues whenever and wherever they like, but the Berghain is like the anti-club, a place where the weirder you are the more likely you are to succeed. I was one of the lucky ones who got straight in, helped, no doubt, by my friend McDowell, who spoke fluent German, as well as the fact I was in the wheelchair (if you've had trouble getting in in the past, maybe borrow one for the night? – works a charm!).

After you're searched, you're let free into the dark warehouse. Cameras are banned, and if you're caught taking a photo, they'll either kick you out or break your phone on the way out. Once inside, well, my lord, anything goes.

The music was throbbing and the naked bodies pressed against each other at every turn added to the stifling summer heat. The downstairs dance floor was almost pitch black – the club is always dark so you have no sense of time passing. Some people party away the whole weekend and stumble out into the sunshine on Monday, wondering where they are.

Everywhere there were 'dark rooms', where casual, random sexual encounters could take place, and were almost encouraged. I didn't get involved but I did peek in for a look. It was an experience, put it that way, and I really enjoyed myself. One day I'd return.

But after seven months of touring the world and partying like never before, I'd genuinely seen enough for a while. Add to that an extreme lack of funds (legit, $0 in my bank account). Berlin marked the end of the trail. It had been an awesome time, and I recommend that sort of travel to everyone, whatever obstacles you have to overcome along the way. I was returning a more trusting, more confident person than I'd been when I set out. I'd seen that if you need help in life most people will give it to you, and I'd proved that I could look after myself and adapt to whatever life threw at me, while having a whole heap of fun along the way.

Thinking my adventuring was behind me for the foreseeable future, I headed back to Melbourne. I'd only taken a break from my commerce degree, and I expected to go back to a settled period of study. I could never have guessed how quickly those plans would change.

\*\*\*

I came home in September 2013 and, on a whim, decided to pick up my tennis racquet again. I'd once been the number four junior wheelchair player in the world, but this time around I had no real ambition other than to get a suntan and to get a bit fitter to work off the beer gut I'd developed on my trip.

But I found I really enjoyed it, so I started playing every day. At first, I wasn't taking it too seriously, but the more and more I played, the more I thought about taking it a little more seriously and perhaps rejoining the international wheelchair tennis tour. Then, with the support of Australian coach Greg Crump, and with the carrot of the Australian Open just around the corner, I went all in and started training like a professional athlete again.

Wheelchair tennis was invented in the 1970s by American Brad Parks, whose dream of becoming a professional freestyle skier ended when he was paralysed by an accident on the slopes at age eighteen. The sport really took off in the 1980s, and made its first Paralympics appearance in 1992 at Barcelona, where Parks and teammate Randy Snow won gold in the men's doubles. Six years after that, the body running it internationally became part of the International Tennis Federation, making it the first sport to integrate sportspeople with disabilities at that level. The only different rule in wheelchair tennis to able-bodied tennis is that the ball can bounce twice. The first bounce must go in the court, but the second bounce can go anywhere. Players can also hit the ball on the first bounce if they choose.

When I'd played as a junior, I was classifiable for the open category, which was for athletes who had one or two limbs affected by their disability. However, due to the extensive nerve damage in my right hand, things had changed, which opened up some interesting possibilities. The damage to my hand the previous year meant I was now classified in the quad division, the category for wheelchair players with damage to three or more limbs. Having played for Australia at two Paralympics, I started to seriously consider having a shot at a third Games. But this time in a whole different sport.

Luckily for me, it all started to come back, and I picked up the sport again pretty quickly. In basketball, I'd learnt to manoeuvre my chair at speed, a skill that translated incredibly well onto the tennis court. My experience with my Rollers teammates had also given me a strong work ethic, a professional training style and physicality. In basketball, your chair skills are on show for the whole forty minutes of match time. All you do is push and push and push yourself around the court, and I was able to take that mobility onto the tennis court. So, physically, I had a real advantage.

But the mental challenges were much tougher. Every time the Rollers played we went out there as a band of brothers, backing each other up. If you started to cramp up you signalled the coach, who took you off and sent a replacement player out. In tennis, there are no substitutes – you're out there by yourself. If you start to cramp up and can't continue, you forfeit the match.

In basketball, if you miss a shot or make some other mistake, you don't have time to dwell on it. Instead, you immediately have to push back hard into defence to help out your teammates. But in tennis, you're on your own. It can be a lonely place, with your mind often overthinking or overanalysing, resulting in errors and poor thought processes and performance on the court. The best players are those who can completely move on from whatever's just happened and focus on what's coming.

Given my background in tennis as a junior, I felt pretty confident I could fast-track my way into some important tournaments. Still, even though I'd won Paralympics gold for wheelchair basketball, would it translate onto the tennis court? There was only one way to find out.

At the end of December 2013, I entered a few tournaments in Australia and New Zealand. I didn't win them, but it seems I played well enough to catch the eye of Australian Open staff. Because in a decision I could hardly believe, I was granted a wildcard into the 2014 Australian Open.

# 9

# *living out my tennis dreams*

NOT MANY TENNIS PLAYERS can say they have a Grand Slam tennis tournament in their very own backyard. Unless you're from one of the select four cities that hosts one, you don't get the luxury. I'm one of those very lucky people.

Ever since I was a little kid, the Australian Open tennis tournament was my favourite two weeks of the year. As soon as I was old enough to know what it was, I'd beg my parents to take Zack and me. There was something about being so close to the action that drew me to it. Even with a ground pass, you could be inches away from the best players in the world hitting serve after serve at 200 or more kilometres per hour. And when the Open was on, there was an energy in the city that was electric. All of Melbourne seemed to embrace it, and I loved everything about it.

When, at sixteen, I made the decision to quit wheelchair tennis, I had to accept that my dreams of playing in the Australian Open would now never come true. It was a tough call to make. If you'd told that same sixteen-year-old that in seven years' time he'd be rolling out at Melbourne Park to represent his family and his country at the greatest Grand Slam of the year, he wouldn't have believed you. But that was what was about to happen.

It was in early December 2013 that I'd received the news tournament director Craig Tiley and Tennis Australia had given me the wildcard to compete in the 2014 Australian Open. I'd been training madly in the lead-up, trying to cram as much tennis knowledge as I could into a small amount of time so I could put my best foot forward when the competition started.

Unlike in wheelchair basketball, this time I'd be out there by myself, with no one to lean on, so switching to tennis required a mental shift that took a little getting used to. The other thing I had to adjust to was the fact that tennis is one of the few sports without a game clock. In basketball, if you're up by 20 points with two minutes to go, you can simply maintain possession of the ball until the buzzer goes and you win. But in tennis, you can be up 6–0, 5–0 and still lose. You have to do something to win it.

But after a lot of hard work – both on court and off – I felt like I was ready. One of the best things about wheelchair tennis is that it's one of the few sports that (at select tournaments like the Grand Slams) is fully integrated with the able-bodied players. We share everything – the same restaurants, courts, transport, locker rooms – everything. It's a very cool experience.

Locker rooms at Grand Slams are very exclusive places. No media, no families, just players and their coaches. It's a place where players can escape the circus that's going on outside and relax and prepare to compete. So it was a huge buzz the first time I went into the locker room at Melbourne Park, knowing that I'd be sharing it with some of the greatest players of all time. Safe to say, though, things didn't go down as I'd expected.

The wheelchair tournament starts in the second week of the tournament, meaning we gain access to the locker room on the second Monday, the eighth day of the two-week tournament. When I first went in, I met the locker room attendant, who showed me around, gave me the tour and then asked which locker I wanted.

I randomly pointed at one. 'That'll do,' I said.

'Ah, Mr Alcott, you've got locker 61. That's a good locker. A very good locker.' He returned to this point, saying again how lucky I was to have it.

I just nodded. All the lockers were identical, so I had no idea what he was talking about.

I put down my tennis bag and racquets, opened up locker 61, and loaded in my gear. I wanted to get my racquets restrung, so there I was, head in the locker, looking for some string. Eventually I found it and pulled my head out of the locker. Standing there, completely naked, basically with his penis on my shoulder, was one of my tennis heroes. It was Roger Federer. I couldn't believe it. I just sat there, stunned.

The Swiss maestro looked down at me. 'Hi, I'm Roger,' he said.

'Hi, I'm Dylan,' I said, thinking to myself the whole time, *Eyes up! Eyes up! Eyes up!* It's not every day you get to meet your idols, let alone in the nude, but I was pretty impressed about how my first day at the Australian Open went down.

On the court, the Quad Singles event featured the top three ranked players in the world and me, the wildcard recipient, in a round robin format, with the top two players at the end of the round robin stage competing in a final. In a Grand Slam wheelchair competition, only the top players in the world are invited to play. In non–Grand Slam tournaments, any player can enter and will receive entry if their ranking is high enough.

I felt very privileged knowing that a big contingent of my family and friends would be there supporting me when I made my Australian Open debut playing against American David Wagner. He'd become quadriplegic at the age of twenty-one when he and some friends were playing beach Frisbee in California. He'd dived into shallow water for a catch but landed headfirst in sand, breaking his neck.

Now, at thirty-nine, he was the world number one, the defending Australian Open champion and a veteran of the game. He'd won singles silver and doubles gold at the Athens Paralympics in 2004 and had claimed the Australian Open Quad Singles title in 2011 as well as 2013. A fierce competitor, safe to say he isn't the biggest fan of mine. He gave me the impression he hated the way I'd 'come out of nowhere', and wasn't giving me many smiles when we shook hands at the net before we started the match. Fast forward to today, and we've played nearly fifty times in five years, and it's always a great battle.

Sitting in the locker room, moments before heading out to play, I was the definition of shitting myself (it seems to be a common thread here! Nerves are a good thing!). One of the tactics I've always used to get in the zone and relax is music. As a result, I started what has become a locker room ritual that I carry out before every game, and listened to my favourite Wu-Tang Clan song – 'Protect Ya Neck'. It's a song that would change my life forever, and you'll find out why soon enough. But before playing my very first match at an Australian Open, the song helped me get into the right headspace.

Out on court, Wagner won the toss and chose to serve. It took a while for my nerves to settle, and pretty soon Wagner was leading 4–1 in the first set. He played a few mind games, trying to rattle me by stalling at crucial moments (he's the master of this). He also made very few errors, which meant I had to force the play.

But once I settled, I hit back to snatch the opening set 6–4, reeling off five games in a row. I continued on my merry way in the second set, eventually leading 5–3, 40–love, with three match points up my sleeve. *My god, are you about to beat the world number one at the Australian Open on your first attempt?* I asked myself. What a huge mistake that was! As soon as I had that thought, a huge knot of nerves developed in my stomach. It was immovable, I couldn't calm down, and I let all three match points slip, letting Wagner win the second set in a tie-break.

In the third set, I was cooked both mentally and physically. Wagner was proving tough to crack, and cramp took over my racquet hand. In the end, he won 4–6, 7–6, 6–3.

Matt King/Getty Images

I was devastated, but happy I'd been able to compete until the end. Regardless, and most importantly, I'd bloody loved every second of it. This was where I wanted to be.

The tournament continued and I had nothing to lose. I had to keep enjoying myself out there and really soak up the experience because you never know how many Australian Opens you're going to get. I played Andy Lapthorne next and held on for a thrilling 6–4, 5–7, 9–7 victory, keeping my Australian Open dreams alive.

The following day Lapthorne's second successive loss saw him exit the tournament, while I went up against 27-year-old South African Lucas Sithole, a triple amputee who was the reigning US Open champion. Lucas is a very cool dude, and one of the most impressive people on the tennis court you'll ever see. When he was twelve, he'd been helping the owner of an agriculture storage business move some bags when he fell onto railway lines just as a train was coming and was run over.

He lost both his legs and most of his right arm. Seven years later he started playing wheelchair tennis, and it's a sight to see. He serves by throwing the ball up with the same hand he holds the racquet with, and pushes his chair with his stump. He's a Zulu and a professional singer in his home country of South Africa. His last name sounds dangerously like something else.

Unfortunately for me, Sithole won 2–6, 6–2, 8–6. Once again I'd won the first set but then I fell in a bit of a heap when it mattered most. I'd let another close one slip away and was very upset.

After the match, I was in the players' cafe looking pretty dejected, when Pat Rafter came up to me. Pat was another of my great sporting heroes, my first, in fact, and had been a huge influence on my choosing tennis as a sport when I was a junior. I just loved the way he went about his business. He was intense, wanted to win, but was the most gracious person, whether he won or lost. I modelled myself on him, and hoped that one day people would view me in a similar light as Pat. He was also a very good-looking rooster with his own underwear ads, where he'd get his rig out on TV. Maybe I could do that one day, too, yeah?

Pat was also super talented on the tennis court. He'd won the US Open twice, made the final at Wimbledon twice and had reached the semi-final at the Australian Open and the French Open. I remember watching him lose the 2001 Wimbledon final in heartbreaking fashion to Goran Ivanisevic (I was ten and I'm pretty sure I almost teared up). Despite the look of agony on his face, he was all class. As a kid, I had a big signed poster of Pat on my wall. What a fan boy. But now, there he was in front of me talking to me about my match.

We analysed what I could have done better. He told me I had to be more proactive in my play and less reactive. I couldn't settle for just trying to hit the ball back and hoping my opponents made mistakes. At this level it didn't work. I would have to do something to win.

In other words, I had to find a different approach in tennis to the one that had served me well in basketball. You can't expect to maintain a lead in tennis by shutting down the opposition as you can in basketball. The fact that you have to do something positive, not defensive, to win, even if you're 5–0 up, means there's always the chance that you can blow a lead under pressure. It's advice I still call upon regularly to this day.

It's a very tough mental challenge at the top level, but my performance in the tournament had convinced me that, with some hard work and focus, I could make a second career out of the sport that had been my first love. I hadn't been this happy for a long time. I was back as an athlete – but this time as a tennis player.

\*\*\*

Kick-starting my tennis career catapulted me into an awesome 2014, with great things happening off the court too. Back in 2010, I'd met a girl who I immediately strung up a connection with. Her name was Kate Lawrence and we met at the Melbourne Spring Racing Carnival through a mutual friend of Zack's. Kate was American, brown-haired and beautiful, and she immediately got my attention. We hit it off, and I loved getting to know her, but there was one problem – I knew she was a faaaaaair bit older than me.

I was nineteen at the time, and she was twenty-four. A five-year gap. I knew this was going to be an issue, but I didn't want to jeopardise my chances, so I lied about my age, and said I was twenty-two. She bought it (well, I thought she did, though she claims deep down she knew) and we had a great time together. Unfortunately, though, when she found out my true age, it fizzled out, and Kate returned home to the USA for the next three years.

We stayed in touch, though, and fast forward to the start of 2014, I heard she was back living in Melbourne. I was so happy and immediately wanted to rekindle what we'd had. She wasn't sure to start with, but, luckily for me she gave it a crack. Kate was more beautiful than I remembered, both inside and out. It was the start of a great relationship.

Two months after the Australian Open, my tennis comeback continued when I hit Tucson, Arizona, for the USTA Desert Classic. Having made the most of my wildcard opportunity in the Australian Open, I was slowly creeping up the world rankings. As expected, Wagner, who was still ranked number one, reached the final easily. Somehow, I had made it there myself.

Wagner won our final after three tight sets, setting a pattern he would follow for much of the year. But I took a lot of positives out of Arizona. I'd scored some good wins over highly rated players, so I was happy enough.

Next was Baton Rouge, Louisiana, for the Cajun Classic, where I made the semi-final of the singles and, with Lucas Sithole, was runner-up in the doubles. I wasn't snaring any titles but I was rising fast in the rankings, and was now approaching the top ten in the world.

That wasn't going to be enough to pay the bills, though. Fortunately, I was able to supplement the small paydays from the tennis tournaments – a couple of thousand dollars here and there – with my growing career as a motivational speaker, as well as some important personal sponsorships, namely from Tennis Australia, OCS Group and Melrose Wheelchairs. It all helped cover the costs of life on tour, which was great because I loved being on the road.

In May 2014 I made the semi-finals of the singles and doubles at the Japan Open. Then it was back home for a tough training block. People often ask me, 'What training can you do in a wheelchair?' Well, we can do pretty much everything. This training block consisted of a two-hour-long tennis session every morning, six days a week, in addition to three or four gym sessions. A lot of people may think that being in a wheelchair would prevent you from working out in a gym, but this couldn't be further from the truth. Sure, there are some things you can't do (hey leg press!), but with a few adjustments, you can actively complete a full workout that includes bench presses, chin-ups, dips – the lot. I also did hill sprints at the MCG, boxing sessions, swimming sessions, sprint sessions on grass for added resistance – I did everything.

The training block was important, because I was preparing for a seven-week stint in Europe playing in the French, British, Swiss and Belgian Opens.

First up was the BNP Paribas Open de France (not the Roland-Garros French Open – quad wheelchair players don't play that one yet). Up against Lucas Sithole in the semi-final, I won 6–2, 6–3 to progress to the final. I'd be playing David Wagner. Due to heavy rain, the match had to be played indoors. Our first set was hotly contested but the change of setting had thrown me off a little, and, as usual, I choked when it counted. Wagner tightened his grip and beat me yet again, making it six for six and claiming his seventh Open de France title.

To rub salt into the wound, the 7–6, 6–1 scoreline marked Wagner's third successive straight-sets win over me. I knew that to have any chance of beating him, I had to sort myself out mentally.

I was pretty shattered but I headed to London and set to work even harder in training.

Even though I was no longer a Roller, I still took a keen interest in the progress of my mates and it gave me a boost when I heard that the team had won the World Championship, beating the USA in South Korea. Five days after their victory I was in Nottingham, England, for the British Open, a tournament that was as important as a World Championship to me. It was a breakthrough moment. Having made it to the final, I beat Andy Lapthorne 7–5, 6–1 to claim the magnificent silver plate. Taking out the British singles crown was the biggest tennis victory of my career to that point, and I left Nottingham certain that I had what it took to go all the way to the top.

The following week that belief was put to the test in the final of the Belgian Open. Once again I was up against David Wagner. But this time the result went my way, 6–4, 6–1. Wagner had beaten me in seven successive finals. Now, the monkey was off my back and I knew that if I played my best I could beat absolutely anyone.

By now I'd spent six months as a full-time tennis player, and I knew it was the life for me. But even at the top, the money for the wheelchair game was peanuts (costing more to travel to an international tournament than the prize money you'd receive for winning it!). Still, I knew that becoming a successful athlete in two sports would be huge, both on the field and off it. Already, I had it in my head that I wanted to become a disability advocate. I wanted to help normalise disability and improve the lives of people with disabilities all around the world. Hopefully, my sporting successes would give me the platform I needed.

But before I went global, I wanted to help some people who were very close to my heart. I think it's important to give back to people who helped you get to where you are or who are less fortunate than you. A lot of people had helped me throughout my life, especially two charities – the Starlight Foundation and Variety, the Children's Charity.

The Starlight Foundation came into my life in 2000, when I was in hospital recovering from the botched surgery that robbed me of six months of my life. I was very depressed, and it was tough on my family, too. So the nurses at Monash Medical Centre nominated my family and me for an all-expenses-paid trip to the Gold Coast for three weeks. We swam with the dolphins at Sea World, met Batman at Movie World (still not sure if it was the real one or not) and had an all-round awesome time. That trip was a lifeline, and something my family and I really needed.

Variety, the Children's Charity, gave me a very important gift – if I hadn't received it, I'm not sure I would be doing what I'm doing today. Wheelchairs are really expensive, and a lot of families can't afford to buy the $10,000 wheelchairs their kids need in order to play sport. So while Zack needed a $100 pair of footy boots to play football, I needed a

$10,000 wheelchair. It's a huge barrier to entry, and you can see the dilemma. Luckily, someone at Variety had read a newspaper article about me and recognised the problem. Variety donated my first ever sporting wheelchair so I could train and compete.

I'd always wanted to do something to repay these wonderful organisations in some way. Then I came up with the dumbest idea of my life, something that would be far more demanding than anything else I'd ever done. It would push me to the outer limits of exhaustion and leave me on the verge of collapse.

The idea came to me one night on the way home from Kate's place. My route took me past Melbourne Park, home of the Australian Open. Its lights were ablaze, and I remember thinking, *I never really get to play tennis at night* ... Then I had a lightbulb moment. I was going to play wheelchair tennis for twenty-four hours nonstop to set a world record and raise as much cash as I could in the process. I know – what a dickhead.

My manager at the time was a guy called Winston Rous, who was mostly involved in AFL players' contracts. Winnie was a legend, and he and his partner, Scott Lucas, and their company Phoenix Management Group had taken a risk on me and donated their time to help me when I was a relative nobody. It was something I will be forever indebted to them for. So I rang Winnie and told him what I was planning.

His reply was blunt. 'Are you crazy?' But, as always, he did everything he could to help me make it a reality. After a few months of arduous planning, I announced on social media and via a media release that, on 11 December 2014, I would attempt to set a world record by continuously playing wheelchair tennis for twenty-four hours nonstop. The plan was to raise $100,000 for the two charities. It was ambitious, I know, but, hey, you might as well aim high.

Twenty-four hours is a long, long time to play tennis. To put it into perspective, the longest I'd previously played without a break was about five hours. Twenty-four hours seemed like a light year in comparison.

In the lead-up, I trained my arse off, putting in daily marathon hits on the court to get ready. But even then, if I was to last the distance, I'd need help from other people. In fact, I'd need all the help I could get. So we organised for a medical team as well as a bunch of volunteers to be on standby, ready to give me whatever I needed to get through – food, water, electrolytes, caffeine, beers (just one).

I'd also need hitting partners. Friends and family signed up in droves so I'd never be short of people to play with. As well, some big-time celebrities agreed to add a bit of star power, including AFL players Jack Watts, Tom Hawkins, Chris Dawes and Jack Riewoldt, tennis stars Sam Stosur and Sam Groth, and TV personalities Rob 'Millsy' Mills and Lauren Phillips, just to name a few.

Lastly, of course, I needed donations. It was the thing I worried about most, but pretty soon after we announced the event, they began to roll in. A few bucks here and there from generous friends and supporters kicked things off and before long $5000 had been pledged. Then First National Real Estate donated $10,000, followed by Acquire Learning with another $10,000.

Soon we'd reached $26,000, then $30,000. We were going strong. When I talked about the event I referred to it as a 'barrier-breaker' that I hoped would draw attention to wheelchair tennis as well as the deserving foundations.

With a week to go, funds raised topped $50,000, thanks to a $20,000 donation from AGL Energy. This was serious money and I hadn't even hit a ball yet. There were other valuable donations too, with the crew at Damn Good Productions agreeing to provide a live stream of the whole twenty-four hours, while Tennis Australia contributed the venue, staffing fees, catering, security and promotion as well as kicking in $10,000.

It was all such a buzz. I was training five hours a day every day, doing sprints in the chair and weight-training for endurance. Kate and some friends joined me as I pushed my wheelchair through the Melbourne Half Marathon. I needed to be sure I had the fitness to keep going for the full twenty-four hours. I knew it would come down to mind over matter and that the adrenaline would keep me going through the night.

I was chomping at the bit to get started. I wanted it to be a party atmosphere for everyone, so we organised alcohol donations, lights, lasers, food trucks and a DJ, namely my good friend DJ Generik, to create a vibe and help push me through.

Everyone who came to the event would receive an 'I helped Dylan smash the world record' T-shirt.

But as the clock ticked down to start time, I was struck by a wave of doubt. What if I didn't make it? What if I let everyone down? It was too late to back out now. I'd just have to fake it and hope I could make it.

The afternoon before the big day, my massage therapist, Phil Boland, gave me a rub down and I did media interviews with my friends at triple j. Triple j had been hugely supportive of my sporting endeavours over the years, and now they gave the marathon plenty of love too. Who knew it would be the start of a beautiful relationship?

Then the big day was upon me. I had declared to the world I was going to play from 8 am on Thursday until 8 am Friday, with just five minutes off every two hours for a toilet break. Now, in front of everyone, I was about to find out if I could make good on that.

I started slow and steady, hitting against the big-serving Sam Groth, who at that point was still well and truly on the professional tennis circuit. Next up, Liz Cambage took a turn on the other side of the net. Liz and I have been friends since I was eighteen. We met when we both played basketball and, despite a few bumps in the road, have stayed close friends. I feel so proud watching her rip it up all over the world on the basketball court, and am so proud of the person she's become off it. That said, she was easily the worst tennis player I played against that day – if not my whole life.

Following Liz were AFL players Jack Riewoldt, Tom Hawkins and Jack Watts, then, eight hours into the event, US Open winner Sam Stosur came and had a hit, playing first on her feet and then in a chair. Now, we all know she's a great player on her feet, but it turned out she was pretty terrible in a wheelchair! It was fantastic to have her there and she gave me a boost by declaring to a reporter covering the event: 'If anyone is going to be able to play tennis for twenty-four hours it's going to be Dylan. He's certainly got tons of energy.'

American actor Jason Lewis, who played the love interest Smith in *Sex and the City*, was in town to open a nightclub and came down after hearing about the event from friend

Lauren Phillips. He played barefoot for a couple of hours, and the ladies (well, mainly my mum, Resie) loved it! Safe to say, he was a very good-looking unit. Rob Mills arrived late on the Thursday night, fresh from the Melbourne opening night of *Grease*. He took to the court decked out in his black-tie finery before switching to a T-shirt and shorts.

Come midnight, I was knackered. But 500 or so supporters were still there, partying into the wee hours, and I relied on their urging to keep me going. The truth was, though, it felt like my body was falling apart. After so many hours wheeling around the court and hitting the ball nonstop, my arms were wrecked – I didn't know arms could get that sore. While my right wrist was heavily taped it was still killing me, and both my hands were bleeding from the constant friction. When I took my toilet break after the 21-hour mark my right wrist had swollen up to what looked like five times its normal size. I was in so much pain, I actually started to cry. I didn't know how I could keep going, but I knew I couldn't stop.

I wanted to fall out of the chair and lie on the court and sleep forever. I wanted this brutal nightmare to end. Instead, I pushed on through the agony, reminding myself why I was out there and focusing on all the good that would be done with the money we were raising.

As the sun came up, I just kept hitting the ball, wheeling back and forth, hitting ball after ball after ball. Finally, after what felt to my shell-shocked body like weeks, the chant went up. Five. Four. Three. Two. One.

It was over.

I'd done it. I'd set a world record of twenty-four hours straight of wheelchair tennis. It was more gruelling than anything I'd ever done, but I'd got there.

My arms felt like they each weighed a ton but somehow I managed to get them over my head in triumph. I breathed a huge sigh of relief, and tried to exhale the pain from my battered muscles. I was so done in I could barely speak.

Exhilaration battled exhaustion. After all, this had been a team effort, and so many people were still there when I finished. Special mention to Liz and Lucy Wilcox and my family, who all stayed the whole twenty-four hours with me, an unbelievable effort.

We knew that not everyone who wanted to donate had done so, and we kept donations open for another week. In the end we raised more than $105,000, not just reaching but exceeding my ambitious original goal. My heart was full of gratitude to everyone who'd been part of this incredible result. There were ongoing benefits in addition to the funds too, with

Starlight and Variety each receiving promotion that would have cost more than $1 million if they'd had to pay for it.

To everyone who helped, thank you. The pain in my body eventually faded, but the knowledge of the difference we were able to make to the lives of kids by supporting the amazing work of the Starlight Foundation and Variety will last forever.

I vividly remember what it was like to spend weeks at a time in hospital with little or nothing to distract me from the pain and boredom. Now hospitals across Australia have a Starlight Express Room where kids can watch DVDs or play on the Xbox, PlayStation or Wii. They can join Captain Starlight in a musical jam session, have their face painted, watch a live magic show, make balloon animals and take their minds off their treatment.

The brilliant people at the Starlight Foundation have made it their mission to replace pain, fear and stress for kids in hospitals with fun, joy and laughter. The design of the rooms is based on scientific evidence that shows that, for kids, play is one powerful antidote to pain, fear and stress, and is essential in developing resilience, wellbeing and a sense of normality. Which happens to be how I've always viewed sport.

Variety also gives much-needed support, helping kids gain independence and freedom by providing financial support for walking frames, portable hoists and, just as they did for me, state-of-the-art wheelchairs. They provide in-home medical aids, including seizure alarms, and at schools they build all-ability playgrounds and provide transport for children in wheelchairs. I'm intensely proud and honoured to have contributed to this work.

When it came time to deliver the money, I had two large novelty cheques made – one for Variety and one for the Starlight Foundation, each for $52,500. I presented the Starlight cheque to a little girl named Melanie, who was in hospital being treated for leukaemia. She was too young to understand exactly what all those zeroes represented. But she knew that she and the other kids like her hadn't been forgotten or overlooked, that there were people out there who cared and wanted to help.

It was that moment, when I was delivering the funds, that I realised that one day I wanted to start my very own foundation. When or how, I wasn't sure, but from then on it was a dream I was determined to make a reality.

# 10

# *wu-tang is for the children*

MOST PEOPLE AT SOME stage look back on their lives and wonder what could have been. It's only natural – everyone can get tired of life's repetition, and long for change or something new. As they say, the grass is always greener on the other side.

I'm no different. I love my life just how it is, but often I wonder what it could've been if I'd taken a different path. What if I'd become a lawyer or a politician? What would my life be like?

These days, I'm pretty happy I chose sport – I've lived a pretty awesome life of which I'm very proud. But sometimes, just sometimes, I wish I'd pursued a career in music. Usually I'm not one for regrets, but if there's one thing I regret, it's quitting singing lessons in school. As a youngster, I had a pretty good voice. I was in the school choir and was asked to try out for the Australian Boys Choir (you know, the choir in the QANTAS ads). When I reached high school, I still sang a bit and still enjoyed it. I even tried out for *Australian Idol* (thank god there's no video of that!). Mum pleaded with me to take singing lessons, saying that if I didn't I'd regret it down the track. But, fully worried about what the other boys at school would think and wanting to fit in, I told Mum that taking singing lessons would be lame. Play sport. Be cool.

Fast forward to today, and, as usual, Mum was so right. And I do regret it. These days, my voice isn't great. It broke, and it's quite deep and gravelly. I was never trained to sing more deeply, so I lost it.

Now, when I see my favourite artists perform I can't help but feel a touch jealous. There's something mesmerising about watching musicians play live, and having 20,000 people hanging on every word is a feeling I've always wanted to experience. *Maybe I could've done that! If only I hadn't given it up!* I think to myself. But alas, those skills are gone. Playing music, performing to the masses, was nothing but a distant dream. Or so I thought …

*** 

After my twenty-four hours of tennis, I was absolutely cooked. Wrecked was an understatement. I couldn't even push my wheelchair. Kate had to lift me into the car and take me home. I remember diving into bed, no shower, and falling into what was the best sleep I've ever had in my life. Eighteen hours nonstop. The body is an amazing thing, but it doesn't respond so well to that much punishment. The physio had given me a wrist brace to wear to bring down the swelling, but I could barely put any weight on my wrist.

Every part of my body was sore. But I had a bigger problem, and I wasn't sure how I was going to get through it: I was about to head to my favourite music festival, the Meredith Music Festival.

The Meredith Music Festival is held annually in early December on private land in the bush, halfway between Geelong and Ballarat. It started out as a friends' getaway twenty-eight years ago, and has evolved into a brilliant event that runs from Friday morning to Sunday afternoon. Numbers are capped to keep it special, with punters having to register in a ballot to get tickets. It only has one stage, 'The Supernatural Amphitheatre', and from the first year I attended, I was hooked.

So, although I was in agony, I wanted to go. Besides, I'd worked so hard, I felt I deserved to blow off a little steam. As well, one of my favourite rappers of all time was performing, Ghostface Killah from the Wu-Tang Clan, and there was no way I was going to miss him.

So, after much deliberation and against doctor's orders, Kate, Liz, Lucy and I jumped in a car and made the 120-kilometre trek from Melbourne to Meredith. Heaps of my friends, including Zack, were already up there – they'd all left straight after I finished the fundraiser – so I was super excited to see them and to have a celebratory frosty libation.

When we arrived, I was overwhelmed by the number of strangers who came up to say congratulations about my world record. I wasn't particularly well known back then, so it was super nice to discover that the event had made an impact, especially for the two charities involved.

But as the day went on, I was struggling, *really* struggling. My swollen wrist was still giving me a heap of pain, and I contemplated driving home on multiple occasions. But I hung in there, determined to wait it out until I saw Ghostface. Then I'd leave. Perfect.

I waited all day. Then, a few minutes after 5 pm, the moment I'd been waiting for arrived when Ghostface came on for his forty-minute set.

Now, I've been a massive Wu-Tang fan ever since I first discovered them at thirteen. If you don't know, the Wu-Tang Clan is an American hip hop group from Staten Island, New York City, originally made up of East Coast rappers RZA, GZA, Ol' Dirty Bastard, Method Man, Raekwon, Ghostface Killah, Inspectah Deck, U-God and Masta Killa. Known for fairly hectic lyrics and storytelling (known as 'Gangsta rap'), the Wu have been one of the most influential hip hop groups of all time. Their album *Enter the Wu-Tang (36 Chambers)* is my favourite album of all time, period (did I already mention that?), and I know most of the words to most of the songs. So I was pumped to see one of the main rappers from the group, Ghostface, rip it up on stage.

Ghost was playing mostly his own solo music, some old stuff and some new stuff. As the set progressed, I grew more and more excited, anticipating that he was about to rip into some Wu-Tang classics, but I was also looking out for something else. I'd seen online that a few members of the Wu, when performing solo, would often pull members of the crowd up onto the stage to rap with them. Nearly every time, the guest rappers bombed it, messing up the lyrics when it counted most. My plan was, if Ghostface was to get someone from the crowd up on stage at Meredith, I'd do everything in my power to be that person, even if I made a fool of myself.

The set had almost finished. It looked like Ghost wasn't going to get anyone up, and I was pretty bummed. But, oh well, I'd just enjoy myself. Then, out of nowhere, Ghostface shouted: 'We need two motherf*ckers to get up here and help us with this next track "Protect Ya Neck"!'

It was my moment, my song, the last song I listen to every time I play a tennis match! 'Get me up! Crowd-surf me in my wheelchair!' I yelled to Zack and some other mates.

I was that pumped they obliged. Now I was probably 75 metres away from the front of the stage and well out of the eyesight of Ghostface on stage. I needed to get closer. So the boys started passing me over the crowd, edging me to where I'd be in sight. But Ghost had already picked two other people to rap with him. I was devastated. I'd missed my shot. I couldn't believe it. So close!

But then – music to my ears – the two people Ghost had chosen said they didn't know the words (suckers). I was still in with a shot. By now the whole crowd had seen me crowd-surfing, and they pleaded with Ghostface to choose me. After what felt like an eternity, he saw me, but his response wasn't what I was after. 'He won't know it! He won't know the lyrics!' WHAT!? I knew every word. Come on! But after a few cheers from the crowd, he gave in. The security grabbed me and hoisted me up on stage.

Ghostface stood over me. 'Do you actually know this? Are you going to f*ck this up?'

'I know all seven verses, mate,' I said. 'Just tell me which one.' Safe to say I was being a touch ambitious – I didn't know them all. But Ghostface bought it and said I'd be rapping the Method Man verse from the group's most iconic song. This was actually happening.

Zack and my friends couldn't believe I was up there. Zack told me later that one of our mates turned to him and said: 'Mate, I know Dylan likes attention, but what the hell's he doing! He's going to embarrass himself!'

It wasn't far from the truth. What the hell *was* I doing! I'm an athlete, not a rapper! I looked out at the crowd, 13,000 people deep, and thought, *What if I choke*! I'd never live this down.

My mouth was dry like the Sahara Desert, so Ghostface's hype man gave me a bottle of Hennessy to skol. I took a big swig and almost vomited, but I was ready to go.

Ghostface launched into the song. The guy looks like a heavyweight boxer and has the same intimidating presence. He was off and running, spitting fire as usual, which meant my moment was only a verse away. I sat at the back of the stage desperately practising the lyrics. But there was no time – very soon it would be my turn. Ghost's hype man gave me a mic, patted me on the back, and said good luck.

Thirteen thousand people fell eerily quiet. I suspect they were expecting an absolute car crash, a guy in a wheelchair embarrassing himself live on stage. But they were so intrigued they couldn't look away. Ghostface finished his verse, and it was time.

Holy shit. Here we go. I started rapping. As soon as I spat out those first two lines, the crowd went *absolutely mental*, both excited and shocked that I knew what I was doing. I've never felt, or heard, a crowd like it – maybe because this time I was the one on stage.

Ghostface couldn't believe it either. When he realised I knew every single word he almost fell over. I think he was just relieved I wasn't going to embarrass myself or him in the process! I kept rapping, giving a word-for-word rendition of the original. It was like an out-of-body experience. I just couldn't believe it was happening.

Ask yourself: if you could pick any artist and any of their songs to perform on stage with them, what would you pick? Got it? Imagine how unbelievably cool that would be. Well, that's exactly what I was doing.

To this day it remains one of the best moments of my life. I felt proud that somehow, some way, I managed to nail it. I'd never rapped before, ever, and I was stoked I'd pulled it off. No other way to put it.

I knew Ghostface was happy too. After the set he took me backstage for a drink and told me I'd nailed it and it was one of his favourite moments on stage for years.

Later, people asked me what gangster stuff we'd got up to together. The truth was we just chatted, and then I asked him for an ice pack, because my wrist was killing me from the tennis the day before! How un-gangster of me.

That wasn't the end of it. A few days later, Ghostface said in an interview on triple j that calling me up to perform with him was one of the best things he'd done on stage ever. Then, off-air, he got my phone number and called me to see if I wanted to perform again at his next gig later that week at St Kilda's Esplanade Hotel (the Espy, as it's fondly known). I quickly accepted.

The second stint with Ghostface was awesome too – though the crowd at the Espy was nothing like the massive audience at Meredith – and it wasn't the last time I'd be in touch with Ghostface.

***

The marathon wheelchair tennis fundraiser, along with what went down at Meredith, kick-started a massive period of my life, that was only going to get bigger as I entered the summer of tennis in 2015.

Things on the tennis court were going pretty well, and I entered my second year on the world tennis tour ranked number three in the world. The first tournament of the year was the Brisbane International at Pat Rafter Arena. I'd made it through to the final, but my wrist was still giving me a great deal of post–tennis marathon grief and the blisters on my hands still hadn't healed. But I worked my way back into the game and went on to win the singles 0–6, 6–2, 6–0.

Unfortunately, the presentation ceremony was memorable for all the wrong reasons. I accepted the trophy, then hoisted it aloft for the classic victory photograph. In doing so, I'd forgotten that my tennis bag was hooked to the back of my wheelchair – it's the easiest way to carry it. Now, those things are heavy – six racquets, spare tyres, string, grips, hydration gels and more. So when I put my hands up, the weight of the bag overbalanced my chair and I toppled backwards, arse over head. Smooth, Dyl. Luckily, the trophy didn't break, but safe to say my ego took a fair hit.

I soothed my bruised dignity the following week by winning the Sydney International at Sydney's Olympic Park. I beat defending champ Lucas Sithole 6–2, 6–4, taking my sixth career title since I'd made my debut as a wildcard twelve months earlier. But winning the smaller tournaments meant little if I couldn't back it up at the Australian Open.

Luckily, this time around I was confident I had a real shot at realising two lifelong ambitions – to become world number one and win a Grand Slam title in my hometown in front of the family and friends who'd helped me so much throughout my life.

Sure enough, my ever-growing army of supporters were there, right behind me, when I kicked off my second Australian Open campaign at Melbourne Park on 19 January 2015.

It was, as always, a major event, and the usual big guns were there in the able-bodied stakes: Novak Djokovic, Serena Williams, Andy Murray, Maria Sharapova, Roger Federer and Rafael Nadal. In total, there was a staggering $40 million in prize money, with the men's and women's singles champions each collecting $3.1 million. Not the worst payday in the world.

By contrast, however, the winner of the wheelchair Quad Singles would receive just $14,000. In comparison, if you lost the first round of the able-bodied tournament – in other words, if you didn't even win one match – you'd be paid $50,000. Now, that's a large discrepancy. Not that I'm saying players with disabilities deserve millions for winning. But I do believe that the wheelchair prize money should at least be comparable to the minimum an able-bodied player receives. The good news is, as more people buy tickets to come see us, and sponsors and TV networks become more aware, these days the prize money is trending in the right direction, as it should.

In any case, on that overcast Melbourne morning in January 2015, there was much more at stake than money.

My first match in the round robin opener of the Quad Singles was against Andy Lapthorne. And while I was feeling good about my chances, my wrist and hand were still giving me problems from my accident in 2012 and my world record attempt, and I needed cortisone injections. Regardless, I was prepared to put up with the pain for the joy that might follow.

When I took the match 6–4, 6–4, I knew I had a real shot at winning my first Grand Slam event, even though there was plenty more tennis to get through. First up, I'd need to defeat David Wagner in the next round the next morning. That would be followed by a doubles match in the afternoon, and the singles semi-final the day after. It was a demanding schedule, but nowhere near as demanding as playing tennis for twenty-four hours, so I was ready.

As I'd hoped, my good form continued and I beat Wagner in straight sets, 6–4, 6–4. I was well on my way to the final. In the following day's singles semi-final my opponent was Lucas Sithole, my doubles partner, who is one of the toughest and most determined competitors in the sport. A year earlier he'd defeated me in my first shot at the Australian Open. This time it was me on top, and I won 6–1, 6–1.

I'd learnt so much about the game at the top level in the preceding twelve months. My confidence was high, and I was planning to go all the way. I'd driven past Melbourne Park thousands of times dreaming of playing in the final and winning the Australian Open. Now here I was, so close to making that dream a reality I could almost taste it.

In the final I again faced David Wagner, the defending champion. 'Dylan is probably the strongest player in the division,' David told a reporter before the match. 'With his strength, he hits a big ball. He's fast, he's got solid hands with touch and feel, so he's an all-round strong player.'

It's always good to know that your opponents rate you as a threat. I just hoped I could stay true to form and get the job done for everyone who'd backed me. I wanted to make them proud.

Sitting in my dressing room, I tried to stay calm. I was about to play one of the biggest matches of my life. Sure, I'd won a gold medal in basketball in Beijing, but I did so as part of a twelve-man squad, supported by my teammates. This time it would be all up to me.

Outside, a crowd of more than 1000 (which at the time was massive!) had gathered at court 8. At least half of them were my friends and family, all there ready to urge me on to victory. The weight of expectation made me feel nervous, *very* nervous, but I think nerves are a good thing, because they're a symptom of how much something means to you. If you can embrace that feeling and enjoy it, you'll perform at your best.

As soon as I got out onto the court the cheers of the crowd calmed me. I was fit, primed and hungry for the win. It was my moment and I was determined to take it with both hands.

I began by claiming an immediate break, before taking the first set 6–2. I was playing great tennis, and could tell that the loud crowd was making Wagner nervous. If you're Australian, Australian fans are truly the best in the world, but they'd be so annoying if you're not. I love that about our culture, that we back each other, no matter what.

The second set began well, and I was up 4–1, ready to take the title. Then, devastatingly for me, it started to rain, completely ruining my moment. Suddenly I was thinking

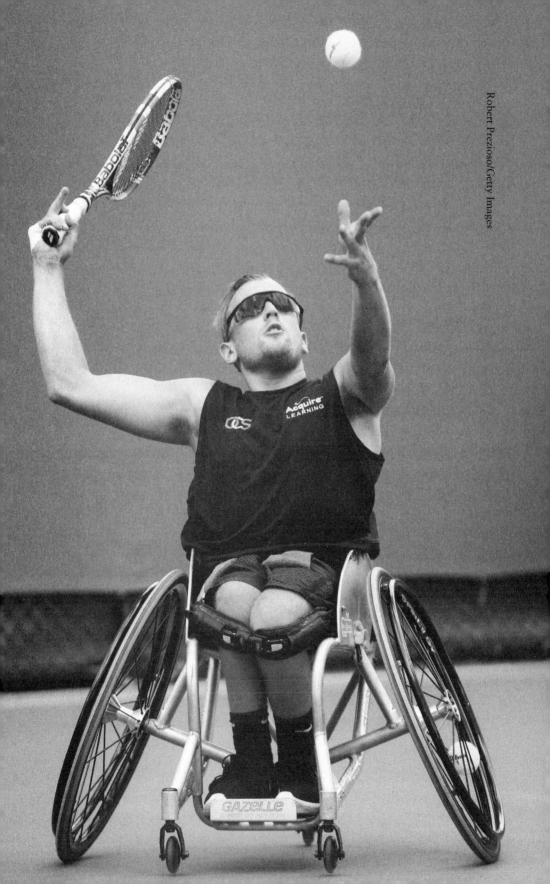

too much, and the weight of the occasion began to get the better of me. After a delay due to rain, I lost the next two games. Now I was leading by just one game, 4–3. *Don't let this moment slip. You can do this!* I told myself. The positive self-talk worked and, in the end, I proved too strong for Wagner and won the second set 6–3.

I'd done it. I'd won a Grand Slam! And it wasn't just any Grand Slam, it was the Australian Open, the championship I'd fantasised about winning since I was a kid wheeling myself around a tennis court for the first time. It was the definition of a dream come true.

People often ask me what it feels like. If you ask any top-level sportsperson they'll give you the same answer – the initial feeling is one of relief. Relief that you didn't let the opportunity pass. Relief that all the work was worth it. Relief that you didn't let your supporters and team down. It's like a giant, metaphorical weight off your shoulders. It's the best feeling in the world.

Soon after, the relief turns into utter jubilation. The sheer number of smiling faces in the crowd was overwhelming. To have 500 (no exaggeration) of my friends and family there to support me is something I never take for granted. Seeing how pumped they were was overwhelming. You really are nothing without the support of the people around you, so to be able to share it with so many familiar faces meant the world to me. I also easily drank about thirty beers out of the trophy that night and have never been so hungover in my life the next day! But hey, that is what a champion should do, right?

Winning the Australian Open title in 2015 boosted my profile, and for the first time the Australian media properly reported my successes on the court. Channel Seven broadcast highlights of the final during the prime-time coverage of the men's final, the first time something like that had been done. Other media agencies were taking note too. It was gratifying that people were interested in what I was doing, but not even I could imagine the heights it would reach in coming years.

# 11

# *king of the hill, top of the heap*

ONE OF THE BEST things about playing competitive sport, at whatever level, is the people you meet. There's something about camaraderie, competition and teamwork that bring people together. Everyone is working towards a common goal and having fun in the process.

I've never underestimated the huge role that sport has played in my life from a young age. Not only did it help with my health and fitness, encouraging me to get out of the house and get my heart rate up, but it also introduced me to a bunch of people just like me. For the first time ever, I met people who were in the same situation as me and who were smiling, happy, competing, travelling. It gave me a new perspective and hope that I could live a normal and happy life. But most of all, it gave me friends who were similar to me, not least the first ever friend I'd met through sport – Heath Davidson.

As you might remember, Heath was my first doubles partner, back what I was ten years old. He's four years older than me, and we'd played and trained together for years.

I'd always loved hanging out with Heath, not least because he was a naughty kid. He was always getting into trouble, always had girls around him, and always used to kick my arse at tennis. He started getting tattoos at a pretty young age too (and my god they're some of the worst tattoos you'll see – tribal tatts and all – and he'll agree with me!). Being four years younger than Heath, I always aspired to beat him, but I also loved it when he invited me over to his place to play video games, so I could see how older teenagers in wheelchairs did it. You learn a lot from other people with disabilities.

Unfortunately though, when I quit tennis, Heath quit tennis too. However, we did it for completely different reasons, and while I was retiring to focus on a Paralympic career in wheelchair basketball, Heath's life took a turn in another direction.

Heath's family life wasn't always perfect, and I'd feel sorry for him when he was in the middle of a family argument, which happened a bit. Hey, my family wasn't perfect either, but Heath was always such a legend to me, I worried about him, even back when I was a teenager. Then, after Heath decided to take a break from tennis, he started getting into partying, and pretty quickly his life spiralled out of control. We lost contact and barely said a single word to each other for years, for no other reason than we were mixing in different circles and weren't doing the same things anymore.

But Heath often crossed my mind, and I would wonder what he was up to. To be honest, I thought I might never see him again. So if you'd told me at the start of 2015 that I was about to get a new doubles partner and his name was Heath Davidson, I would've told you to get stuffed.

But the world works in mysterious ways, and during the 2014 Wimbledon TV coverage, Heath's fiancée, Darcie, had asked him why he'd given it up. The very next day, realising he'd given up for no good reason, Heath texted our old coach Marco Persi to arrange a hit. By the end of the week, he was back in the old routine and before he knew it he was in love with the sport in a way he'd never been as a junior.

Darcie encouraged him – she could see how much tennis was helping Heath turn his life around. Three months later, while his form was far from what it had been, the potential was there and he was still playing. So when he gave me a call and said that he wanted to have a hit, I jumped at the chance. I was so happy to see him back in the sport, and even happier to have him back as a friend. That first hit was a new beginning for both of us and led to a great partnership down the track. We've trained together every day since.

*\*\*\**

Following my win at the Australian Open, I headed to the United States in early March. With a freshly minted world number one ranking next to my name, the pressure was on to maintain my form. First up was Florida's Pensacola Open, where I defeated David Wagner in straight sets. At the New Orleans Cajun Classic the next week, however, I lost to Andy Lapthorne in the final.

In May, I headed to Fukuoka for the Japan Open, one of my favourite tournaments of the year because I speak a little Japanese from my school days. There, I got the win over David Wagner pretty easily in the final. But for the entire trip I was studying and writing, because there was something big on the horizon. As soon as I got home I was going to give a TEDx Talk to 5000 people at the Sydney Opera House.

Not that I wasn't looking forward to it. I was – along with sport and music, my great passion is public speaking. It's a skill I picked up at school, and it's always been something I love doing. Many would find that weird – giving a speech is probably one of most people's greatest fears – but for me it was the opposite. As you can probably tell eleven chapters in, I like the attention, and I always had a pretty natural knack for it.

A career I'd been pursuing outside of sport was motivational speaking. Now, I want to make clear that I actually hate that term 'motivational speaker', because it sounds like someone who forces their agenda down your throat, or makes you compare your life to theirs, causing you to cry and break down in tears. But for me, it's not about that. For me, a good speaker is someone who shares their story but doesn't force their thoughts or feelings upon their audience. It's up to the people listening to interpret that story any way they wish. If they feel motivated, great. If they laugh, even better. If they hate it – well, hey, at least it only lasted an hour.

My speaking career had been pretty small fry to start with, giving talks at schools and honing my craft on kids. Kids are great because they always ask the best questions, questions that adults are too scared to ask. 'Why are your legs small?', 'Can you drive?', 'You have stupid hair!' (not so much a question, that last one, but you get the gist). From there, I'd graduated to giving a few talks for the Victorian Institute of Sport, which was mostly telling my story to people taking tours of the place in Melbourne. But I'd always dreamt of cracking the big corporate market, going to the biggest companies all around the world, sharing my story and helping create positive social change for people with disabilities. I wanted to break down negative stigmas that are associated with my community, and change the way people with disabilities are perceived. But I was young, too young, and no one ever took me seriously.

That was until 2015, when I was asked to do the TEDx Talk at the Sydney Opera House. If you don't know what TEDx Talks are, well, let me put it this way – they're the public speaker's holy grail. Speakers get ten or so minutes to talk on a topic of their choice, and if you nail it, they go viral. *Very* viral. TED and TEDx Talks have been viewed tens of billions of times. It's a huge platform.

To be offered the chance to present a TEDx Talk at the age of twenty-four was a huge deal for me. I'd watched these talks for years (TED is branded 'Ideas Worth Spreading', of course) and had always dreamt of sitting on that red carpet dot and presenting one of my own. So when I received the call in March 2015, I legit almost crashed the car. What a freaking huge opportunity. *You better not f\*ck this up*, I thought to myself.

The topic I wanted to discuss was the idea of 'mainstreaming disability', the notion that we need more positive role models of people with disabilities in mainstream media to change the negative way we're perceived, to make people more comfortable and to normalise disability in the process. It's always killed me that whenever I saw anyone who looked like me on TV, they were viewed in some negative, devastating way. For example, in road safety ads, they'll follow a shot of a speeding drink driver crashing their car with an image of someone in a wheelchair, just like me, in tears because their life's over. Just the other day I watched a movie called *Me Before You*, in which a *hot*, famous billionaire who has everything going for him is hit by a car and ends up in a wheelchair. So now he is: 1. still hot; 2. still a famous billionaire; and 3. in a wheelchair; and 4. Khaleesi of *Game of Thrones* wants to have sex with him. That's the plot, which sounds bloody all right to me! So what does he do? He kills himself because he's in a wheelchair and feels he's a burden on society. What does that tell people about my life? People think I feel the same, but it couldn't be further from the truth.

I want to change that and help people with disabilities all around the world. So I decided at that very moment, sitting in the car, that I was going to put as much effort as I possibly could into this talk. I began writing, sharing stories, opening my heart, writing hooks, writing jokes, everything. If I say so myself, I was pretty sure I'd nailed it, and I went into my first Skype rehearsal with the TEDx director and producer full of confidence.

Safe to say it didn't go as well as I thought it would. In fact, they hated it. They said it wasn't even close to being good enough for the main stage. Shit. I needed to inject more 'me' into it, they said, and I understood what they meant. Often people try too hard to do things they think they *should* do and to say things they think they *should* say, rather than backing themselves in and doing what's authentic to *them*. I needed to speak more in my language and my tone, as opposed to trying to impress an older audience. So I did. I started speaking from the heart. Talking about how being bullied made me feel. About what it meant to never see anyone like me on TV. How it made me feel to be a Paralympian. And finally my talk started to come together. The whole process took about two months, but it was totally worth it. I learnt how to create a more substantial and effective piece of communication. *With a bit of luck*, I thought, *I may just be able to pull this off.*

So the week before, which I spent in Japan and in transit back to Sydney, I did virtually nothing but practise, doing non-stop ten-minute rehearsals, trying to memorise what I wanted to say. There are no notes allowed for TEDx Talks – everything has to be 'off the dome', as they say in rap music. It was going to be a big ask, but I thought that I had it in me.

The night before I had to give my talk, I had one of the worst sleeps of my life. Words were flying through my head, nonstop, as I tried to remember every last syllable of my speech.

When it was time, I walked from my hotel to the Opera House and met up with Mum and Dad, Dana, Zack, Kate and Liz Cambage, who had all flown up to support me. Seeing them before heading onstage helped calm my nerves. But now it was show time. My turn had come.

As soon as I hit centre stage, my mouth became as dry as the Nullabor in drought. Boom – thousands of eyes were on me, and my hands began to shake. It was probably one of the most nervous moments of my life. One way that I calm my nerves at big events like the Paralympics is to find my family in the crowd. Not sure why, but it always works. So that's what I did, and once I found them, I relaxed a little. And once I got to the front of the stage, I took a breath and launched in.

The time passed quickly. I was on autopilot, but somehow I nailed it, hitting every line and every joke. Near the end, I actually began to enjoy myself. Educating such a huge crowd about something I felt so passionately about was an experience I'd dreamt about, and one I'll never forget. The highlight, easily, was the 5000-strong standing ovation at the end – it gave me goosebumps. How ironic – a standing ovation for a guy who can't even stand.

That TEDx Talk opened a lot of doors for me, and suddenly I was travelling across the country, delivering motivational talks for some of the biggest businesses in Australia. Banks, financial institutions, car companies – I did them all, and still do to this day.

\*\*\*

Things were also changing for me on the tennis court. I had a new coach – François Vogelsberger – who I'd met after he moved from England to Australia with his family. As you can tell by his names, François is French (who would've thought!), and we immediately clicked. He's one of the best blokes you'll meet both on and off the court. He's also pretty handy on the eye (both Zack's girlfriend, Em, and Tim's girlfriend, Anna, have crushes on him). François's coaching was taking me to another level, and I was loving it.

In June 2015, I was back on the road again, heading to Europe for a summer of competition. I love playing the big events around the world, especially the Grand Slams, but a lot of wheelchair events are in small venues with no crowd and no media. I still play them because I need the world ranking points, and it's important to support and promote the game as much as possible, wherever possible. But I always struggled to get pumped up for them.

My first stop was the BNP Paribas Open de France in Paris, where I made it into the final, to defeat David Wagner 6–1, 6–2.

I celebrated by taking in all the sights of Paris, a city that's steeped in history. One of my favourite places is the Louvre, the great art museum that holds some of the world's most precious masterpieces. However, this time, my visit didn't go to plan. The elevators there are really hard to find, so I took matters into my own hands and wheeled onto the escalator. Escalators are pretty easy to use in a wheelchair, you just grab onto the sides with your hands and let the belts and stairs take you up. If you're going down, you turn around, grab the belts with your hands, and head down backwards (going backwards is a lot gnarlier and scarier). I nailed my ride in the Louvre, but a security guard saw me, grabbed me and, despite my attempted protests, escorted me out of the building for using the escalator in my wheelchair! Ah, the French.

Next stop was London to watch Sam Groth put up a gutsy fight against powerhouse Roger Federer in the third round at Wimbledon. Grothy had given me player box tickets, and it was awesome to be there to see him win a set on centre court against the great man. Unfortunately, back in 2015, Wimbledon didn't have quad wheelchair tennis, which sucked, and I wondered what playing on the most famous grass in the world would be like. One day I hoped to find out for myself.

Soon afterwards, Andy Lapthorne bundled me out of the British Open at Nottingham. The following week, I set out for the Swiss Open determined to do well enough to retain my world number one ranking.

Unfortunately, I lost to David Wagner in the final. Now he was world number one, and I'd slipped to number two. It stung. I wanted it back.

After six weeks in Europe, I headed back to Melbourne, where I spent five weeks preparing for my first shot at the US Open. I was ready for a red-hot go at winning the US title at the famed Flushing Meadows. This was my first Grand Slam tournament outside of Australia, and New York City was one of my favourite places in the world. I couldn't wait to get there and get underway.

But when I eventually arrived in New York, I couldn't seem to do anything right in practice. With the tournament just a few days away, I became worried and confused. I simply couldn't figure out what was going wrong. The more mistakes I made, the more tense I got. It was no fun at all.

Finally, out at dinner one night, it dawned on me – no fun was precisely the problem. I was taking it all so seriously, I'd temporarily forgotten how to enjoy myself on or off the court. It was time to remind myself who I was, and bring my personality to the court.

Kate, Dad and Dana arrived and I consciously decided to make the most of the city with them. And when I arrived at Arthur Ashe Stadium, inside the vast Billie Jean King National Tennis Center, I was raring to go.

For all its fame, the venue has quite a sterile feel compared to Melbourne's Rod Laver Arena. I think the problem is that it's a thirty-minute train ride from Manhattan, out in the borough of Queens. It would have a very different atmosphere if it was in Madison Square Garden, smack bang in the middle of the city.

David Wagner and I were hotly favoured to make the finals. As if the US Open title wasn't big enough in itself, we also knew that whichever one of us was victorious would finish 2015 as the number one player in the world.

Wagner started the tournament in style, beating his friend and doubles partner Nick Taylor 6–1, 6–0 in a mere thirty-four minutes. Their head-to-head record was an astonishing 72–7 in Wagner's favour.

Interviewed afterwards, Wagner explained that he was hugely motivated to win what he hoped would be his fifth Grand Slam singles title and third US Open crown, because the timing of the following year's Rio Paralympics would rule out participating in both events next year. Despite being forty-one, he had no plans to retire – something he attributed to yours truly. Our rivalry, he said, had propelled him to new heights: 'He makes me have to play the best I can play every time I step on the court. He's definitely changed what I have to do, as my training continues and my game plan moves forward. What I love about the sport is the ability to adapt and become stronger and better. Players that have the strength that he has definitely raise the bar in our division.' Ours was a fierce rivalry, and its intensity made any victories all the sweeter.

I started the Open well, defeating Andy Lapthorne 6–3, 6–3. I dispatched Nick Taylor next, which put me into the final against Wagner. It would be the twentieth time I'd gone up against David Wagner in only eighteen months of competition.

I started fast in an attempt to throw him off his rhythm. Kate, her cousins, Dad and Dana were there, and Jannik Blair had made the trek from Alabama, but there was only a small contingent of Australians in the crowd, so it surprised me to realise that a lot more people were cheering for me than for Wagner, despite the fact he was American.

The crowd response and my own burning desire to reclaim the number one position propelled me through a rapid-fire first set, which I claimed 6–1 in just nineteen minutes. Wagner hit back hard to take the second set 6–4.

I began to feel tight all over, and at the start of the third and final set, I was cramping quite badly. It wasn't long before I had to stop and call for the trainer. The problem was my right hand, which had become a permanent weak spot due to the nerve damage.

I was in all sorts of trouble and by the time Wagner was up 2–0, I feared I was done for. Then, just when I needed it most, I hit an unbelievable backhand down the line, pretty much with my eyes closed. Fluke or not, my dad claims it was and still is the best shot I've ever made. It put me right back in contention. I clawed my way back two minutes shy of three hours since we'd begun and I took out the third set 7–5 to be crowned US Open champion for the first time.

The feeling was amazing. Winning the Australian Open at the start of the year had been a great personal triumph but now, eight months later, here I was, the US Open champion. I thought my day couldn't get any better. I was wrong.

Previously, I'd received some free tennis apparel from Nike Australia. Nike was my favourite brand, and although it wasn't really a sponsorship – just a helping hand – they gave me some kit to wear in matches. It was very nice of them, so I thanked the company in my acceptance speech.

Not long afterwards, some guys approached Dad. 'Do you know that kid? We want to speak to him,' said one of them.

It turned out they were from Nike Tennis Global. 'Nike might not have been sponsoring you before the match, but it is now,' they said. True to their word, they did, and I've been sponsored by Nike ever since. Now they send me enough gear to clothe an army, including an unlimited quantity of shoes, which is funny for a brother in a wheelchair who definitely won't be wearing them out anytime soon!

The lesson from that event? It pays to be nice, and it pays to say thanks.

Kate and I had just celebrated our one-year anniversary, and after the US Open, we stopped off in San Francisco, Kate's hometown. She'd just bought an apartment in inner-city Melbourne and her parents lived in Melbourne too. But a lot of Kate's family still lived in San Francisco, so it was a great opportunity to meet her grandmother, aunts, uncles and cousins. They were lovely, caring people, just like her, but we'd never be moving to San Francisco – holy shit, those hills are murder if you're in a wheelchair!

\*\*\*

As 2015 drew to a close, I was back in Australia preparing to defend my Australian Open title early in the new year. But my sights were on the 2016 Rio Paralympics. The Games may have been nine months away, but excitement was already building, led by the Seven Network, which had bought the Australian broadcast rights. In addition to the usual Olympics glamour-sport coverage, they were putting the spotlight squarely on the Paralympics. It was the first time the Paralympics would be shown on a commercial network.

Life was great, with one sad exception. Unfortunately, our beautiful little cat Chad had finally passed away. Given his age, it wasn't a surprise, but, still, the whole family was devastated, especially Mum.

Chad was such a cool dude. When, as a kid, I suffered immense pain after my back surgery, Chaddy was always there to brighten my mood. Everyone who met him, loved him. He'd been with the family almost my whole life and we would all miss him terribly.

But there wasn't much time to mourn, because 2016 beckoned, and it was shaping up to be the biggest year of my life to date.

# 12

# *from f1s to oprah*

IT WAS LATE 2015 and the Australian Open was just around the corner. But while the Aussie Open was important to me, I had one eye on the ultimate goal for the year – singles gold at the Paralympic Games in Rio de Janeiro.

Just the thought of Rio made me excited. There was nothing I loved more than the Paralympic Games, so it was hard not to get ahead of myself and dream about what it would be like to win gold in a second sport. I had to keep a lid on it, though, as there was still a lot of hard work to do if I wanted to be in the best position come September.

The summer training block – from December through to when the tournaments start in early January – is the time when tennis players get most of their training done. The tournament schedule, for both able-bodied and wheelchair players, is packed. Week in week out, there are up to ten tournaments to choose from all around the world. For example, in a week in May there could be tournaments of varying competition level in Chile, Sweden, New Zealand, China, the USA and South Africa all at the same time. So players play a lot of tournaments, and training blocks are few and far between.

This was going to be my last big training block before the Rio Games in September, so I wanted to make the most of it. Luckily, there's nothing better for your fitness than training in the Australian sun. It's *hotter* than anywhere in the world at that time, and the stress it puts your body under prepares you for anything you might face, perfectly prepping you for the gruelling tour that awaits.

With the Paralympics on the agenda, I had a huge summer of preparation, training twice a day, if not three times, and leaving no stone unturned. I also tweaked a couple of things in my game, namely my serve and my net play.

My improved net play, in particular, came about in unexpected fashion. Thanks to the rich history that tennis has in Australia, I've been surrounded by a wealth of tennis knowledge over the years. But in the past, I'd never been brave enough to ask some of the great Australian able-bodied players for advice on my game. Sure, we'd chatted, but never in a one-on-one coaching sense. However, that all changed in my lead-up to the 2016 Australian Open when I approached a couple of my heroes for some tips.

About two weeks before the Australian Open, Pat Rafter and another Aussie great, Wally Masur, were having a hit on the court next to me. There was nothing much out of the ordinary about that – some of the former tennis pros like to keep themselves in good nick. One of the weaker parts of my game was my volley, and it was something I'd always wanted to improve. But how? What did I need to do? Well, why not ask two of the best volleyers in history, who happened to be playing right next to me. I approached their court, asked them, and they happily obliged.

So there I was getting a tennis lesson from Pat Rafter, my childhood hero, and Wally Masur, one of our great Davis Cup captains. As it turned out, their tips were priceless.

People tend to think you have to punch the ball when you volley, with not much follow-through. In fact it's often drilled into you – DON'T FOLLOW THROUGH! But Wally taught me something that Tony Roche had taught him – once you make contact with the ball, don't stop your stroke there, but instead give it a *tiny* little follow-through in the direction you want the ball to go. Not much, but enough to gently caress it to where you want the ball to head.

We practised it for an hour together and it worked. From that day on, I've been a different player at the net, something for which I'm forever grateful to those two incredible players. Even now, if I know Pat's in the crowd when I play, I find myself giving him a wink when I hit a good one.

\*\*\*

With my training block over, I headed up north to the Brisbane International, eager to defend my title. Heath Davidson had really developed since his return to the sport twelve months earlier, and he'd qualified for the tournament too. It was one of his first major tournaments since his comeback. Heath and I would each play in the singles and play together in the doubles. To say I was excited to have him there would be an understatement.

In his Brisbane debut Heath won his first round match but lost in the next round to Britain's Jamie Burdekin. I came up against Jamie in the final and defeated him to claim the Brisbane International Quad Singles trophy for the second year in a row.

That tournament also marked another milestone for me, too, when, for the first time, I did live commentary of an able-bodied professional tennis match for the Seven Network. I'd showed interest in commentating to the network during the previous year, and was stoked to get my first opportunity behind the mic. For the team at Seven, namely Chris Jones, Nick Barrow and Hamish McLachlan, who made the introductions, to back me in and give me a crack meant a lot, and I was pretty pumped that I didn't embarrass myself on my first showing! At the conclusion of the event, they invited me to join the coverage for the 2016 Australian Open, an offer I gladly accepted.

Following Brisbane, it was on to the Apia International Sydney, where I again defeated Jamie Burdekin and Japan's Mitsuteru Moroishi before a straight-sets win over Andy Lapthorne in the final. There was no time to rest, though, because the following day I was in Melbourne ready for the Australian Open.

The Open was a lot different for me this time around. For the first time in my sporting career, people were starting to recognise me, and to care about my career. Sponsors began to take a small interest, and my new relationship with the Seven Network meant they were pushing my commentary and matches on their channels. With this, in turn, came added expectations, and I was desperate to make it two Australian Opens in a row.

Week one kicked off with training and work behind the mic, an opportunity I relished. I got to commentate matches and interview players (namely Gregor Dimitrov), and was even the subject of a few media stories myself. Jeez, how things had changed!

My on-court campaign started in the second week with a convincing win over Andy Lapthorne. The following day I beat my old rival David Wagner 7–5, 6–1 and followed it with a 6–4, 6–3 victory against Lucas Sithole. Once again (can you see a common thread here?) I would meet Wagner in the final, in what would be the twenty-second match between us. Our battles had started out very one-sided, as he'd wiped the floor with me every time. But my performances had improved, and the ledger now sat at eleven finals victories to him and ten to me. I was determined to even it up here on my home turf.

A big crowd turned out, by far the biggest crowd I'd ever played tennis in front of, and on paper I should have come out firing. But instead I was soon down 2–0. It was as though I'd forgotten how to play the game. My god, I was nervous! *This is going to be bad*, I thought to myself, and for a brief moment I began to spiral into self-doubt. I started my breathing routines and tried to settle down.

Relaxation is such an important skill in sport, in particular the ability to clear your head. As my manager Mark Jones once told me, 'It's not the best player who wins the big matches, it's whoever has the clearest thought process.' I couldn't agree more. That's why so many sportspeople play well in practice but struggle to reproduce it in big matches. In training it's easy to think, there's no pressure. In big matches, it's a whole different story.

Eventually I settled and stopped over-hitting the shots. My subtle touch returned. I began to play well and started steamrolling him, taking the first set 6–2. Up 5–2 in the second, I broke Wagner's serve to love to win the match in sixty-six minutes. Two in a row, baby! The year had begun perfectly.

My success on the court was accompanied by success off it. A week after defending my Australian Open title I was appointed an ambassador for Swisse vitamins in the lead-up to the Paralympic Games. It was humbling that big brands were starting to see the benefit of supporting Paralympic athletes, and not just to get a warm fuzzy feeling in their stomachs. They were beginning to understand the benefit to their brand and the return on investment, thanks to our abilities on and off the court due to our interesting stories.

The Swisse deal came with a couple of added bonuses, namely the opportunity to hang out with one of the most famous people on the planet. Oprah Winfrey was in town completing her world motivational speaking tour, and Swisse was the major sponsor of the event. A group of about sixty people were invited to attend an intimate meet and greet with her before she hit the stage at Rod Laver Arena, and I was one of those very lucky people. From the moment Oprah walked into the room, she was mesmerising. Everyone fell dead silent – you could hear a pin drop – and a feeling of calm descended. I couldn't look away from her. That's Oprah!

She then proceeded to tell us stories about her life for half an hour before getting up to leave. On her way out, she spotted me in my chair out of the corner of her eye (the wheelchair's great for getting people's attention!), and made a beeline towards me.

After introducing herself she asked me what I did. I could barely speak, but I managed to mumble that I played tennis.

'I love your energy,' she said before posing for a photo with me. From there, she worked the room then was gone.

The most memorable thing I learnt from meeting her was how incredibly kind and lovely she seemed, proving that no matter how much money you have or how famous you are, it's important to stay true to who you are, and how powerful that can be when you do.

Not long after, Swisse invited me to do a lap in the back of a Minardi two-seater F1 car at the Australian Grand Prix in Melbourne. Every year they do it. The car is driven by a professional driver, and the passenger sits in the back and gets taken on three hot laps of the track. There'd been concerns about my disability and whether I'd be able to do it. Until then, no one with any form of disability had ever been allowed in the car, but I assured everyone I'd be fine. I was already a paraplegic, anyway – what else could happen?

After some discussion, the team at the Australian Grand Prix, Minardi and Swisse gave me the go-ahead – it was on. Sitting in the back of the F1 car waiting to do the laps was a weird feeling. I didn't know what to expect. I'd been in a fast car before, sure, but this felt like a whole different kettle of fish. But there was no turning back now.

We took off slowly out of the pit lane and then BOOM! – zero to 200 kilometres per hour in about four seconds. ARE YOU KIDDING ME! My whole body was pushed against the back of the seat, and no matter how hard I tried to move, I couldn't. We took corners so fast, my neck was thrown around like a rag doll's (no wonder these dudes have such thick necks!). The acceleration of the car was intense, but nothing compared to the braking. We went from 300 kilometres per hour to under 100 in about one second. ONE SECOND! The force it put my body under was intense. It was exhilarating, but after three laps, it was over and I was quietly happy to return to the comfort of my wheelchair.

It was an experience I'll never forget, though, and thanks go to everyone who made it happen. (I have to apologise to my dad, Martin, because to do an F1 lap was the number one dream of his whole life, and I stole it! Sorry Dad!)

Things were ticking along nicely. But there was more excitement to come, this time in the form of the greatest band ever, the Wu-Tang Clan. I might have been training for the Paralympics, but nothing was going to stop me catching the Wu, who'd announced a three-city tour back in December.

Ghostface, Raekwon, RZA, GZA, U-God, Inspectah Deck and Masta Killa were coming to Australia and it would be the first time the whole crew had been here in five years. Along with hip hop fans around the country, I couldn't wait.

But there was a hitch. Ghostface, Masta Killa, U-God and Inspectah Deck had been in trouble with the law when they were younger and there was talk that they might not get visas. For Ghostface, the problem was a charge of attempted robbery in New York in 1995. For some reason this hadn't been a problem when he came out by himself for Meredith, but suddenly it was an issue when the rap sheets of all four guys were reviewed ahead of the tour.

My friend Lozi Hughes was working for the touring company and asked me if I'd write a character reference for Ghostface to try to help him get his visa approved. She didn't have to ask twice; after all, not only was I a fan, but I knew what a lovely bloke he was. I was happy to help.

I wrote a character reference for Ghostface and the others that was to be submitted to the Department of Immigration, and, boy, did I put some mayonnaise on it. I pulled out all the cards I had – mentioned my OAM and gold medals, said the Wu-Tang music helped me get through hospital, and the rest. I sent in the letter, and the next day, out of nowhere, they got their visa! I suspect my letter made absolutely no difference, but the Wu (with some high praise from Lozi) seemed to think it played a big part, and they invited me to perform with them at Melbourne's Margaret Court Arena.

This time was super special as the whole of the Wu-Tang Clan was there. And after 'we' played 'Protect Ya Neck', Ghostface told the crowd: 'Make some noise for my motherf*cker mate, Dylan, right here in the building. The motherf*cking tennis champ. Listen, he made the phone call the other day for me to enter this country, you understand. Because of this man I got through. Make some f*cking noise.' For a lifelong rap fan, it doesn't get any better than that.

\*\*\*

As we counted down the 200 days until the Paralympics, Heath and I were putting in some huge training sessions to get ready. I'd already qualified for the Games, but Heath's ranking fell outside the qualification cut-off, meaning he would have to impress the International Tennis Federation to be granted a wildcard. We were desperate for him to be there so we could play doubles together, so we were pushing each other to the limit. In one session we almost wore our arms off as we pushed and pushed our way through two hours of hill sprints outside the Melbourne Cricket Ground. Kill me.

Then, around Easter, Heath, François and I got on a plane and headed for South Africa, where Heath and I were to compete individually and together in the Gauteng Open and the South African Open. These would be two of the last tournaments before the cut-off for the Paralympic Games, so Heath and I needed to impress on the doubles court if he was to win that wildcard to Rio.

In Gauteng, Heath won his opening singles match, but went out in the second round. I struggled a bit with the thin atmosphere 1600 metres above sea level (about the same as Denver, Colorado), but worked my way through the field to face David Wagner again in the final. I got the win.

Heath and I did well early on in the doubles too, and did enough to get through to the final, where we were up against David Wagner and Lucas Sithole. We got *pumped*, 6–0, 6–0. I'm not going to lie, it was a bad sign. To get our arses kicked hurt our confidence. I thought all that training would have paid off, but it hadn't. If we played like that at the Games, there'd definitely be no doubles medal for Australia.

However, a week later, in the South African Open in Johannesburg, things changed, and drastically. I was lucky enough to win the singles tournament, but it was in the doubles that things really rocked. We ended up playing the best doubles of our lives, beating Wagner and Sithole in the semi-final in straight sets, and then Jamie Burdekin and Andy Lapthorne (the UK pair) in the final for our first big victory as doubles partners.

It was a huge turnaround from the week before, and I was so proud of how well Heath had played. He was like a new man, solid as a rock, giving our opponents nothing. It was a significant win, given that we'd beaten the world's best teams, and it was the first time I thought we might be in with a shot for gold in Rio together. But that was still a long way off.

In May, we headed to Japan for the last tournament before the qualification cut-off for the Games. A lot was on the line. We'd been playing together for eighteen months, and now we were starting to click.

In Japan, I won the singles and Heath and I won the doubles. Two in a row. We were building a good case, but a big test was on the horizon – the BNP Paribas World Team Cup.

This event is the wheelchair equivalent of the Davis and Federation Cups. It's the biggest event of its kind in the world, drawing fifty-one teams from twenty-nine nations. You might remember I went to a bunch of these as a junior player, but this was the first time I'd played in the senior competition. Australia was making its debut in the quad category, and Heath and I were honoured to have been chosen to represent our country.

In our first singles pool game, Nick Taylor got the USA away to a good start, beating Heath, but I pulled things back our way, beating David Wagner. In the doubles we fought back from a slow start to defeat the USA before defeating Japan and then Israel to take Australia through to the quad final.

Heath was getting used to the pressure and the speed of the game at the top level, and I was stoked by how he was progressing. He wasn't winning too many singles matches, but we were cleaning up all opposition in the doubles. One reason for our success was how relaxed we were out there together. We were always smiling, partly because we're mates, but mostly because we'd found we played our best tennis when we were having fun.

Getting our country through to the finals on debut was pretty special. We went up against Great Britain under lights after rain had delayed the start of play. Jamie Burdekin beat Heath in the singles 6–3, 6–4 but I got past Andy Lapthorne 6–2, 6–4. The winner of the deciding doubles would lift the World Championship trophy.

It was easily the biggest match of Heath's career, and the largest stage we'd played doubles on together. It was fantastic to see that Heath was not at all overawed. He genuinely loved the competition and said he felt like he was out there having fun, hitting tennis balls with a mate. It's true that we played an eccentric brand of tennis compared to most of our rivals, but it kept the British guessing.

With our shared dream of reaching the top of the world, we were seriously motivated. In the end we easily accounted for the Brits, Heath and I creating our own little piece of tennis history with Australia's first victory at the World Team Cup in our classification. As we hugged and then proudly posed with the magnificent trophy, we both knew we were in with a real chance for an even greater reward in a few months' time.

But first, we had to nervously wait to hear whether Heath would gain a wildcard entry to the Paralympics. Surely after our recent victories, there was no way he could be left out, and it was with huge relief that we finally heard he'd be on the plane to Rio. The thought of having one of my best mates alongside me at the Paralympics, especially given where he'd come from, was extremely special.

The celebrations were quite short following our World Championship win. Sure, it was a great feeling, but both Heath and I had bigger fish to fry. Our eyes were on the prize, and the prize was a gold medal.

# 13

# *going for gold again: rio 2016*

IT'S IMPORTANT TO TAKE risks in life. And I've always been one to put a lot on the line. Within reason, of course – I try to make sure I take educated risks. Because, in my book, the biggest risks bring the biggest rewards.

But a lot of people shy away from getting out of their comfort zone or pushing themselves to do new things, preferring to stick to the status quo instead. I guess we all get stuck in our routines, which is fair enough, because taking risks can sometimes lead to failure – even disaster. Back in 2012, after the London Paralympic Games, I found myself being one of those people, living day to day, not pushing myself to do or be better. I needed to take a risk and set myself a new challenge. I needed to put it all on the line.

In the end, I decided to make my move to tennis. But if I was going to do it, I needed an end goal, an overarching challenge that would mean everything to me. For me, that challenge was to win the singles gold at the 2016 Rio Paralympic Games. Only a select group of athletes have won two gold medals in two different sports across two Olympic or Paralympic Games. I wanted to be one of those athletes.

I could have pretty easily stuck with basketball and had a great career with the Rollers, something I loved. But I wanted to go all in and challenge myself. Who knows? I might have failed miserably at tennis and may have never been able to get back into the basketball team. I may never have qualified for the Rio Games. I may have lost my sporting career all together. But those were all risks I was willing to take. I wanted to challenge myself to see if I could do it.

In the weeks leading up to Rio, I was absolutely annihilating myself on the training track, working my arse off, and so was Heath. I was training so hard – so that when the time came and I got out on the court in Rio and looked across at whoever was on the other side of the net, I'd know for sure that there was absolutely no way they could have worked as hard as I had. There was no way they'd spent more hours preparing than I had. Because, as my Tennis Australia high-performance manager, Alex Jago, once said, in moments of pressure, you don't rise to the occasion, you sink back to your habits. My thinking was, if my habits were better than theirs, thanks to hours of preparation, I couldn't lose.

By most measures I was fit, but there was still room for improvement. So I switched to a ketogenic diet, no longer eating carbohydrates and sugars and getting all my energy from fats. Everyone's different, but the diet worked for me, helping me to get in the best shape of my life.

My training regime was more intense than ever, consisting of five hours a day, six days a week. I'd spend two and a half hours on court in the morning and then do speed and agility drills later in the day. I also did three or four intense weight sessions a week with my high school friend and trainer, Eddie Espinosa. Eddie is a legend, and he was giving me personal one-on-one sessions to get me ready for the Games. He would *kill* me – boxing, ropes, sled pushes, chin-ups, weighted dips, everything – but my god it worked. Thanks to Eddie, I was feeling incredible. The crazy part was he never took a single cent in payment. He just wanted to be part of the journey, and to this day he still trains my whole family every week.

The lead-up to Rio also involved quite a lot of media attention and events, which were tough to juggle but something that I always enjoyed. As Paralympians, we didn't get paid the mega bucks some of our Olympic counterparts were paid. As a result, I always felt it was essential to hustle for media attention. If I didn't, no one cared about us. But thanks to years of persistence, the attention was now there, and it was enjoyable to be part of it.

I was doing regular interviews with my good friends at triple j, as well as a number of pieces for the Seven Network, who was broadcasting the Paralympics for the first time. One of the most enjoyable gigs was being interviewed by the great Bruce McAvaney (BRUUUUUUCE!) about the upcoming Games on an episode of his show *Off the Record*. I shared the episode with Paralympic swimmer and friend Ellie Cole. Safe to say, it was ... special.

Another one of the cooler things I did was have dinner with the Vice President of the United States, Joe Biden. Kate and I were invited by the Governor of Victoria, the Honourable Linda Dessau, and it was an opportunity too good to pass up. When I saw Vice President Biden's cavalcade of more than thirty cars turn up, I couldn't believe how freaking long it was! There were fire engines, police cars, SUVs and a pair of limousines flown in from America especially for the Vice President's use. I'd never seen security like it. There must have been eighty guests at Government House, plus easily forty security guards especially for him, all talking into microphones and adjusting their ear pieces.

Before entering, guests were schooled by the Governor's staff on correct protocol. Our names were to be read out to the party, including the Governor, the Premier and the Vice President, and then we were under strict instructions to proceed into the room and to address Mr Biden as 'Mr Vice President'.

The Vice President came into the room with an air of confidence. Kate was introduced to the honoured guests before me.

'Hello, Kate,' Vice President Biden said as she walked in.

'Hey Joe!' Kate replied. What happened to the protocol?!

I cracked up laughing and couldn't stop. The Vice President liked it too. As Kate was American, we both very much enjoyed the night and felt privileged to be there.

After dinner, the guest of honour got up to leave, accompanied by Governor Dessau. Vice President Biden walked past everyone else before stopping by me.

'Dylan's about to head off to the Paralympic Games in Rio for wheelchair tennis,' Governor Dessau said to

Vice President Biden. 'Good luck!' the Vice President said. 'Who's your biggest competition?'

'An American,' I replied.

'Well then, not too much luck then,' he said before walking off. What a cheeky guy.

In July 2016 at a ceremony in Melbourne, Heath and I were 'officially' named in Australia's Paralympics team to compete in both singles and doubles. The other three members of the wheelchair tennis team were Ben Weekes and Adam Kellerman in the men's open singles and doubles and Sarah Calati in the women's singles.

Heath and I made a lightning visit to the UK to compete in the British Open. Heath didn't have much luck in singles, losing in his first game, but once again I faced David Wagner in the final and won in straight sets.

We didn't end up playing in the doubles because we missed the sign-in cut-off by one minute. Brenda, our team manager, wasn't happy. Sorry Brenda! But with the busy schedule we had, I didn't think the rest would hurt our chances too badly.

Back home very briefly, we did final prep for the Games. Physically, I was ready, but I was always working on ways to improve my mental game. I wanted to come up with a tactic for when I started to feel the pressure in Rio. The Games and winning gold meant so much to me, I knew I was going to feel the pressure more than ever before. I talked to my sports psychologist, Anthony Klarica. Anthony used to be the head psych at Tennis Australia, but now works for the mighty Carlton Blues. My aim was to develop some tools to ensure I didn't freeze up on court, or 'choke', as it's known. I wanted to be able to perform at my best, no matter what might happen.

Anthony asked me to think of something that always made me happy, something that had no negative connotations tied to it at all. I told him that the one thing in the world that always made me feel happier, no matter what mood I was in, was my cat, Chad. No matter what was going on, thinking about Chaddymoongies would always put me in a good mood. Anthony told me to think of Chad as a tool to clear my head, to relax, and to smile. It would be a tool that would come in handy in a couple of weeks' time.

It might have seemed as though I didn't need these little tricks and last-minute sessions. After all, I was going into the Paralympics ranked number one in the world for Quad Singles. But as every top athlete knows, rankings mean very little once you're out there. It all depends on what happens on the day. At that level, absolutely anyone can beat anyone. That's why you get upsets, when newcomers and long-shot players turn into giant killers. So I wanted to leave no stone unturned in order to be ready. Also, winning silver in London was rarely far from my mind, and I never wanted to have that feeling again.

It had been sixteen years since Australia's previous and only Paralympic gold in wheelchair tennis, won by wheelchair tennis legend David Hall in Sydney. I planned on adding to that tally.

*** 

On 25 August 2016, the Australian Paralympic team left Australia. Our journey had begun. However, rather than fly straight to Rio, the team spent a week at a training camp in Miami, acclimatising to the humidity and heat, which was similar to what we'd experience in Brazil. The training camp went off without a hitch, and by the time we arrived in Rio, we were ready for our assault on gold.

At the Rio Paralympics there were 4342 athletes representing 159 countries. Like every other visitor, we Australians were blown away by the amazing spectacle that is Rio. From Copacabana Beach to Christ the Redeemer, Rio is unbelievably picturesque. However, in terms of the infrastructure, it was probably the most underprepared of all the Games I've competed in. These Games didn't have the mega budget of Beijing or London, and many parts of the athletes' village and competition venues weren't fully completed up to standard. I'm not one to complain, though, and it was an honour to be there regardless. I was ready to roll.

We arrived in the village about a week before the Games were due to get underway, but it didn't feel real until the day of the Opening Ceremony. There was a total party vibe, and the ceremony was filled with dancers, colour and light, but the most special moment for me was entering the stadium behind Brad Ness, captain of the Rollers, who carried the flag for our country. I couldn't think of a better person to represent us and symbolise what the Paralympics were all about. I felt immense pride, wheeling into the stadium behind him.

I also felt buoyed by support from Aussies back home, who flooded us with messages, as well as those who'd flown halfway around the world to be there. Twenty of my friends and family had flown in from all over the world to support me in the flesh. It cost all of them a lot of time and money to do so, and having them there meant the world to me. I was hoping that the chance to be among the elite athletes who'd won gold in two Paralympic sports would not only justify the effort I'd put in over the past few years, but would reward my life-long support crew who'd been there through everything, the highs and the lows. I wanted to make those people proud of all the work they'd put into me.

I opened my campaign at the Olympic Tennis Centre by beating Israel's Shraga Weinberg 6–0, 6–0 in the singles. It was the perfect start, and filled me with confidence for the rest of the tournament. I was also extremely pumped for Heath, who, after dropping the first set against American Bryan Barten, came back to win and make it to the quarter-finals. Unfortunately for Heath, Andy Lapthorne defeated him in their singles quarter-final, but I was running hot, beating Nick Taylor in the quarters, and Lucas Sithole in straight sets, 6–0, 6–3, in our semi-final. Meanwhile, in the doubles, Heath and I defeated the Japanese pair Shota Kawano and Mitsuteru Moroishi to make the doubles semi-finals. We were victorious here, too, blasting Brits Jamie Burdekin and Andy Lapthorne 6–1, 6–2.

I'd made it through to the finals of both the singles and doubles, putting my dream of dual golds in different sports firmly within reach. The other members of the Australian wheelchair tennis team in Rio had played great, but unfortunately had been eliminated before the medal rounds, so the hopes were firmly resting on us.

In a relatively big upset, Andy Lapthorne beat David Wagner in their semi, so I'd be facing Andy for the singles medal. Lappo and I got on quite well, so it was going to be a very entertaining final. But before that, my focus was firmly on the doubles gold medal match, which was scheduled the night before.

As expected, Heath and I were up against Nick Taylor and David Wagner from the USA. Taylor and Wagner were favourites going into the match, given that they'd won three successive gold medals prior to Rio. In fact, they'd never lost a match in the history of the Paralympics. Never. It was a very impressive record. Our final was scheduled after the women's semi-final match on centre court. Unfortunately, that match ran nearly four hours, which meant our final was delayed. By the time the Netherlands' Aniek van Koot finally prevailed over Japan's Yui Kamiji, it was night time. There was one upside to this: our match was being telecast live back in Australia. Now, instead of it airing in the wee hours, it would be broadcast at breakfast time back home. That allowed over a million people to watch, which would give our profiles a real boost.

The match finally began, and Heath and I started badly. He was nervous and I could sense that, and I responded by overplaying, trying to do too much and finish points too quickly. We lost the first set 6–4. We were still in, but something had to change, and change quickly.

Unfortunately for us, nothing did, and before we knew it, we were down 4–1, 40–0. Wagner and Taylor seemed just minutes away from securing the gold medal. At this point, no word of a lie, I thought we were cooked. I actually found myself starting to think about what I'd eat after the game, to give myself energy for the singles final the following night. I also felt a sense of embarrassment that we'd just got pumped live on national TV. It really wasn't going to plan.

But suddenly Heath and I came together, and for the first time in the whole match, we actually had a laugh and a smile at how bad we were going. It changed everything. We relaxed, starting making balls, and slowly clawed our way back. We got it back to 4–2. Then 4–3. Then 4 all. Then, in a flash, we took the second set 6–4. The match had so far lasted fifty-nine minutes, and we were in prime position. But there was one problem: we were both busting for a pee. So we took a toilet break. Bad move.

We lost all our momentum and found ourselves down 3–0 in the third set. What idiots! Why did we take a toilet break? Once again, I thought we'd stuffed it. But luckily, we pulled it together. I began to take control of the net and Heath started hitting some big winners. Facing a double break, we fought back again to 3–all, then 4–all, then 5–all.

Heath was serving at 5–all but I could see the nerves had hit him again. I rolled over to him. 'Mate you've got this,' I said confidently. 'Just give us four first serves.' I was putting on a brave face, but deep down, if I'm honest, I thought the moment would get the better of him and he would completely stuff it. Instead, Heath nailed his serve. And again. And again. And again. We won that game to love. We were up 6–5. At the point, I knew the gold was ours.

Wagner and Taylor were shattered. Now it was us who seemed just minutes away from gold, and this time there was no twist in the tale. Wagner was serving to save the match. At 30–30, Nick Taylor floated a ball into the net and we were one point from gold. Heath and I pumped our fists. Then I smashed a winner and, two hours and forty-five minutes after we'd started, we took the final set 7–5.

We'd gone from two fat kids with no friends to, sixteen years later, Paralympic gold medallists! I honestly couldn't believe it.

Ecstatic, Heath and I embraced on centre court and shed tears of joy on each other's shoulders. I was so unbelievably proud of him and how well he'd played. It was his first major tournament, and he'd showed nerves of steel in the biggest moment of our lives. We were both shocked that we were Paralympic champions.

Our amazement was pretty understandable. If you played that match one hundred times over, from the position we were in, down 4–6, 1–4, you'd lose it ninety-nine times. To pull it off the way we did, winning five games in a row, then being 3–0 down in the third set and still triumphing, well, I'm just so proud of what we achieved.

It was one of the best thrills of my life to be beside one of my best mates, and to fight the way we did. Our victory was shared with every single one of the thousands of people who had helped us get there. Our gold medals were a tribute to all of them.

Not surprisingly, I didn't sleep very well that night. It was a huge high to come down from, but I needed to prepare myself for my next challenge, the gold medal singles match against Andy Lapthorne. Although the gold medal in the doubles was incredible, it had come as a bit of a surprise because we weren't expected to win. However, it was a different story with the singles. All the expectation was on me – I hadn't lost a singles match for more than a year, and had arrived at Rio with an eighty-game winning streak. As well, winning that singles final meant more than anything to me, and if I lost it, I knew I'd leave Rio very disappointed, with a hollow feeling.

\*\*\*

It was show time. The stands were packed with supporters, and the vibe in the stadium was electric. My family and friends were up and about, and Lappo had an equally big mob who'd come over from the UK. They were just as passionate as my crew, and from the moment the match started, the atmosphere was not too dissimilar to an English soccer game, with both sides chanting loudly for their man. It was a fun vibe, but on the court the atmosphere was serious.

I won the first game of the match and then prevented Andy from getting in front for the whole set. When I took the first set 6–3, I was happy with how the match was progressing. But I knew I had a lot of work still to go before the singles gold was mine.

In the second set, I got off to a great start, and was soon leading 5–2. Now I was just one game away from singles Paralympic glory. That's when the nerves hit. Next thing I knew, it was 5–4, and I started to get stressed. We'd been

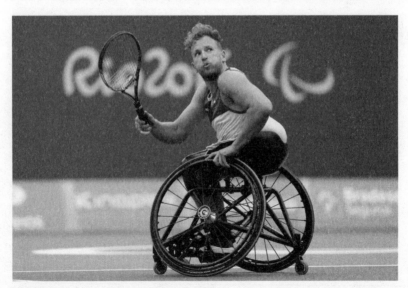

Matthew Stockman/Getty Images

playing for ninety-two minutes when, at 5–4, 40–30, I served on match point for the gold medal. But Andy Lapthorne wasn't giving up. He wanted this victory just as much as I did, and hit a big winner to get it back to deuce. I grimaced at the lost opportunity.

Our supporter groups were chanting louder than I'd ever heard. Thirty seconds later, Lappo's face erupted into a huge smile as he lobbed one past me. Advantage receiver. Union Jacks waved in the stands as he fought back with everything he had.

I managed to dive on a shifty little drop shot he plonked over the net, sending it into the far corner of his court. I was back in the game. Deuce.

Then came a wide serve, followed by Lappo's backhand return and a big forehand winner from me. Once again it was my advantage.

Again the nerves hit. I was shaking, barely able to hold the racquet. This was make-or-break and the tension surged within me. I needed to relax. Then it dawned on me – I had the tools to do so. I sat there, with my eyes closed, and thought of my cat, Chad. No word of a lie. I painted a picture of his little face in my head, and I immediately felt a weight off my shoulders. I was ready. I was serving for the ultimate prize. It was, in fact, the biggest moment of my life.

I opened my eyes, bounced the ball a few times, tossed it high and hit it with everything I had. The serve went straight down the middle. Lappo tried a backhand return but it was too quick for him. I'd served the biggest ace of my life.

The scoreboard flashed up 6–3, 6–4. I'd done it! The gold medal was mine. .

Up in the grandstand Mum, Dad and Kate were in tears. Everyone was on their feet, cheering. François had a look of immense pride on his face. And I was proud that I'd done it.

Overjoyed, I stretched my arms out wide in victory, then clasped the top of my head and held it tight, as if trying to make sure that this memory never escaped. I now had three gold medals from two Paralympic sports in two different Games. I'd been thinking of this very moment, picturing it, for three and a half years. I was overcome with happiness, and relief.

Lappo and I wheeled ourselves to the net and embraced. I kissed him on the cheek and told him how proud I was that we'd brought out the best in each other. I wasn't surprised when he began to cry, either. No one understood better than me how much hard work and emotion and sacrifice it had taken for him to get here. Now it would be four long, frustrating years before he could go for gold again. As thrilled as I was to win, I felt for him, because I'd been in that position four years earlier.

He gave me great praise after the match. 'This guy is the best in the world and a brilliant tennis player, and he came out and proved why tonight,' he said. 'Me and Dylan are going to go at it for the next four years. I'll see him on the centre court at the Paralympics in Tokyo and we'll have the rematch.' It meant a lot to hear his kind words.

When it was time for my interview I, too, choked up. I was just so proud and grateful for everybody who'd helped me get to this historic moment.

'This one is for them,' I said. 'To have so many friends and family here, it's amazing. Sport has done everything for me. I was once really insecure about my disability and now to travel the world and play sport, it's a dream come true … the Paralympics is a beautiful thing, where for two weeks people with a disability rule the world, and to share it with the wider world means everything to me.

'It was real tough out there and Andy played incredibly. Any able-bodied person who hasn't watched Paralympic sport: you don't know what you're missing, because not only are we inspirational, we're entertaining, elite athletes who put on a show every time we compete. I'm so proud to be a Paralympian and I'm so happy that I made everyone in Australia proud.'

I meant every single word that I said. It still stands today as one of the best moments of my life.

# 14

# *smashing glass ceilings*

ACHIEVING AN ULTIMATE GOAL is the best feeling in the world. Every single day for nearly three years, I had dreamt, lost sleep over, and thought about winning gold at the 2016 Rio Paralympic Games. At last I'd done it. Not everyone gets the chance to achieve their number one dream so I wasn't taking this for granted. I knew I was extremely lucky to be able to live out my boyhood dream, not once, not twice, but three times, and my elation was indescribable. So much effort, time and sweat had gone into winning those two gold medals in Rio. Now, with the hard work over, it was time to celebrate and enjoy the moment with the people who meant most to me.

My first stop, gold medals dangling from my neck, was the athletes' village food hall, to grab a quick bite before heading out on the town. All week, I'd been eyeing off the all-you-can-eat free McDonald's, but I'd refrained, keen to ensure I was in peak condition to compete. Now I was done on the court, I launched in. All week, Heath and I had discussed how many nuggets we could eat in one sitting. *Stuff it*, I thought, and ordered 200 chicken nuggets. Why? Just because I could. When else would you get the chance to order that many? You don't get free McDonald's every day. But I failed miserably and only ate about fifteen.

Heath and I were young and riding high. With François and our team manager, Brenda, we headed out to join my friends and family. We were in one of the world's great party cities, however I was booked for a TV interview with the Network Seven team first thing in the morning (7 am!), so Brenda had set a 2 am curfew. It was a good call.

We began by celebrating in a restaurant on Copacabana Beach. Coincidentally Andy Lapthorne and his family were at the same place. It was really nice to be able to sit back, post-competition, with each other's families and share a toast. Safe to say, we had a few. Brazil's deceptively potent national cocktail, the Caipirinha, goes down way too easily, and, before we knew it, it was 4 am. Only a few hours until my interview. Ouch.

I got a few hours of sleep, but was definitely worse for wear the next morning. I woke up, wearing nothing but my gold medals, to the sound of my Australian phone ringing (we also had Brazilian numbers which we kept on us at all times for security reasons).

It was my best mate, Tim. 'Where the fuck are you?' he yelled. 'Channel Seven have been saying every ad break that you'll be up next but you haven't turned up!'

SHIT! I was an hour and a half late! I quickly got dressed and raced downstairs to the Australian Paralympic team media room to sort out a car to get to the studio.

Luckily, I made it just in time, with about fifteen minutes to go in the broadcast.

'Where have you been? You're late!' was the first question.

'I just won two gold medals – where do you think I've been?' I said, channelling every Aussie sporting winner ever.

Luckily, the team at Seven didn't hold my tardiness against me. They actually saw the funny side, and I spent the rest of my time in Rio doing interviews and story packages for both them and the Australian Paralympic Committee. It was a great opportunity to test my broadcasting skills in an unfamiliar environment, and I loved every minute. I went rolling around the famous Ipanema Beach talking to locals. I visited an orphanage for Brazilian kids with disabilities, and showed them my medals. I interviewed some of the best performing Australian athletes from the Games, namely para-canoeist Curtis McGrath, who'd won a gold medal and been chosen as our flag-bearer for the closing ceremony. Curtis has an incredible story – just four years after losing his legs in Afghanistan after standing on a land mine, he'd won a gold medal.

I was also lucky to chat to the great Kurt Fearnley after his last Paralympic marathon. Kurt has been a good mate since I first met him back in 2008, and I loved to see him succeed. His work both on the sporting field – winning copious gold medals and World Championships to boot – and off has always impressed me, and is something I've tried to emulate in my own career. Kurt helped put the Paralympics on the map in Australia, and has always been a strong advocate for equality for people with disabilities across the country. And, coincidentally, we also look alike. Well, we're both in wheelchairs and we both have beards. That's enough to confuse anyone.

It happens a lot. The first time was at Flemington Racecourse on Melbourne Cup Day in 2012. A bunch of security guards came up to me, shook my hand and asked for a photo. Back then, I was barely known so it was extremely rare for this to happen. Safe to say I was pretty chuffed. So there I was, full of confidence, a beaming smile on my face, just happy to be getting some recognition for my sporting achievements. Photo op over, I pushed off.

'Thanks, Kurt!' they yelled after me.

I'm not going to lie, I was devastated! Oh, yes, my ego took a beating.

Kurt's also famous for tackling the Kokoda Track, an intense test of endurance for even the fittest able-bodied person, let alone a paraplegic wheelchair user. Kurt's solution was to crawl the whole excruciating way. I have no idea how he did it, but somehow he managed to finish it (he is a madman). Now, occasionally when I'm out, people come up to me, ask for a photo, and say: 'When you crawled Kokoda, that was incredible! Can I buy you a beer?' My response is always the same: 'Thanks, mate, it was really tough. That would be great!'

Lately, though, as my profile has increased, the same thing has happened to Kurt. He reckons at least once a week people tell him he's great on triple j, or ask him if he wants an egg sandwich (in reference to my ANZ ads). Luckily we're mates and can have a laugh about it. Also, being mistaken for Kurt, one of the greatest athletes of all time, well, it could be worse.

\*\*\*

As for all good things, they must come to an end, and the closing ceremony marked the culmination of two amazing weeks. It had been the best two weeks of my life, bar none, and as I boarded the plane with those two precious gold medals around my neck, I was so proud and so grateful.

When we arrived back home, life was a bit different. Because the Games had been on commercial free-to-air for the first time, a whole lot more people had seen them, resulting in plenty of interest. I'd only been home a few days when I learnt I'd made the shortlist for the Don Award, one of Australia's most prestigious sporting accolades. It's named for cricket great Sir Donald Bradman, the inaugural legend inducted into the Sport Australia Hall of Fame, and each year it's presented to Australia's most inspirational and best performing sportsperson.

International golfer Jason Day had won the previous year, and I was honoured to be on the 2016 shortlist along with Curtis McGrath, rugby league's Johnathan Thurston, swimmer Kyle Chalmers, rower Kim Brennan, cyclist Anna Meares, the Australian women's sevens rugby team, and the eventual winner, jockey Michelle Payne. It was great to see two Paralympians up there with the biggest names in Australian sport.

The celebrations continued on AFL Grand Final day, when Heath and I had the unbelievable experience of being included in the sporting legends' lap of honour at the MCG before the Western Bulldogs' epic victory over the Swans. Zack is a big Bulldogs fan, so it was great to be able to take him to the game and see his team win (he actually teared up – how cute). There were a few Paralympians doing the lap of honour. It was Heath's first time, but I'd been lucky enough to be included back in 2008, after the Rollers won gold at Beijing. On that day though, my lap around the ground hadn't gone completely to plan. As I was going to be on TV, I put my brand new pair of $400 Ray Ban sunnies that Dana and Dad had bought me to celebrate my victory into a hat they'd given us to wear. As we drove off the field (I was sitting next to my teammate Justin Eveson), he threw his hat into the stands, so I did the same. Except my brand new sunnies were inside it. Some lucky person in the crowd must have thought, *Gee, that Paralympian kid is generous!*

Then, the following week, thousands of supporters lined Melbourne's Bourke Street Mall as Victoria's Paralympians were honoured with a state parade. It was a great opportunity to meet all those people who'd given us incredible support throughout our campaign, in particular a lot of young people with disabilities, who'd never before been exposed to the Paralympics. At the parade I met a little guy in a wheelchair named Noah. He couldn't stop smiling as I put one of the gold medals around his neck and told him to follow his dreams, just like I did, so he could win a gold medal too one day. It's moments like these that really make all the training and effort worthwhile.

The support we received that day was a reflection of how much the Paralympics had moved into general consciousness. In the past, events like that were mostly populated by our families and friends, going virtually unnoticed by the general public. However, it was heartening to see how things had changed. It helped that Australia's Paralympic team did so well in Rio, winning eighty-one medals, including twenty-two gold, and finishing fifth on the overall medal tally for the fourth consecutive Games. We were proud of what we'd achieved.

So considering how well the team did, I felt enormously honoured to be named Australia's Paralympian of the Year for 2016. The list of previous winners is star-studded, and includes Louise Sauvage, alpine skier Michael Milton and swimmer Matt Cowdrey, just to name a few. There was any number of star performers in the Australian Paralympics team that year, and the award could have gone to any of them, so I was humbled to be the one chosen. Receiving that award will always be, for me, a high point of my career.

As a result, Australia Post honoured me with my own $1 commemorative stamp, featuring a photo of me holding my singles gold medal. If you ever wanted to lick my face, well there's your chance (I know you're out there!). For the next twelve months, whenever I received a parcel through the post and saw my face on the stamp, I did a double-take. I never did quite get used to it. Mum still has the stamps framed and hanging up at home. I know she was very proud of that one.

Then at the end of 2016, at a lavish black-tie ceremony in Sydney, I was named *GQ Australia* Sportsman of the Year. Other winners of this coveted award, bestowed by the high-end men's fashion and culture magazine, include boxer Jeff Horn, surfer Mick Fanning, motor racing ace Daniel Ricciardo and golfer Adam Scott, so I was in great company. This award really meant a lot to me – Zack and I got a lot of style tips from *GQ* magazine back when we were teenagers. As well, people with disabilities don't exactly litter the pages of high-end fashion and lifestyle magazines. So it was incredible that *GQ* had taken a leap and given the award and a four-page spread to an athlete in a wheelchair, something I acknowledged in my speech. To make it even more special, the award was presented by Ian Thorpe, one of the greatest Australian athletes of all time. I was just stoked Thorpie even knew my name! I was star struck.

I'm not one to think too much about these things – I do what I do because I love doing it. However, to be recognised for my achievements in Rio, especially considering the calibre of people who had come before me, was special. Then, in early November I heard that for the second year in a row I'd been nominated for the Newcombe Medal. This is the highest honour in Australian tennis, awarded to 'Australia's most outstanding elite tennis player and ambassador for the sport'. For me, it was the big one.

You can't put yourself up for this award – nominees and the eventual winner are chosen by a panel of experts. Some of the biggest names in Australian tennis have input, including Pat Rafter, Craig Tiley, Wally Masur, Alicia Molik and Lleyton Hewitt, in addition to Newk himself. So it really was terrific to be a contender.

In the past, athletes with disabilities had never really been up for contention for the main awards at events like this. The Athlete of the Year category was normally specifically for 'able-bodied' athletes, while athletes with disabilities fought it out for the Athlete with a Disability category. However, I've always viewed myself as an elite athlete, first and foremost, who just happens to have a disability. When it comes to sport, there's no reason in my mind why athletes with disabilities can't be viewed as equals to our able-bodied counterparts.

Call me biased, but I was astonished when I learnt that athletes like Kurt Fearnley and Louise Sauvage had never been awarded Athlete of the Year for their incredible achievements. They'd won a swag full of Athlete with a Disability awards, but they'd never been in contention for the top gong. I wondered whether it would be the same for me.

This time around, the field for the Newks was strong. Nominated were Daria Gavrilova, who had teamed up with Nick Kyrgios to give Australia its second ever win in the Hopman Cup and had an impressive year herself; John Millman, one of the nicest guys in tennis, who had reached the third round of the men's singles at both the Australian Open and Wimbledon; John Peers, the doubles ace who had won Grand Slams and the ATP World Tour Finals that year; Sam Stosur, who reached the semi-finals of the French Open for the fourth time, claimed the record for the most number of years representing Australia in the Federation Cup and played her fourth Olympic Games; and Jordan Thompson, who broke into the world top 100 for the first time and competed in the French Open, Wimbledon and the Olympics.

The winner would be announced at an awards function at the Palladium at Crown, in Melbourne. The place was buzzing, with great tennis names past and present among the guests, including Evonne Goolagong Cawley, Tony Roche, Todd Woodbridge and Frank Sedgman. Kate, Mum, Dad, Dana, Zack and his partner, Em, Heath and Tim Biggin and his partner, Anna, were all there to back me up. I was trying to keep a lid on it – I was determined not to get my hopes up too much. Still, when the time came for the winner to be announced, I must say I was pretty nervous.

John Newcombe, the medal's namesake, winner of seven Grand Slam titles and former world number one, was on stage, ready to read out the list of nominees. He opened the envelope. My chest tightened. There was not a sound in the big auditorium. 'The winner of the Newcombe Medal for 2016 is ...'

The pause seemed to last forever.

'... Dylan Alcott.'

Wow. I couldn't believe it.

Newk's words were still swimming in my ears as Kate kissed me, and my friends and family cheered with joy. Now the whole room was on their feet. As I made my way to the front, I looked around to see so many familiar faces, people who'd helped me on my tennis journey.

I pushed up the ramp onto the stage. There was Newk, beaming at me, the medal in his hands. He put it around my neck, then bent down and gave me a hug and a kiss. Nothing like a bonus face massage from one of the nation's most famous moustaches.

It was an incredibly important moment for me, personally, but also, I hoped, for anyone with a disability who'd ever thought they were 'less than', anyone who felt we were always in the shadow of our able-bodied counterparts.

I was choked with emotion as Rove McManus, the host of the night (what the!?), handed me a microphone.

'I'm so proud to be a Paralympian, proud to have a disability, and I'm not going to lie, I really wanted to win this award. We have an Athlete with a Disability category and that's a huge honour. But I see myself as an elite athlete, first and foremost, who just happens to have a disability, who uses a wheelchair to play. This week is International

Day of People with Disability, and to have this award given to a disabled athlete in an able-bodied dominated world, it means a lot to me and the Paralympic movement.'

As my dad said to me after, it felt like a glass ceiling had been smashed. For too long, the recognition of achievements by athletes with disabilities was always capped, considered to be outclassed by our able-bodied counterparts. But, for one of just a few times around the world, an athlete with a disability had taken out the major prize. I was humbled and extremely honoured, I really was. At last things were really changing, as athletes with disabilities began to be recognised as elite sportspeople, but also as disability and Paralympic sport became more and more mainstream.

That award really did top the lot and I have to thank Craig Tiley, Tennis Australia and Newk himself for taking a bit of a risk, for challenging the status quo and being a part of it.

\*\*\*

At the end of 2016, most of the partying and events were done, and it was time to get back to work. I was back into training, getting ready for the 2017 Australian Open. But there was more on the horizon.

Triple j radio station had offered me a presenting role for 2017. Ollie Wards, the head of content at the time, knew I had aspirations to work there. I'd been a triple j fan for years, so I jumped at the chance. The only problem was I'd never done any radio before, and, at triple j, presenters do *everything*, pushing the buttons, mixing the music, taking the callers. There are amazing producers who help along the way, but a lot of the panelling is done by the presenter. We agreed I'd start in February, after the Australian Open was done and dusted. In the meantime, I could have a few sessions on how to work the panel.

I also now had sponsorship deals with ANZ and Toyota. (People often ask me, 'Can you drive?' The answer is yes. I often tell people that I do it using two bricks and a piece of string. But in actual fact, paraplegics drive with their hands using hand controls that are built into the car. Being able to drive is crucial for independence, so it's great that technology is advanced enough to give me the opportunity to drive. I am still working on my 'Oh what a feeling!' jump for the next Toyota campaign. I reckon we'll be waiting a while!)

The sponsorship deals had been put together by my management team, and I'm forever grateful. I'd met Mark Jones and Rod Reid in early 2016 through a family friend and another athlete, snowboarder Scotty James. Both said that the team at the Sports Group (Mark and Rod's company) were second to none. So when they offered to manage me, I quickly said yes.

Having people who understand you, back you and support you is essential if you want to get your message out there, and signing with Mark and Rod was one of the best decisions I ever made. When I first started working with them, they did it all for free, as I wasn't earning any money to be able to pay them. That didn't matter to them – they just wanted to be involved in my journey. They were in it for the long haul, which meant a lot to me. And now, as things picked up, it was awesome to have them on board.

The lead-up to the Australian Open kicked off in the usual fashion, with tournaments in Brisbane and Sydney.

However, this campaign was a little different. This time, I was doing some work behind the microphone. By the end of the Sydney International, I'd interviewed Grigor Dimitrov (one of the best blokes going around), and hosted the Fast4 Tennis event in Sydney, where I interviewed Rafa Nadal, Dominic Thiem and Nick Kyrgios.

Back home in Melbourne, I fulfilled some promotional duties at the Kooyong Classic before giving Novak Djokovic a hand with the charity event he was staging just days before he attempted to defend his Australian Open title. A charismatic personality, Novak has been a strong supporter of wheelchair tennis, being a good friend of Andy Lapthorne. He had no trouble attracting some of the biggest names in Australian sport to help him raise money for the Novak Djokovic Foundation, which supports early childhood education (so essential to giving kids a good start in life).

It was very cool to be asked to host 'A Night with Novak', especially because it wasn't your usual black-tie do. Instead, Novak made good use of his guests, tennis great Roy Emerson, cricketers Shane Warne, Aaron Finch and Meg Lanning, netballer Sharelle McMahon, Max Gawn of the Melbourne Demons AFL side and Melbourne Victory football great Archie Thompson, by taking them on in their own chosen sports in front of a big, appreciative crowd at Margaret Court Arena.

Novak had varying degrees of success. He had a reasonable idea of how to kick a soccer ball, for instance, but when it came to bowling leg breaks like Warnie, he looked like he might pull his shoulder out of its socket. In saying that, everyone looks average next to the great man, who is one of my favourite Australian athletes of all time.

As the end of the night neared, it was my turn. I wheeled out onto the court. 'Novak, I think it's time we took you back to tennis, and I'm going to take you on,' I said.

'Okay,' he said. 'I'm going to play with the Olympic champion right here.' I'm not an Olympic champion, I'm a Paralympic champion, but I let that one slip.

Cheered on by the capacity crowd, we hit a few balls. As agile as I am in the chair, safe to say he was a bit too good for me on his feet. I wanted to even the odds. 'I reckon this is a bit unfair for me. Novak's got his perfectly working legs, but who wants to see him try to beat me in a wheelchair?'

There was an enormous roar of applause.

'Yes, bring it on!' Novak shouted, running with eager enthusiasm towards a wheelchair conveniently parked on the sideline.

'I tried wheelchair tennis once, you remember?' he asked as he sat down.

'Yeah,' I said, deadpan. 'You were awesome.'

We both cracked up. Wheelchair tennis is extremely hard. The toughest part is holding the racquet while pushing the chair. It stumps everyone, so I was pretty confident I could kick his arse.

'You get two bounces,' I explained. I gave him a few pointers on how to manoeuvre and spin the chair and then we were away.

For someone who can stretch to the absolute limits on his feet, Novak was pretty immobile in the chair.

'If I beat you I'm never playing you again because it's 1–0 me for the rest of my life,' I called over the net.

The poor bloke just couldn't take a trick. 'This is, like, the hardest workout I've ever had in my life,' he said. At one point I hit the ball straight at his feet and he couldn't budge to make a return. 'I have so much admiration for you.' It was a pretty nice compliment from one of the best players of our generation.

We had just one more point to play. 'Winner takes all,' I announced. 'If I win, I get all your Grand Slams and the prize money. All $100 million. Cool. Let's go.'

But Novak wanted something in return. 'Okay, and if I win, I get your two gold medals.' Deal. It was on.

Novak served as hard as he could from the chair. I lobbed one back towards his feet and he leapt up out of the chair to smash one of the biggest winners he's ever hit. Great tactics by him, and the crowd loved it. Luckily, he let me keep my medals.

\*\*\*

I was loving doing interviews and hosting gigs, and every chance I got was an opportunity to hone my skills and prove myself. One interview I'll always remember was with Andy Murray. We'd had lunch together one day in the lead-up to the Open, and I asked him if he'd be up for it. I was stoked when he said yes.

Andy's one of the nicest guys I've met on the men's tour. He's always had time for me, and contrary to what people in the media might think, he's a very cool guy with a pretty funny and witty personality. Same goes for his brother, Jamie, one of the best doubles players in the world. At the time, Andy was in a great place, having just reached world number one and soon to be knighted. The chat went great – it always does when there's mutual respect.

Andy told me that hitting top spot in the world had been a relief after twelve long years on the tour, most of which he'd been stalled somewhere between number two and four. I pointed out that his brother Jamie had enjoyed a great year as well, making it to number one in the world in doubles. 'If your Mum Judy had to pick a favourite son,' I asked, 'who do you reckon she'd pick?' Andy couldn't help but crack it for a laugh. 'I think I'm my mum's favourite and Jamie's my dad's favourite,' he said with a big smile. 'They'd tell you that they love us both equally but that's how I feel.'

I asked him if he knew what Scotland's national animal was, which he didn't (it's the unicorn!), and whether it could beat a boxing kangaroo in a fight. We both agreed the kangaroo would win. Andy agreed that it would be good to use the plastic samurai sword I'd brought along to the interview for a trial run ahead of the awarding of his knighthood. Practice makes perfect, and I think our run-through definitely helped a month later when the Queen officially made him a Sir.

But now it was time to get down to business. I went into my own 2017 Open campaign happy with my preparation, having won the APIA Sydney International singles for the third year in a row, beating Heath, Andy Lapthorne and David Wagner to the title. It had been so hot when we were playing – 43 degrees with 80 per cent humidity – that the wheelchair rims scorched our hands and we were literally burning rubber out on court, fragments of our tyres peeling off on the fiery playing surface. The Australian sun in the summer is extremely gnarly to play tennis in at times, so I'm glad I grew up with it. I always feel sorry for my competitors who come from the Northern Hemisphere winter – from zero degrees and snowing to 40 degrees and scorching would be a tough pill to swallow.

My hope was to build a long run of victories at Melbourne Park, and I began the competition buoyed by all the good-luck messages and support from people across the country. Unfortunately, my first win came at Heath's expense. He was making his Australian Open debut that year and his first match was against me. I beat him in straight sets 6–1, 6–4.

Next up was Andy Lapthorne, and he came out strongly while it took me some time to get going. I was hitting the ball all right but making a lot of errors – I think the fact that the match was being broadcast right across the country got me a little excited. It got better and I was happy with the way I came on strong in the second set, to take the match 6–4, 6–1. Viewers really responded, with countless tweets saying how good wheelchair tennis was to watch. It meant a lot to us.

My last round robin match was against David Wagner. It looked like I was all set to cruise to the finish line when I grabbed an immediate break in the second set, but Wagner got back on serve before I broke him again in the eleventh game. I finally prevailed 6–1, 7–5, setting me up to face Andy Lapthorne, who had accounted for Wagner and Heath in the group phase, in the final.

Due to the growing interest in wheelchair tennis, the outside courts at the Australian Open had become too small to contain the crowds. It was a far cry from when I was a junior, when the only people there watching us play were our parents and our coaches. Now, courts with 2000 seats weren't big enough. It was astonishing.

As a result, when I made the final, I went and saw Tennis Australia boss Craig Tiley and campaigned for our match to be played at Rod Laver Arena before the able-bodied women's final. My argument was pretty straightforward – it was simply a case of supply and demand. Demand was higher than ever, meaning we needed to supply enough seats for people to come watch. I had estimated up to 5000 people might attend (ambitious, I know), and I wanted everyone to be able to get in.

To Craig's credit, he had the foresight to see that it could work and so Tennis Australia agreed to give us star billing on their biggest stage. It would be the first time a wheelchair final was played on centre court of a Grand Slam. This was another watershed, another glass ceiling smashed by Craig and the whole Tennis Australia team. And it was another dream come true for me.

Lappo and I would face off for the Australian Open Quad Singles title on Saturday, 28 January 2017. But no matter who finished with the trophy, wheelchair tennis was going to be the real winner, having received more mass media coverage in Australia than it ever had before.

Spectators could get in with just a ground pass and I put out a call on social media for tennis fans to come and watch some high quality play. When our 2 pm match time rolled around, there were 5000 people in the stands, eager to see a replay of the Rio Paralympic gold medal match, but this time for the Australian Open title. It was also a wonderful birthday present for my mum, Resie, who had put in so much effort over the years to give me every opportunity she could.

I received some stirring messages to boost me and, along with the excitement of the occasion, they really fired me up. I wasn't going to let this one slip. After just sixty-nine minutes,

I was able to see off Lappo, to win my third consecutive Australian Open singles title 6–2, 6–2.

Andy was gracious in defeat, saying in his post-match on-court interview, 'Congrats, Dylan, you're by far the best player in the world at the moment and you deserved the victory. I apologise for today's performance. It wasn't one of my best – maybe the moment got to me a bit. But we'll go again. Centre Court at a Grand Slam — I may have lost this one but I'll remember this match forever.'

So would I. And it was cool to share the moment with Andy.

It was my third consecutive hometown Australian Open title. The trophy was presented by my first tennis hero, Pat Rafter, whose signed poster was still on my old bedroom wall in Mum's house (I've asked her to take it down but she loves it, and I can't reach it to take it down myself). I was so excited about the result and the historic importance of the match, I grabbed Pat and gave both him and the big silver trophy a hug and a kiss. I don't think Pat minded too much. Just another reason why he'll always be a hero in my eyes.

# 15

# *ends and beginnings*

I'VE BEEN EXTREMELY LUCKY in my life and things seem to have worked out pretty well for me. As I said, I don't take it for granted. But I firmly believe you do make your own luck – things don't just fall into your lap. What I've found is, when you put yourself out there, good things tend to happen. And when you don't put yourself out there – when you stay guarded, or protect yourself – you're not in a position for luck to occur. Unfortunately, luck doesn't often strike when you're sitting at home and not pushing yourself.

Ever since my teenage years, I've always backed myself. Sure, I have a pretty loud personality at times and I'm sure it's annoyed some people over the years, but if *you* don't back yourself, then who the hell will?

Whenever I'm asked to do some work in the media I jump at the chance for two reasons. One, I bloody love it. I relish the opportunity to share other people's stories as well as my own. And two, I see it as an opportunity to push for one of the biggest passions of my life – the inclusion of people with a disability in every part of life.

So when I was first asked to join the team at triple j, it was another dream come true. I'd absolutely loved the station growing up. On the ride to school I'd beg Mum to put it on, and she'd oblige. Mum could see how much I enjoyed it, and she'd let the odd swear word slide like it didn't happen. Thanks to Zack, I've always been into indie music, especially hip hop, and triple j was the place to get it.

As my sporting career progressed, I found myself being interviewed on the station more and more. The first time I was on was with Lindsay 'The Doctor' McDougall during his 'Secret Skills of Sports Stars' segment back in 2012. Our mutual friend Liz Cambage introduced us, and he asked me to come on his show to chat about my crowd-surfing escapades. Hearing myself on the radio for the first time was extremely weird, especially given it was my favourite station.

Then Matt Okine and Alex Dyson interviewed me on the breakfast show a couple of times, after which I did my first extensive interview on the station, this time with Zan Rowe. The interview with Zan was on her 'Take 5' segment, in which she asks guests to pick five songs that best represent them and the topic she's chosen. In my case the topic was 'Dylan's songs to smashing it'. It was the first opportunity I'd really had to tell my story on radio and introduce myself to the faithful triple j audience, and I owe Zan a big thank you for picking me for the segment. To put it into perspective, other 'Take 5' participants include Paul McCartney, Mike D from the Beastie Boys and Josh Homme of Queens of the Stone Age, just to name a few – not bad company.

I picked five songs that represented my life at different stages, including Bomfunk MC's 'Freestyler', the first song I ever 'love loved' and the first song I put on my Sony MiniDisc; Jurassic 5's 'What's Golden', the last song my teammate Justin Eveson and I listened to before every game when we won gold at the 2010 World Championship; and of course Wu-Tang Clan's 'Protect Ya Neck', the song that had changed my life in the biggest way.

Zan made me feel so comfortable, I felt like I could talk to her about anything. She was incredibly well researched, and allowed me to open up about my ambition to work in the media, not only because I'd love the challenge but also to continue to pursue my main goal of mainstreaming disability on a nationwide, if not global scale. I think that interview may have planted the seed in the minds of the team at triple j that maybe I could work there one day, but, to be honest, I thought it was a pipe dream that would never happen.

So when I'd received the call offering me a role as weekend afternoon presenter, with fill-ins and regular appearances on both the breakfast and drive programs, I grabbed the opportunity with both hands.

My first shift at triple j was just days after my 2017 Australian Open victory. Following a couple of lessons on how to run a full-on national radio show – buttons, panel and all – it was show time. I was absolutely packing it. Nervous is an understatement.

I'd tried to set expectations at the right level by asking my social media followers to tune in to some 'sweet, sweet tunes and to me hopefully not making a fool of myself'. My love of music was deep and genuine, no problem there. But with just two and a half hands-on sessions learning how the control panel worked, I knew I could easily make some glaring error and send the whole station off air. Or maybe my mouth, which was getting drier with every new nervous thought, would stop working entirely.

I was not only trying not to say the wrong thing, but I was also panicking that I'd completely stuff up the buttons, resulting in dead air and me looking like an absolute rookie.

My first on-air break was terrible. I stumbled over my words, and hit play on the wrong song. *Smooth, Dylan*! But once I was underway, I slowly loosened up, and before I knew it my four-hour shift was over. Back to present the same time-slot the following day, I felt pumped, and wanted to get through the show mistake-free. But a very large spanner was thrown into the works. At the time, the ABC studios were being renovated around the clock during weekends. On my second day, a builder was using a jackhammer directly behind the studio, and I could feel the vibrations through the walls. Each studio is set up with soundproofing designed to prevent any on-air disturbances, and it usually does a great job. But that Sunday I was in the middle of my shift, really getting the hang of it, when there was a loud bang just as I started to speak after a track had ended.

Before I could even turn around to see what was happening, the soundproof wall behind me came crashing down and landed on top of my head! Fortunately, the noise-absorption panels were lightweight, but it knocked me over enough to push me out of the way of the microphone. The result was about twenty-five seconds of dead air while I wriggled out from under the wall that had landed on me.

I managed to get back to the mic and the panel and fired off another song. A couple of dudes in high-vis vests were walking past, and they dusted me off and quietly carted away the pieces of wall.

It was the definition of a baptism of fire. Ollie and the triple j team said that if I could handle that on week one, I'd be able to handle anything. And before too long, I was covering during the week for the prime-time shifts, taking over from Zan when she was on holidays, and being entrusted to host her 'Take 5' segment, the very segment that had kicked off this journey. Before long I was teaming up with two incredibly talented ladies, Gen Fricker and Brooke Boney (who are now two of my best mates – love you guys!), and hosting triple j breakfast when usual hosts Ben Harvey and Liam Stapleton were on break.

Hosting breakfast was incredible, especially being given the keys to 'Like a Version', one of the most popular segments in Australian radio, where artists come in and do a stripped-back version of an original and then a cover. If you've never seen or heard of 'Like a Version', go to YouTube now and have a look. You'll be there for hours watching some of the best live music performances you'll ever see. My personal favourites include Tasmanian band Luca Brasi's cover of the Paul Kelly classic 'How to Make Gravy' and DMA's cover of Cher's 'Believe'.

Starting work at triple j was a game changer for me, and I immediately noticed that more people were coming up to me in the street and saying hello. Connecting to listeners on a weekly basis was easily the best part of the job. I received thousands of beautiful texts from people showing love (and sometimes hate – my favourite text of all time was from a bloke called Sam, who texted in and said: 'Who gave Darryn Lockyer his own radio show – eat a Strepsil you F*ckwit!!!' in reference to my gravelly voice), requesting music and just stopping by to say hello. It's the best part of the job, so to anyone who has come up in the street to say hello or texted in, good or bad, I say a big thank you.

The year 2017 was going really well but it was extremely busy. I hadn't quit tennis to do radio, so I was still training and competing, as well as smashing out weekly on-air radio on the weekends. Then, just when I thought my life couldn't get any more chaotic, a new challenge presented itself.

As I've mentioned a bunch of times already, my true passion in life is changing the way people with disabilities are perceived in our community. Due to biases of the past, negative stigmas and low expectations are still regularly placed on people with disabilities, providing the biggest barrier to what they can achieve. Sure, it's annoying when you don't have accessibility features such as ramps and captions, but there's always a way to get around that. However, in my opinion, it's low expectations and a lack of understanding of people with disability and what we can really do that's the biggest obstacle we have to overcome.

Most people would think that, these days, I wouldn't have this problem – after all, people might have seen me on TV and recognise my face. But I do, and far too regularly. Only a few months ago I was out ordering a coffee after a radio shift when a lovely lady came up to me in tears.

I thought to myself, *Oh my god, are you okay? What happened?*

Looking into my eyes, she said, 'It's so inspirational to see you here getting your own coffee.'

'It's inspirational to see you get your own coffee too,' I replied.

Now, she was just trying to be nice, I get it. She didn't have a mean bone in her body. But her expectation of me was that I couldn't do anything. So imagine if she was an HR manager or a recruiter. Or the school teacher of a little girl with cerebral palsy. Or the mother of my future partner. These low expectations make it really hard for people with a disability to get out and live the lives they want and, more importantly, deserve to live.

So while I was really proud of what I was doing and happy with my life, I knew that, for too many people with a disability, this wasn't the case. Luckily, winning the Australian Open had given me opportunities to make a real difference where it was needed. One such opportunity was a filmed promotion I did for one of the sponsors of the Open, in which I answered questions from fans while riding around the streets of Melbourne.

People asked me things like, what's my favourite social media (Instagram) and favourite music (giving me the perfect opening to rap the Method Man's part from 'Protect Ya Neck'). Then one fan asked me what advice I'd give to someone with a disability.

Well, I was really glad to get that question, and I spoke from the heart. 'Don't worry if you have a disability. I don't care that I'm in a wheelchair – in fact, I love it. Go to work with what you've got. I live the best life ever. Please get out there and enjoy life. Even though it's a bit different, being different is definitely good.'

I guess I was saying, embrace your disability. Because, the truth is, I've met a lot of people who clearly have a disability, but deny it. I reckon they do that because the word 'disability' still has negative connotations. They deny they have a disability, even to themselves, because they don't want to be discriminated against. They don't want to be denied opportunities that should be open to everyone.

The short of it was, I wanted to do something to help fix the issue and I had an idea. There's always been a gap in the market for a resource to educate governments and corporates to not only better understand people with disabilities and what they need, but to understand what incredible employees they can be and the positive impact they can have on the bottom line.

So, in April 2017, I approached my friend Nick Morris, a 1996 Paralympic wheelchair basketball gold medallist and one of Australia's leading accessibility consultants. Together with my dad, Martin, family friend Mark McCoach and the Simonds family we co-founded our company, Get Skilled Access, with the intention of completely revolutionising the way governments and business deal with accessibility and disability. We aimed to be more than just a flash in the pan – we wanted to impact generational social change, and, for the first time, make disability a key issue for large organisations and governments.

Because, truth be told, for too long disability has been the one stream of diversity that no one really cared about. Don't get me wrong, gender, racial and LGBTQI equality are all extremely important and deserve the coverage they get. But disability never really gets the coverage it deserves in the mainstream. Yet, on sheer size, it should, because you'll be shocked to read that there are over 4.5 million Australians with some form of disability. That's more than one in five people!

Around the world, it's more than 1.3 billion people, a huge number. And all of these people deserve the right to be able to work, shop, bank or travel, to do all the things and make all the independent choices that able-bodied people tend to take for granted. Still, many organisations neglect to understand the needs of people with disabilities, and the organisations are missing out because of it. After all, not only do we make great, loyal customers, we also make great workers. With Get Skilled Access, we wanted to open their eyes to the fact that people with disabilities can work, and work well, and dispel the myths that get in the way of truly inclusive recruitment.

But the question was, how do we do it? Why do people not care to learn, or see the opportunities in front of them? What we found was, the whole sector had a dusty, old-school, 1970s old-person-on-a-zimmer-frame approach, which hardly inspires people to want to emotionally invest enough to care about it. Why can't disability be sexy, fun, humorous or emotional? We needed to jazz it up, make it interactive and disrupt the status quo. But how to do that?

Ever since I was a kid, it's bothered me when able-bodied people speak to other able-bodied people about how to treat and understand people with a disability. All you have to do is look at our parliaments right across the country to see that all the decisions, all the policies associated with people with a disability, are made by able-bodied people. I firmly believe if you want to speak about somebody at a table, they need a seat at that table. So, we decided that all of our content and all of our training would be written and delivered by people with a disability. Because, after all, I have no idea what it's like to be blind, or to have autism, so I'm not going to tell you. Someone who does should.

We've now been up and running for more than a year. Dad and Zack work with us as part of a great team that includes some familiar faces, including Heath Davidson, Brad Ness, Jannik Blair and Kelly Cartwright, and the organisations we've worked with include ANZ, Coles, NAB, Bunnings, Medibank and Australian Unity, just to name a few, as well as multiple state and federal governments. It's super rewarding to know we're starting to get real cut-through, as we see companies start to invest in people with disabilities and start to employ them, not out of some sense of 'worthiness' but because they recognise it makes good business sense, delivering a healthy return on investment and an increase in the productivity and profitability of their organisations.

\*\*\*

With so much happening off the court, life was incredibly busy, but it was important for me to fit in tennis somewhere. So May saw me head back to the Japan Open to chase my third successive singles title there.

There were thirty-two players in the singles draw and purely by coincidence my first match was against Heath. It's always weird having to play each other in singles, and Heath's development post-Rio had been rapid. He gave me the biggest scare I've ever had playing him, and I was lucky to get the win in three close sets. I progressed pretty easily through the rest of the tournament, reaching the final, where I was up against the usual suspect, David Wagner.

Wagner had won seven straight titles at the Japan Open up to and including 2013. Now he was intent on denying my bid for a hat-trick there. He'd reached the final with three successive straight-sets wins, so he was in hot form, and keen to take the number one ranking from me.

Wagner isn't the kind to roll over, so when I took the first set 6–4, he hit back hard to take the second 6–3. In the end, though, I prevailed, winning the third set 6–3 and holding on to top-of-the-world ranking for a few more months. Heath and I backed it up with a win in the doubles also, beating Wagner and Lucas Sithole in the final.

Back in Australia, my media career was hitting its straps, with a lot of commitments all across the country. Triple j was going incredibly well, capped off by an opportunity to host the 2017 Splendour in the Grass broadcast for the station, interviewing big acts like Haim and Powderfinger, just to name a couple. Get Skilled Access was also starting to take off, meaning a lot of travel and keynote speeches. I also got to live out a childhood dream shared by many Aussies, hosting an episode of ABC-TV's *Play School* (that's right, *Play School*!), a favourite of generations of kids. It was a pretty surreal moment, having Little Ted sit on my lap while I read out a bedtime story called *The Very Itchy Bear*, about a bear and a flea who end up becoming great friends despite their differences. Very fitting.

All of these extra-curricular activities were really hurting my tennis career – I wasn't getting in the training hours I needed for peak performance. As a result, when the US Open came around in September, I got absolutely pumped, losing my first round match to Andy Lapthorne 6–4, 6–1. It was my first loss since January 2016, and I was bundled out of the tournament. I was embarrassed – I hadn't lost that badly in years, and I knew I'd let everyone down from my lack of preparation. But everything has a silver lining, and it was the wake-up call I really needed. Up until that point, I thought I could get away with doing the bare minimum of training, but I had not only underestimated my competition but had overestimated my own abilities. From that day on, I was going to prioritise my training; otherwise, I'd have to give away the sport.

Tennis wasn't the only part of my life I was struggling with. My relationship with Kate was also not going so well. As much as we cared for one another, things seemed to have stopped working. I was to blame for it – there was a growing distance between us, mainly because I was constantly away. We'd had three awesome years together but unfortunately we were being pulled in opposite directions. It was a tough time because, while I recognised things weren't working, I still loved her and didn't want to let go. We both thought we might have spent the rest of our lives together, but in September 2017 we decided to break up. It was really tough, and moving out of her house was one of the hardest decisions I've ever had to make. Kate is one of the most – if not *the* most – caring and amazing people I've ever met, and although we haven't seen much of each other since, I still hope we can reconnect and remain close.

But life had to go on, and my focus turned to qualifying for the 2018 Australian Open. It had been an incredibly productive twelve months for me off the court, but I'd been so busy with other things that, with the end of the year in sight, I'd played only four tournaments in 2017 – the APIA Sydney International and the Australian, Japan and US Opens. My results had been okay, but competing in so few events meant I hadn't racked up as many competition points as I had in previous years. As a result, my ranking had slipped from number one to number three in the world.

If my ranking slipped further I'd be in danger of not qualifying for the Australian Open, where only the world's top four Quad Singles players compete. So, at the end of November, Heath and I made a quick trip to Bath in England to ensure our qualification. It was a successful trip for both of us – we won the doubles together and I made the singles final, though I lost to David Wagner. Although it was annoying to lose, both Heath and I did enough to guarantee our spots in the 2018 Australian Open.

Back in Melbourne in December, I was honoured to serve as patron for the International Day of People with Disability. But, more and more, I was focused on defending my Australian Open title the following January. I wasn't in the shape that I needed to be, so I worked incredibly intensely with a guy called Jimmy Kostaras, who was fitness coach for the Melbourne Demons Football Club. Jimmy put me through so much boxing training I felt like I was ready for a championship fight, not just a tennis tournament.

As the old year gave way to the new, Heath and I made a flying visit to Queensland to give an exhibition of wheelchair tennis at the Brisbane International before heading to the Sydney International Wheelchair Open, which I managed to win, defeating David Wagner in the final to lift the trophy. It was the perfect prep for my assault on a fourth straight Australian Open title.

But with my public profile on the rise, this Australian Open was going to be different. Media and sponsorship interest in me had increased dramatically, which was a good feeling, and I was determined to make the most of it to lift the coverage for Paralympic sport in our country. So when the ANZ bank asked me to be the face of their brand during the summer of Australian tennis, I jumped at the opportunity. Previously Novak Djokovic had been ANZ's main tennis ambassador, but that relationship had come to an end.

The centrepiece of the campaign was an ad. The filming process was incredibly cool. I'd never done much acting before, so to be on set for two whole days was something I really enjoyed. I couldn't get over the sheer size of it all – 300 extras were there all day for two days. It was like being on a movie set, and I felt pretty important.

Safe to say, once the ad was released, it was everywhere, and I mean *everywhere*. Billboards, TV, newspapers, radio, the side of trains, buses – you couldn't get away from me. People still come up to me in the street and ask me where my egg sandwich is.

Being in the ad meant a lot to me for a couple of reasons. First, for one of the biggest organisations in Australia to back an athlete with a disability over an able-bodied athlete to be the face of their brand was a real game changer for myself and the movement. It showed that athletes with disabilities are first and foremost elite and can also give a great return on investment to sponsors (if not more than our able-bodied counterparts) when backed in and given the opportunity. But, even more than that, the ad helped me achieve one of my lifelong goals, which was to see inclusion of people with disability in the mainstream. You might remember that, growing up, I really struggled with the fact that when I turned on the TV, I never saw anybody like me. There were no people in wheelchairs living their life, succeeding –

doing anything at all. Now, at last, throughout that month of January 2018, I saw someone like me on TV (who just so happened to be me!).

When ANZ presented someone with a disability as the face of their brand they did a really powerful thing, taking a risk and challenging the status quo. They didn't follow the usual narrative, either – you know, scripting a commercial about my 'inspirational journey from the hospital bed to centre court' or something. They thought, stuff it, we're going to let Dylan be Dylan, very importantly allowing me to be a character and a consumer. They were just proud supporters of me, wheelchair and all. It really meant a lot to me, more than anyone would ever know.

And easily the best bit about being a part of the commercial was the thousands of messages I received from people with disabilities and parents of young kids with disabilities about how much the ad meant to them as well. Seeing themselves represented on TV for the first time, during every single commercial break of the tennis, showed society that it's okay to have a disability, and that you can still achieve what you want to achieve. I even received a video of a little boy in a wheelchair who rolled up to the TV and hugged it every time the ad came on. Seeing that made me emotional. Thinking about it today, it still does, and that's why I get out of bed every day.

Due to the sheer size and scope of my involvement with ANZ, the 2018 Australian Open was crazy for me and like nothing I'd ever experienced. The first week of the Open was filled with photos, signatures and hundreds of people coming to watch me practise. It was surreal. Nothing could have prepared me for it, but I was enjoying the ride. Then, as the first week of the Open drew to a close, things got a hell of a lot bigger again.

There's always plenty of star power at the Australian Open, in the stands as well as on the court. Some celebrities are huge tennis fans and fly in specifically for the event, especially when the big guns like Roger, Rafa or Serena are firing. Others take advantage of being in Australia at the same time to come along and experience one of the world's great sporting events live, and a man by the name of Will Smith did exactly that at the 2018 Open.

I've been a fan of the rapper turned actor all my life, and I know every word to the theme song of his hit TV show *The Fresh Prince of Bel-Air,* even though it debuted a few months before I was born. Will was in Australia to promote his new movie and to train for his next one – his physical trainer is an Australian – so he decided to pop down to Melbourne from Sydney to watch Nick Kyrgios play Jo-Wilfried Tsonga in the third round. It so happened that I was sitting next to him, so I said g'day, and he seemed like a lovely bloke.

Kyrgs is a big Will Smith fan (who isn't?!), and later said he became really nervous when he found out Will was in the stands. 'I just wanted him to watch me and think I was the coolest person ever.' I don't blame him – I would've been crapping myself too. So imagine how I felt when I got a call at midnight that night telling me that the Oscar-winner himself wanted to have a hit of tennis the following day and since neither Nick or Jo-Wilfried could do it, I was up.

I was told to meet Will at 10 am on the indoor courts at Melbourne Park, where the Australian Open is held. I had no idea what to expect – I'd only had a very brief chat with him, so I was interested to find out what he was really like.

I think that when you're as famous as he is, it can either go two ways – you can be a legend, or you can be guarded and a bit of a wanker.

Safe to say he was an absolute legend. When we were reintroduced, I went for the handshake, and he went for the hug – he was that kind of guy. I was impressed too that he'd clearly done his homework – he knew I was a motivational speaker and asked me about my work outside of tennis. But he was every bit as funny as you'd expect.

While Nick couldn't make the hit, his doubles partner Matt Reid could. Will had us all cracking up when he said he'd never played tennis before. In fact, he said he'd never even held a racquet, but (talking himself up in his trademark hilarious way) he was still sure I could make him a pro in three lessons.

As we got ready, he had a great time geeing us up and telling us that he didn't want any little pitty-pat stuff. Unless the ball was coming at him at 100 miles an hour or more, he said, he just couldn't find his groove. So Matt cranked up a 195-kilometres-per-hour (121 miles-per-hour) serve that sounded like a gunshot. It hit the star smack in the middle of the chest. Will called for security. I asked someone to call an ambulance. It was great fun.

Will then jumped in the chair and gave wheelchair tennis a crack. As expected, he was horrible at it, but I gave him a few pointers, including how to manoeuvre the chair by pushing one hand forward and the other hand backwards in order to turn. Surprisingly, he turned out to be better at wheelchair tennis than he was on his feet, and by the end of the session he was hitting the ball pretty well.

When he asked me to name our new duo, I said off the cuff, 'What about "Willin and Dylan"?' Get it? Wheeling and Dealing? Not going to lie, I was pretty happy with myself with that one! Think he was pretty impressed too.

We ended up spending more than an hour together before we exchanged phone numbers and I told him I was happy to come to Hollywood to make *Men in Black 4: Wheelchair edition*. Unfortunately, I'm still waiting for that call.

But after all the fun and games were over, it was time to knuckle down and get serious. The second week of the Australian Open had begun, and my chance to go four in a row had arrived.

# 16

## *digging deep*

THE AUSTRALIAN OPEN IS my favourite tournament of the year, but I'd never been so nervous as I was in the lead-up in January 2018. Competing in previous Australian Opens had meant a lot to me for sure, but back then we'd played on the back courts, and there'd been far less interest in the sport than there was now. As usual, I wanted to make my support team, friends, family and fans proud, but this time around I felt I had a lot more riding on it. I wanted to prove to myself that I could do it, which added to the pressure.

Still, everything in my preparation was going smoothly. I was feeling fit, determined and as relaxed as you can be heading into the first Grand Slam of the season when you're attempting to make it four in a row. My first match was scheduled for Wednesday, 24 January, and everything was looking good. Until, all of a sudden, it wasn't.

It was on the Saturday night, the same day I'd had the awesome experience hitting with Will Smith, that I started to feel really unwell. When you have a disability, feeling a bit crook from time to time is not unusual. Normally, I just battle on and it goes away. But on this occasion, I was really nauseous and just not right. The next morning, I woke up with a bad fever. Uh oh. I couldn't stop sweating or shivering, so I headed in to the tournament to see the doctors at the Open to find out what was going on. They noticed that my right leg was extremely swollen, and that something strange was going on in my body. My temperature was high, so they recommended I head straight to hospital to get some tests. Much to their dismay, I said that I didn't want to go – I had prep to do before my Open campaign kicked off in a few days. Just give me some oral antibiotics, I said, and I'd be fine. Big mistake.

That night I didn't get a minute's sleep. I was shaking and vomiting all night, and when Monday morning came, I knew I had to head to the hospital to sort myself out. I'd been a fool to go against doctor's orders. Now I was in an extremely bad way.

At the hospital, doctors told me the sickness was caused by a little cut on my right foot that had become infected, and I was diagnosed with a bacterial infection called cellulitis. They immediately put me on a drip. 'No chance of playing in the Open on Wednesday,' the doctor said firmly.

As you can imagine, I took this news badly. Absolutely nothing was going to stop me from competing on Wednesday, even if it meant ripping the drip out of my own arm and driving myself there. I agreed to stay in hospital for two nights and to get as much IV antibiotics into my body as

I could before reassessing my situation come Wednesday morning.

Those two days in hospital were absolute hell. Not only was I in serious pain and constantly vomiting, but the thought that I wouldn't be well enough to compete and defend my title was excruciating. Added to this, I was one of the faces of the Open, and not being able to line up and give back to everyone who had followed my journey was a tough pill to swallow. I couldn't sleep, my body was wrecked, and I began to doubt I'd make it to day one of my campaign.

The only people who knew I was in hospital were my housemates Dan and Lucy. My coach François, Heath, my manager Mark, even my family had no idea I was in hospital. I just told them I was getting a cold and had decided to rest at home. I guess I didn't want to make a big deal out of it, or get any sympathy. It was my fault I was in there – I'd pushed myself too hard and had no one to blame but myself. Also, the tennis world is small, and I didn't want my competition knowing that, if I did make it to the tournament, I was going in underdone.

When I found out I was to be in the first match on Wednesday morning, I knew I had to convince the doctors I was well enough to compete. I pleaded that I was fine, and eventually they agreed I was in no great danger if I went off the drip for a few hours, played my match, and immediately returned to get back on the antibiotics.

THANK. GOD!

Early Wednesday morning, after they'd removed the drip from my arm, I went home to shower and collect my gear. Then I headed to Melbourne Park for my first match. Just being there was a weight off my shoulders, and although I was still weak, the feeling of relief put a pep in my step. I was ready to take on Andy Lapthorne in my opening-round match.

Putting the last couple of days behind me, I rolled onto the court ready to play. Luckily for me, Andy came into the tournament with a niggle himself, having battled an injured hand over the summer, which had already forced his withdrawal from the Sydney International and the Melbourne Open. But, aware of what a great player he is, I knew I'd have to be on my game to get the victory and advance. Much to my surprise, I blitzed it, strangely playing some of my best tennis to defeat Andy 6–1, 6–0 in fifty minutes. Maybe I should go to hospital more often!

After the match, once the adrenaline had worn off, I fell in a heap. My body still wasn't right, so I decided to tell Mark and Zack what had happened over the past few days. I'm so glad I did because, rather than ridicule me for not looking after myself, they were really supportive, and escorted me to hospital to get back on the drip. I spent the night in hospital receiving a dose of antibiotics every four hours. But the following morning, I felt even sicker than I had the day before. Once again the doctor insisted there was no way I could get up out of my bed to play tennis. I knew he had my best interests at heart, but I told him if he didn't rip the tubes from my arm I'd do it myself. There was no way I'd forfeit an Open match in my hometown in front of my fans and family and friends. Seeing how much it meant to me, he grudgingly obliged, and once again I headed to Melbourne Park to take on the then world number one, David Wagner, in my second round robin match.

I was really in no condition to play, but I did my best. However, Wagner is a great competitor, and he prevailed

6–4, 6–7, 6–4, guaranteeing himself a place in the final. Luckily for me I still had one more chance to join him there, when I was to take on Heath for a place in the final.

My day wasn't over yet. Next Heath and I were facing off against Lapthorne and Wagner in the doubles final. I was in a pretty bad way, but remembered that Lappo himself was battling with his injury. He was here competing, but he was far from his best. He'd already lost to both me and Heath in the singles, and was out of the tournament, so I knew we had a shot, but I was going to have to heavily lean on Heath for the result to go our way. In addition, and Heath will attest to this, my record in Grand Slam doubles play was *horrible*. I'd never even come close to winning a Slam before, always falling well short when it came to the crunch. Heath often gave me shit about it! So he'd need to bring his A game for us to have a chance.

Luckily for us, he did.

Heath came out on fire, smashing winners left, right and centre, and we took the first set 6–0 in just twenty-three minutes. Could it be that my doubles Grand Slam drought was about to be broken? Well, not quite.

Lapthorne and Wagner weren't going to give in that easy, and they hung tough in the second set. It was back and forth all set, but we came up big when it mattered most, and we won the second in a tiebreak, forcing the match into a deciding match tiebreak (for anyone who doesn't know, this is a first to 10 points tiebreak, and has recently been introduced into doubles matches all around the world).

I was feeling extremely average, and couldn't wait to get back on the drip.

By this time, Heath knew I was sick, but he told me to pull it together for just 10 more points. From 5–3 up in the match break we were pegged back to 6–6, until a run of 4 points finally landed us a 6–0, 6–7 (5), (10–6) victory.

Even though we'd won a gold medal together, this was our first Grand Slam doubles title as a team, and the first one of both of our careers, so it really meant a lot to us. A big crowd had come out to support us, and we received a huge reception from enthusiastic Aussie supporters who were as happy as we were that we'd gotten the job done. After the match, we also found out that Seven had broadcast the whole super tiebreak to over a million people in their prime-time coverage before the men's semi-final got underway. The feedback online was fantastic, and I was so happy to see Heath revel in the spotlight, enjoying a victory that had been many years in the making.

I was pumped up after our stirring win and feeling a lot better, so I didn't want to return to hospital. Instead, I thought I felt well enough to head home for the first time in a week and get a good night's rest before my singles semi-final against Heath the next day. But when I told the doctors at the Australian Open of my plan, safe to say they weren't impressed. They suggested I go back to the hospital for another dose of the IV antibiotic drip before going home to sleep in my own bed. I wasn't going to go against their orders a second time, so I agreed, and off to the hospital I went for the fourth day in a row.

I'm glad I listened to their orders, because the next morning I felt like a different person, almost back to 100 per cent. I owe a huge thank you to the Australian Open medical team and the team at the nearby Epworth Hospital for guiding me through that really tough week, and also for putting up with my abuse when I told them I was leaving each morning. Without them, there's no chance I would've been one singles win away from my fourth Australian Open final in a row. I was ready, I felt great. However, nothing could have prepared me for what was to happen next.

My semi-final match versus Heath was the fourth match scheduled for court 7 on Friday, 26 January (Australia Day, fittingly), with the first match beginning at 11 am. Apart from the first match of the day, tennis matches don't have an exact start time, because no one knows how long a tennis match will run for. As a result, there's often a lot of waiting around at tennis centres.

At about 1 pm I reached the courts. I had a warm-up scheduled for 2.30 pm, and estimated that Heath and I would be on court battling it out around 4 pm, give or take about half an hour. Everything was going to plan and I was really excited, albeit a little nervous to be up against a best mate for a spot in the Australia Open final. Heath and I had played each other before Grand Slams, but never with this much riding on the result. It was going to be interesting to see how we both handled it.

Four pm was approaching and the match in play was coming to a rapid conclusion. It was almost go time. Heath and I were in the locker room getting ready, sticking to our routines to get ourselves primed to play our best when it mattered most. Heath was doing his thing, while, as usual, I was listening to music and keeping my hand-eye coordination sharp by throwing ball with our coach, François. (As coach of both of us, François always sits in the middle of the stadium when we play each other.) Roger Federer was also in there, getting ready for his singles semi-final against South Korea's Hyeon Chung on Rod Laver Arena.

I always take note of how top players prepare for battle behind closed doors. Every athlete is different and uses different methods to calm down and stay relaxed, while remaining ready to go once their match is called. Roger seems so calm, cruising around the locker room, talking to people, doing his hair in the mirror – you'd have absolutely no idea that perhaps one of the biggest matches of his career is only seconds away. It's his style, and clearly it works well for him, given he is, in my opinion, the greatest tennis player of all time.

In contrast, someone like Rafael Nadal has a completely different approach. He's *very* intense, pacing around the locker room, running on the spot, taping his hands frequently, listening to music and not really communicating with anyone. Outside of just-before-game-time, he's a super lovely guy, but when he's in the zone, *he's in the zone*, and is someone you don't want to get in the way of. It's super cool to see.

So there we were, doing our own thing as we waited for our matches to start, when it started absolutely pouring down rain. There'd not been a single drop during the entire two-week tournament, then, out of nowhere, it was like a monsoon had hit (we ended up having almost 30 millimetres in four hours). Unfortunately, court 7 doesn't have a roof, so now we would have to wait for the rain to pass, if it was going to pass at all.

As Heath and I sat there on opposite sides of the player lounge, trying to rest and pass the time, Roger headed to Rod Laver Arena, which has a roof, for his semi-final against Hyeon Chung. Chung went into the match under a serious injury cloud, due to a 3-centimetre-long blister on his right foot. That thing was HUGE, and must have been causing him some serious discomfort every time he stretched or ran down a ball.

The match started, and you could see that Chung was in serious pain. He quickly went down 6–1 in the opening set. Outside it was still pouring with rain, so I decided to take a quick nap until our match was called – or called off, which was looking more and more likely.

While I was napping however, Chung decided he could no longer play on due to his injury, pulling out midway through the second set. Federer would be advancing to the final. With the match cut short, there was suddenly a huge gap in the coverage, both for the 18,000 ticket holders who were in Rod Laver Arena, but also for the millions of people who were watching the coverage around the world.

Craig Tiley and the Australian Open team had to make a quick decision: What match should they throw on to Rod Laver Arena to complete the schedule? There were only three matches still to be played – the two mixed doubles semi-finals scheduled on Margaret Court Arena, and Heath's and my match on court 7. Can you believe it? They went with us.

I woke up to find Craig Tiley standing over me. I was momentarily lost – where was I? When Craig told me that the match on Rod Laver had finished and that he was putting Heath and me on live in front of 15,000 fans, live on Channel Seven and live to millions of people around the world, there were only two words I could muster.

'Get stuffed!' I honestly didn't believe him.

But it was real, and we had just five minutes to get ready. Heath had disappeared and I had to call him and tell him what was happening and that he better hurry the hell up, otherwise we'd miss our chance. Heath came sprinting into the locker room, adamant that I was bullshitting him. I wasn't, of course, and it was what dreams are made of.

Once it had sunk in, safe to say we both got extremely nervous. We were shitting bricks, to put it lightly. My heart was racing, but I felt a little bit better when I looked at Heath – he'd turned a shade of green, almost as if he was ready to puke. Luckily, we were quickly whisked away to Rod Laver Arena so we didn't have too long to dwell on it all.

As I wheeled out onto the court I was absolutely filled with pride. An all-Aussie semi, on our national day, being televised in prime time from the Rod Laver Arena, with Roger Federer as our lead-in. We genuinely couldn't have asked for anything more. I could hardly believe it was happening.

I did a quick scan of the crowd to try and familiarise myself with my surroundings, and all I could see was people – *a lot of people*. I reckon more than 12,000 people had stuck around to see us play, and there were some pretty high-profile people amongst them – Eric Bana, Mark Webber, Evonne Goolagong Cawley and James Tomkins were there in the crowd. Heath and I were determined to give them plenty to cheer about.

I started horribly. I was super nervous, and all of a sudden, out of nowhere, Heath looked relatively calm. He spanked a few forehand winners and quickly took a 2–1 lead, and I started to think, *Uh oh*. Imagine my first loss to Heath coming on this big stage. I'd be devastated, but I'd also never live it down! I needed to dig deep and find a way to get it done. I practised some mindfulness, thought of my main man Chad, and was able to settle down into the match and finally play some good tennis. Meanwhile, Heath started to get really tight and nervous, and I was able to reel off five games in a row to win the opening set 6–2.

The second set went in similar fashion, and before I knew it I'd reeled off eleven games in a row to complete a 6–2, 6–0 win in fifty-five minutes.

In the post-match interview on court, I was on the verge of tears. 'I absolutely love it out here,' I told the crowd. 'Thanks to everyone who stayed. It means the world to me to change the way people perceive people with disabilities – to see us as athletes first and foremost; we just happen to be in wheelchairs. To get the opportunity to do that not only in front of you all, but also to millions of people around the world on the broadcast, and to do it with my best mate, Heath Davidson, it's a dream come true.' I meant every word.

It was a real game changer for Craig Tiley, the network and the whole Australian Open team to trust us and back us and showcase wheelchair tennis to the world, one that I am forever thankful for. Later, Craig told me that it was one of the highlights of his ten years as tournament director of the Australian Open. For him to say that, considering all the amazing things that have gone down at the Open over the past decade, shows how far wheelchair tennis and Paralympic sport have come.

After the match, I rushed off court, recovered and headed straight home, because the very next afternoon I would be back at Rod Laver Arena for the singles final against David Wagner. Hopefully I could make it four years in a row. A big crowd had turned up for the final, too, with about 5000 packing into the stadium to help me bring it home. Of these 5000 people, one of the biggest things I noticed was the huge number of little kids in wheelchairs that had made the journey to come down and support me. I'd never seen so many kids in wheelchairs in one spot, and it was heartwarming to see. Hopefully these little boys and girls dreamt that maybe one day they might be on that court competing. Being the person that they were watching meant a lot to me, and remains one of the reasons that I play – to show them that they too can do it.

Heading into the match, I had the sentimental advantage as usual, with the home crowd heavily on my side, but Wagner was ready to rumble and he went in tough from the start. He was doing pretty well until I broke his serve in the ninth game, but he countered by breaking right back in the tenth. The set had reached 6–6 – now for the tiebreaker. Wagner held his serve on the first point but I raced away with the next seven to claim the set.

'C'mon, baby!' I shouted, pumping my fist and pushing my wheelchair into overdrive. I was ecstatic – who wouldn't be, competing for a fourth Australian Open title in their very own backyard?

The second set started in the opposite fashion to the first, and I gained a convincing 4–0 lead pretty quickly. Wagner looked tired – the heat was getting to him – and I knew I had his measure. When I ran down a drop shot with a last-gasp winner, bringing up match point, I knew it was mine. I was one point from victory, and with a forehand winner down the line off his serve, I took the match in ninety minutes 7–6, 6–1.

I'd done it. Four Australian Open titles in a row.

Considering where I'd been all week, I honestly couldn't believe it. It was the sweetest of my Australian Open wins by a long shot.

'It has been a big two weeks. A crazy two weeks,' I said in my speech. 'I'm pretty glad I could top it off with a win. I do love this trophy. It's beautiful. It's been a whirlwind five, six years. A lot of hard work. But the best decision I ever made was coming back to tennis.

'I love playing basketball,' I went on, 'but playing tennis has changed my life. Now I think it's starting to change the lives of some other people, as well. That's what I've always wanted to do, get people out of their homes and playing sport, being comfortable with their disabilities and proud of who they are. Sport is a great medium to do that, I think … So many kids with disabilities were here today in the stands. It was packed. That makes it all worthwhile.'

I thanked all the people who'd helped me get to where I was in that beautiful moment in the Melbourne summer sunshine in the greatest tennis stadium in the world, from my coach François Vogelsberger and manager Mark Jones to those closest to me. Thanking my beautiful family and friends I told them: 'You're the reason I am who I am, and I don't forget that.'

Finally I thanked every single person who had come along to see wheelchair tennis live or watched it on TV, knowing how much that support meant to me and my peers but also to the generations following us. Change really was happening, you could feel it in the air that day, and I felt so lucky to be a part of it.

\*\*\*

The year 2018 featured more tennis firsts for me, starting with another memorable star encounter a couple of months after the Open. This time I was playing tennis with Arnold Schwarzenegger. I absolutely love the 1987 action movie *Predator*, in which big Arnie co-stars with Carl Weathers, who's playing a character called Dillon. It's spelt differently to my name, obviously, but said the same way, which used to delight me as a kid.

It so happened that the fitness advocate and former governor of California was in town for Melbourne's annual Arnold Sports Festival, which is Australia's largest fitness expo and multi-sport festival and draws more than 60,000 visitors over three days. So when I was invited to attend the festival and have a hit of tennis with the great man, I was delighted to accept.

I mentioned to the event organisers in passing that I was a big Arnie fan and how *Predator* was a particular favourite of mine. They must have clued him up, because when he greeted me with a muscular handshake, he gave me a personalised version of one of the movie's lines: 'Dylan, you son of a bitch!'

I honestly squealed with delight.

He went on. 'The CIA got you pushing too many pencils?'

Life made!

I was in shock. 'Oh Arnie, baby, that's gold!' I squealed, hugging him like a long-lost best friend. It was a fairytale moment. A big, muscly Austrian fairytale.

I was also able to realise my dream to compete on the hallowed grass of Wimbledon. Although the Australian Open is my favourite tournament of the year, there's something about the tradition of the All England Club that draws players to it. The grounds are exquisite – roses line the grass courts, which are immaculately kept, like nothing I'd ever seen before. Up until this point, I'd only been to

Wimbledon as a spectator back in 2014, because back then I wasn't allowed to play.

Wheelchair tennis had been first introduced at Wimbledon back in 2005, but only as an invitation demonstration event. There was a misconception that the wheelchairs would damage the courts and the grass surface would be too hard to push on, so the standard of play wouldn't be high enough for a competition. However, as the years progressed, the All England Club started to come around to the idea, initially allowing a sanctioned doubles wheelchair event, and then eventually allowing singles for the first time in 2016. However, it wasn't fully inclusive, as players in my classification, the quad classification, were left out.

For years it had been a hard pill to swallow. Growing up, all I wanted to do was win the Australian Open, my home slam, and get to pull on the whites at Wimbledon. That was it. And to have one of those things not offered to me, even though I trained daily and put on a show every time I played, was devastating. But I'm not one to take no for an answer, and neither were the other players in the division. I took any opportunity I could to lobby the All England Club to give us the opportunity to compete, promising we wouldn't let them down. So after years of trying with not much of a response from their end, I was shocked and ecstatic when I received a letter in April of 2018 stating that we were going to be invited to play at Wimbledon for the first time. It was to be an exhibition doubles match, but who cares, any opportunity to play on the hallowed grass and prove what we could do was a chance I wouldn't miss.

Arriving at Wimbledon for the first time as a competitor was like an out-of-body experience. It had meant so much to me for so long, and so much effort behind the scenes had gone into this, that it felt surreal to actually be there, playing and wearing the whites. Also, coming from Melbourne, I absolutely hate white clothes, opting for all-black any chance I get. This is also because, being in a wheelchair, I always have dirty hands, which means white clothes always get filthy. (Side note: Have you ever walked on the street without shoes? Yeah, exactly, it's the same thing. People often ask me why I don't wear gloves everywhere. The answer – so I don't look like a creep. Imagine me cruising around in golf gloves all the time. Yuck.) But, not going to lie, I was happy to be rocking the all-white for the first time, and did it proudly.

Unfortunately, Heath wasn't picked to play in the exhibition, because he'd just missed the ranking cut-off. However, he came along as my coach, as did Brenda the manager of the national program, and Mark my manager. Mark was easily the most excited person I'd ever seen in my life, and I'm not sure he's ever really recovered from getting the chance to go behind the scenes at the All England Club.

Our first hit on grass was extremely cool, but also a big relief – I hadn't been too sure how it would go. I'd heard it was tough, but I was stoked to see with my own eyes that it wasn't as hard as they said. In fact, I found grass quite easy and enjoyable to play on, with the low uneven bounce of the ball really suiting my heavy spin game.

We were gearing up for our match on Saturday afternoon, and I really didn't think my week could get any better. But then, out of the blue, it did. On Friday, the day before the match, Heath and I came out of the locker room to find red velvet ropes and a red carpet lining the bridge that connected the men's locker room to tournament control and the player cafe. *That's weird*, I thought. *That wasn't there thirty minutes ago. Someone special must be on the way.* I asked the security guard what was happening and he said that 'two *very* special guests' were on the way. I didn't have to be Einstein to figure out that it was either Prince Harry and Prince William, or the Duchess of Cambridge and the Duchess of Sussex. I extremely hoped it was the latter (shout out to Rachel Zane!), and my prayers were answered.

Heath and I had only been sitting there for all of about two minutes when, before we knew it, the two duchesses were heading straight towards us. The security guards said we could sit there so long as we didn't say anything. Done. I could do that, just sit there and smile. Easy. But as they approached, I caught the eye of Princess Kate, and they both came over to say hello.

Now, on this occasion, unlike the time I met the Vice President of the United States, I hadn't had a protocol briefing on what to say and how to greet them. So when they approached, I tried to remember what to call them. I called upon the only resource I knew – two seasons of the Netflix show *The Crown* – but in the heat of the moment, I came up blank.

So, me being me, I thought, *stuff it*, and put out my hand. 'G'day, I'm Dylan.' What a dickhead. Pretty sure that isn't royal protocol.

Much to my surprise, the two princesses seemed to love it. People often forget that famous people are simply that, just people, and many of them enjoy it when people talk to them normally (unless they're a wanker). So they replied with the same ease and informality. 'Hi, I'm Kate.' 'Hi, I'm Meghan.'

It was unusually hot in London at the time, and they asked me how I was handling the heatwave.

'Aren't you embarrassed to call this a heatwave?' I said to them with a cheeky grin. 'It's only twenty-six degrees.'

They laughed, and for a few more minutes we chatted about Australia, Wimbledon and the Invictus Games, the sporting event Prince Harry created for injured army veterans that would be taking place a few months later in Australia. They even told me I looked good in white. I told Princess Meghan I'd love to catch up when she was in Australia for Invictus, but unfortunately she never took up my offer. She must have lost my number.

Rolling out onto the grass of court 3 at Wimbledon for the very first time to compete was another glass ceiling–smashing moment for me. I love the Australian Open, don't get me wrong, but as the home of tennis, Wimbledon has a very special aura.

I'd teamed up with Lucas Sithole to play Andy Lapthorne and David Wagner. People had come from all over to support us, among them fifty mates of mine. Australians are so well travelled, I feel like I have a home crowd at every single tournament I go to. I'm extremely lucky.

Exhibition match or not, I wanted to win, but Lucas and I hadn't played together for years and things didn't go our way: Lapthorne and Wagner played really well and beat us 6–3, 6–2. There was such a great atmosphere out there, and we impressed enough for Wimbledon to confirm that we would be back in 2019 with a full tournament, fighting for ranking points and all. I couldn't wait.

# 17

## giving back

ONE OF THE BEST decisions I ever made in my life was to make the switch from wheelchair basketball to wheelchair tennis. Sure, it was a tough one at the time, and a risky one at that, and to this day I miss some of my basketball teammates, guys that I'll be best mates with for the rest of my life. But tennis has opened so many doors for me, and given me so many different experiences I wouldn't have had as a basketballer. I owe a lot to tennis, and all the people from the tennis family who have pushed me and believed in my vision for my sport and for people with a disability in general.

So I'll keep playing tennis for a few more years yet, and hopefully I'll win a few more Grand Slam titles, even defend my Paralympic titles at the 2020 Tokyo Paralympic Games, if I'm lucky. That's the dream, but, beyond that, I don't know. I love winning titles and representing my country, but tennis is not my whole life, it's just *part* of my life. There's a lot more to life than tennis courts and aeroplanes, and I don't want to miss out on that. Because, safe to say, I wasn't put on this earth just to play tennis. Instead, what I *really* want to do is help change the way people with disabilities are perceived in our communities. It's what I love doing, and I want to do it all around the world. I want to help young people with disabilities, and show them they can be proud of who they are and do whatever they want to do in life. I want to help people in the way others helped me. Because I know that, without the support of a lot of different people across different stages of my life, there's no way I'd be the person I am today. Everybody, no matter who they are or what they do, needs help to flourish, and I've received incredible amounts of help across all the sections of my life.

It began with amazing doctors, who, when I was only a couple of days old, performed life-saving surgery on me. Without them I wouldn't be here to tell you my story. Next was my family, who never wrapped me in cotton wool, and always backed me and pushed me to be the best version of me. Then it was my awesome group of friends, the best friends in the whole world, who always liked me for me, and always included me even when a lack of accessibility made it a pain in the arse. And, of course, the foundations; first, the Starlight Foundation, who gave my family a lifeline when we needed it most, and, secondly, Variety, the Children's Charity, who gave me my first sporting wheelchair so I could start training and competing. Without them, I wouldn't be the Paralympic champion I am today, period. After that came all my teammates, coaches, managers and support staff, who pushed me every day to strive for greatness on the sporting field. I couldn't have done what I have without them.

One of the most important things I've learnt in my life is the importance of giving back. Giving back to people who are less fortunate than you, or to people who helped you get to where you are today. And having been on the receiving end of a lot of help that's shaped who I am today, I've always wanted do something to return the favour and directly touch the lives of people who need it most.

Which is why, in late 2017, I decided to set up my own foundation, which we called the Dylan Alcott Foundation. It would be a not-for-profit with the aim of helping young Australians with disabilities who feel marginalised – just as I did at their age – fulfil their potential and achieve their dreams in whatever they want to do. As a kid I constantly felt left out because I couldn't compete in sport – if I wanted to, I needed to buy a $10,000 wheelchair. It didn't feel fair. At school and university, there were times when I couldn't go to the library to study because it was upstairs or inaccessible. That didn't feel fair either.

There are too many barriers preventing young people with disabilities from achieving their goals – whether they be vocational, personal, sporting, whatever – and I've always wanted to try to change that. I guess that's what makes our foundation a bit different. After all, there are plenty of feel-good charities out there that brighten the days of kids with disabilities and illnesses, and they do an extremely good job and play a pivotal role in their development. But there aren't too many that help those young people fulfil their potential, giving them the tools they need to be Paralympians, lawyers, doctors, musicians or whatever they want to be. We wanted to build a resource to provide scholarships, grants, equipment and mentoring.

It took a *lot* of paperwork, and a lot of back and forth, but at the end of 2017, the foundation was official and we could start working towards our goals. But like anything in life, without money or funding, you can't do anything. So we needed to come up with an idea to raise funds. As you've probably realised by now, I'm not really your standard, black-tie event kind of guy. I go to them often, and they all feel the same. Instead, I wanted to do something different, that not only raised a heap of cash, but also gave people an experience they would remember for the rest of their life.

I asked myself what was the one place in the world where I felt most included. The one place where no one cared I was in a wheelchair, or cared about anyone's race, gender, sexual orientation, anything. And that one place for me was a music festival. It was the one place where people left their unconscious bias at the door, came together and collectively enjoyed the music. I love them – always have, always will.

But for a lot of people with disabilities, they would have never had the luxury of attending a music festival, due to the often rugged terrain and lack of accessibility. Imagine what that feels like. All your friends, your family, can go to see their favourite music acts or watch their favourite sporting teams but you can't because the venue doesn't have genuine access. It lacks ramps, or pathways, or accessible toilets; there's no sign language or captions; or there's poorly trained staff. These are all huge and glaring issues that prevent events being fully inclusive. How do you reckon that lack of inclusion would affect your life? Your mood? Your relationships?

So what about if we provided that experience for people who'd never had it and raised some money in the process? So Ability Fest was born.

Ability Fest was designed to be a festival for everyone, no matter their age, gender, race, sexual orientation or abilities. Absolutely anyone could come, just like any other festival. The only difference with Ability Fest was that we'd add a number of accessibility features, so people with disabilities could attend and enjoy live music, perhaps even for the first time. We'd have elevated platforms for people in wheelchairs to see the stage, pathways over grass areas, Auslan sign language interpreters signing every single lyric sung on stage, accessible bathrooms, sensory quiet areas – we wanted to have everything, so absolutely no person was left out. And the kicker was, every single dollar raised from the event would go to the Dylan Alcott Foundation, directly to the kids in need.

To pull it off would be a gargantuan task and would require months of planning. But Zack and I had only six weeks.

Six weeks! What was I thinking? I had no idea what I was doing. I'd never organised and run a festival, I'd never even held a birthday party at my house! I was definitely biting off more than I could chew, but we needed to run the event in April 2018, before the festival season ended. Otherwise, no one would turn up. I needed help, and help quickly.

First up, I reached out to some friends who owned a company called Untitled Group, who were experienced in running music festivals and events, including Beyond the Valley Festival, Pitch Festival and a bunch of others. I'd been friends with Nick, Tom, Mike, Fil and Christian since I was about twenty, so I approached them to see if they wanted to partner with me to run the event. I couldn't pay them, I didn't have any money to do so. But when I told them about the idea, they absolutely loved it, and immediately told me they wanted to be involved – completely free of charge. Combined with their team of Lozi, Casey and Pia, they would donate their time and expertise for the entire six weeks in order to make the dream become a reality. I couldn't believe it. It was actually starting to take shape.

Next we needed a venue, somewhere that was accessible by public transport and taxis so patrons could get there, but far enough away and with a really cool vibe, so people could party on the day. I didn't want the festival to look like a hospital – put it that way. I'd been to a few festivals at the Coburg Velodrome, an abandoned-looking concrete cycling velodrome that had been saved from demolition and now hosted day parties. The run-down, industrial-looking surroundings created a super cool environment; however, due to being old-school, it wasn't the most accessible place I'd seen. There were big patches of grass and mud, as well as the extremely steep banks on the velodrome. But we reckoned we could alter it enough to make it perfect for all, and when Chris Gareth and the Coburg Velodrome team donated the space, we locked it in.

After this, we needed artists, because, without music, you haven't got much of a music festival. Due to my work on triple j, I'd built up strong relationships with some of the biggest artists in the country. But, as it was a fundraiser, we'd made it the rule that absolutely no artist would be paid (though we'd cover their costs, of course). I did this not only to raise as much money as we could, but also because I wanted everyone to feel really good about doing something for free to help people. So calling up artists and musicians and explaining my pipe dream and asking them to play for free felt awkward at first. It really did.

I shouldn't have worried, because the response floored me. Nearly every single artist I asked to play said yes, and that they'd love to be involved. No fee – they just wanted to give back. In the end, our line-up was huge, and included but was not limited to Benson, Boogs, Boo Seeka, Client Liaison, Flight Facilities, Harvey Sutherland, Jack River, Japanese Wallpaper, Kingswood, Motez, Tkay Maidza and Willaris K. If those names don't mean anything to you, they should, as they're some of the biggest musical acts in the country. And they were all locked in.

This thing was actually happening. We launched on triple j, and the response, not only from the public buying tickets but also from suppliers wanting to get involved, was

Kate Shanasy

overwhelming. Production teams, lighting, staging, food, security, toilets, donations started flying in. So many people loved the idea and got in touch that we ended up with more than 400 people volunteering to help out on the day. The show of support was amazing.

We worked frantically for six weeks, and as the date drew nearer, I started to shit myself. I was so worried that, firstly, no one would turn up and that it would be crap, and secondly, people with a disability wouldn't enjoy themselves and it wouldn't be accessible enough. I lost sleep over it, but I had to push through and do the best job we could. The last forty-eight hours were manic. Everything was happening.

And then on 7 April 2018, the day finally arrived.

The forecast was for beautiful, clear autumn weather, and when I woke up and saw the sunshine, I was ecstatic. Even though it was the first time the festival had run, I wanted it to be a raging success, one that set the standard for lots of similar events all around the world to follow suit.

Zack and I arrived at the site at about 9 am to make sure everything was in order, and then the countdown was on. Ability Fest kicked off at 2 pm, and to say it was a success would be an understatement. It was easily the best day of my life.

As soon as the doors opened, there was an energy in the crowd I'd never felt before. There was something really special in the air, an inclusive vibe amongst the punters that I'd never experienced at an event like it, and people seemed to really appreciate how much effort had been put in by so many different people. Many were shocked at the sheer size of the event. No 'cost' had been spared, with two stages of the size you'd see at a three-day camping festival like

Splendour in the Grass. We'd installed pathways throughout the place so people with any kind of disability would be able to move around freely. As well, elevated platforms enabled wheelchair users to get a good view of everything. There were sensory quiet areas for people with autism and Aspergers, as well as guide-dog retreat areas, an accessible Ferris wheel – everything!

One of the most overwhelming parts of the day for Zack and me was the sheer number of people with a disability. Of the 5000 people who attended, about 500 of them had disabilities, 300 of whom told us they'd never been to any big-scale event like this before, ever. They were blown away.

Among the crowd were three sisters, one in a wheelchair. I was standing with Zack when we saw them and noticed that the two who were standing were in tears. They were crying with joy at seeing their sister included for once, able to participate in something they'd never been able to share with her before. Zack and I glanced at one another. I struggled to keep the tears down. It was what we'd planned to create, but to see it actually come together in real life was incredible. It really hit me for six.

I'd also been worried that the able-bodied people might be a touch uncomfortable with so many people with different disabilities in one place. For many of the punters, they may have never met someone with a disability, and I hoped that there wouldn't be segregation within the crowd. It turned out I had nothing to worry about. Everywhere I looked, people were mingling, dancing and having a ball. I remember going up to one young guy who was in an electric wheelchair, and was using an oxygen tank in order to breathe. He had four young ladies standing up on the back of his wheelchair, while he was spinning around doing doughnuts in his chair to the music. I asked him how his day was. 'Well, five guys have bought me beers, I just met these four girls, and one of them kissed me. So, yeah, it's going good.'

Brilliant.

Between ticket sales and donations, we raised $200,000 for the Dylan Alcott Foundation, an unbelievable effort from everyone involved. And we gave our very first donation on the night, to an eight-year-old boy called Jin.

Jin and I met at the end of 2017, at a tennis come-and-try day at Melbourne Park. He was born in China, where he was operated on at a very early age to try to correct his club feet. Subsequently adopted by an Australian family, Jin was an incredible kid, and always had a smile on his face every time I saw him. He was a keen wheelchair tennis player and was already working hard towards his dream of becoming a Paralympian, despite having a pretty old wheelchair to compete in, just like I did when I started out. Even the most positive kid can get down if they feel excluded, and just a day earlier Jin had said to his mum: 'I hate having a disability. I can't walk, run or jump like all my friends.' I knew where he was coming from. I'd had the same thoughts as a kid.

As soon as I found out about Jin's story, I wanted to do something to help. And due to all the unbelievable efforts of everybody at Ability Fest, we were able to make his dreams come true.

Jin and I got up on stage before the last act of the night, and as soon as I introduced him by name, the crowd went wild. 'JIN ... JIN ... JIN ... JIN,' they chanted, just like they would for a rock star. It was awesome to be able to present him with a brand spanking new $10,000 tennis wheelchair, so he could progress and follow his Paralympic dream just like I had. That's what it's all about.

The sheer amount of generosity and support that everyone involved in the festival showed that day and in the lead-up really amazed me. So many people got behind the idea and made it a reality, and we plan to bring it back in 2019 in an even bigger fashion. It really did change the lives of a lot of people. But there was one particular story that really hit home for me.

A good mate of mine named James is a doctor at the Intensive Care Unit of a prominent Melbourne hospital, and one night a young guy with muscular dystrophy came in. He'd stopped breathing and needed to be put on life support. Muscular dystrophy is a severe disability where a person's muscles weaken over time, so they eventually can't move, cough, even breathe. It's tough. And when this guy came in, it didn't look good for him. Over the coming days, however, he improved, but his long-term outlook didn't look great.

As you can imagine, this guy was in a pretty bad mood, as you would be when you're twenty-one and you don't know how much longer you have, or what's around the corner. My mate James was doing a pretty intrusive procedure on this guy when he noticed that he had an Ability Fest wristband on. 'Did you go to Ability Fest?' James asked him.

The guy said yes.

'I went too,' James said. 'I'm mates with Dylan. Did you have a good time?'

James said the guy's face lit up with happiness at the memory. 'It was the number one greatest day of my life,' he said.

Because when that young guy got really sick, he started to miss out on life. He said he'd never been to a festival, the beach, a sporting event, nothing. That was the first time he'd ever been anywhere with just his mates, the first time he'd been out and had fun with them. Can you imagine never going anywhere fun with your friends or loved ones for your whole life?

I don't tell that story to brag about how good the festival was, I tell it because I learnt an extremely valuable lesson, and it was this. Making that festival was easy. All it took was a few emails and a little bit of effort to provide an experience that changed someone's life forever. I couldn't believe it. It meant everything to me. And that's why it was the greatest day of my life. I think we all underestimate the impact we can have when we take the time to learn what someone needs, then take the time to deliver it.

That day changed my life forever. And to every single person who made Ability Fest possible, I thank you from the bottom of my heart.

\*\*\*

A couple of months after Ability Fest, I was asked to go on one of Australia's biggest talk shows, *QandA*, to discuss disability. The show is broadcast live on Monday nights, and this particular episode was called 'Enabled'.

On the morning of the show, I was hosting triple j breakfast with Brooke Boney. Brooke had the idea that I could sneak a little something extra into *QandA* in the form of hidden messages, so triple j listeners knew I was thinking of them. I decided that, even though *QandA* was a very serious program and I was super passionate about the subject, I could do it in a way that triple j listeners would enjoy while the regular *QandA* audience wouldn't twig.

We asked listeners to call in with suggestions and a guy called Andy challenged me to drop into my answers as many Wu-Tang references as I could. I agreed, and since I'd said yes on air, it was gospel. I was locked in. To be honest, I couldn't resist, anyway – as you'll know by now, I do love the Wu.

Still, that day, while I was prepping for *QandA*, all I could think was, *What have I done?* Not only did I need to state my case on disabilities as eloquently and logically as I could, I had to somehow weave Wu-Tang references into my answers and not look like a knob doing it. I started to freak out, but Zack reckoned that if I could pull it off it would create heaps of positive PR and might even get people who don't usually watch the show to tune in, and so educate more people about disability.

That evening, I went to the green room at the ABC studios to wait for my call. Also there were my fellow panellists, former disability discrimination commissioner Graeme Innes, who was born blind and became a leading lawyer; Catia Malaquias, a well-known lawyer and human rights activist who has a son with Down's syndrome; the acclaimed actress and disability advocate Kiruna Stamell, who has congenital restricted growth; and the founding father of Australia's National Disability Insurance Scheme (NDIS), economist and disability reformer Bruce Bonyhady.

Our host, silver fox Tony Jones, came in to greet us (he's a stud). I told him I was a bit nervous. 'I'm going to grill you lightly then turn you over and batter you,' he said with perfect gallows-humour delivery. Then we were ushered to our seats in front of a studio audience of around 400 people. Almost another million were watching at home and following the discussion on social media.

Tony began the program by explaining that there were two Australian Sign Language (Auslan) interpreters in the studio for Auslan speakers and that half of the people in the audience had identified themselves as people living with disability or carers. He introduced the five panellists and I made the Wu-Tang Clan symbol – the Wu bat – as I waved to the audience. I was off and running with my hidden task.

The first question to the panel came from a young lady name Steph Travers. 'Hi, my question's for Dylan,' she said. 'Dylan, you've stated that you wish to make disability sexy again. I'm a part-time wheelchair user, and the difference between when I'm standing on my crutches to when I'm sitting in the chair is staggering. Sometimes I'm talked down to, like a child, patted on the head, or ignored completely. I've even had friends in a chair being offered money out of pity. We can't all be elite sportsmen, so how do we actually go about creating a campaign of true inclusion and full awareness to change attitudes against all people with a disability?'

It was a great question and my nervousness melted away. 'Before I was a Paralympian and on radio,' I said, 'I was just a person with a disability as well – I still am. And when I was growing up, I really struggled about the fact that I had a disability. I was really embarrassed about the fact that I had a disability. *It was rough and tough like leather for me.*'

Bingo, a line from Wu-Tang's track 'C.R.E.A.M.'.

I pressed on. 'I struggled to be comfortable with who I was and I really wanted to try and change the way people view people with a disability. You know, people think we are broken, less capable, unemployable, undateable, can't have sex, don't travel, don't do the things that an able-bodied person does. We need more positive role models in mainstream media, breaking down those stigmas and those barriers for people.

'I used to really struggle as a kid, because when I turned on the TV, I used to ask my mum and dad: "Why don't I see anybody like me? I don't know anybody like me." ... I think it's important that people in powerful positions include in our workplaces, in our advertisements, everywhere, people with a disability, so we don't have a *QandA* special about disability – it's just normal, it's a normal part of life.'

'That was an uninterruptible answer, if I may say so,' Tony Jones remarked after I'd finished. Usually, answers on the show are kept to 60 seconds, but mine had run a bit longer than that.

Kiruna Stamell related her battle against prejudice and misrepresentations of people with dwarfism, and then we moved onto the topic of the National Disability Insurance Scheme. It gave me the opportunity to use a couple more Wu-Tang lines: '*cash rules everything* around the NDIS' (ding!), and a lot of people involved in funding, namely both sides of parliament, were trying to '*protect their necks*' (and another!).

The next question came from Fiona Bridger, with the assistance of an audio device. 'I'm thirty-five and have an undergraduate degree in visual arts, a Master's degree in art administration, and a postgraduate diploma in politics and public policy. I've applied for graduate positions with Commonwealth departments, but was unsuccessful. I applied for a graduate position with the NDIA (National Disability

Insurance Agency). I thought, as a disabled person, I might have stood a chance there. I received no feedback at all. I have come to the realisation that I may never get a job. What does the panel consider should be done to encourage employers, agencies and government departments to give physically disabled people a fair go?'

'That makes me bloody upset,' I responded. 'And I think there's this misconception about people with a disability that we're unemployable, can't do a role as well as somebody else, have a lot of sick days, we're going to miss a lot of time off work. And they're all not true.

'Deloitte did a study saying that people with a disability are 90 per cent more likely to be equal to, or more productive than, an able-bodied person. Telstra commissioned a study over fifteen months that said people with a disability have eight less sick days than an able-bodied person. They stay in a role a whole extra year than an able-bodied person. If you take away the fact that they've got a disability, that sounds like a bloody good candidate to me. That sounds like an awesome candidate. And I think that's like *the cream of the crop*' (another lyric from 'C.R.E.A.M.').

There were more great questions, including one from Ben Paior-Smith, a member of the South Australian Special Olympics team, who asked about mainstream schooling versus the push to keep people with disabilities separated in 'special schools', another subject I feel passionate about, since schools should be a snapshot of our community, not just part of it. However, I said, governments are *'stingy with short arms and deep pockets'* (bang!) when it comes to funding kids in school with disabilities, and it needs to be rectified.

As Tony Jones thanked us all at the end of the hour, I flashed one more Wu-Tang symbol. I'd done it! Eight Wu-Tang references, without looking too much like a dickhead!

No doubt, some would think that sending those messages was a childish thing to do. But I completely disagree. Heaps of people sent social media messages saying they watched the whole show just to see me do it. As well, triple j cut together a video highlighting my Wu-Tang references in the context of the relevant questions and answers. It was watched by more than two million people worldwide, the majority of whom didn't see the show itself. They were happy to watch a Wu-Tanged version and learn about disability and inclusion along the way. Check the video on YouTube!

I was a bit concerned my side game might have stretched the tolerance of the show's creators, but executive producer Peter McEvoy and the managing director at the time, Michelle Guthrie, *loved* it. They said that, while there'd previously been some great musicians on the show, I was the first panellist to weave the lyrics into my answers.

'He's a champion – basketball, tennis, broadcasting and now, as he proved last night, he's making disability sexy,' Peter said.

And why not?

# *epilogue*

ONE OF THE GREATEST lessons I ever learnt is that events don't dictate the life you live; rather, it's how you perceive those events that determines the path you take. It's a lesson I live by every day.

Recently, I was on a TV show called *The Interview* with Andrew Denton. One of the questions he asked me was: 'Do you ever dream of what life would be like if you could walk?' It was the first time I'd ever been asked that, and the answer came to me quickly.

'No, I don't.'

It's a fair question, and one that I suspect a lot of people would love to ask me. After all, people think that life in a wheelchair must be tough compared to life for an able-bodied person, right? And sure, parts of it is.

When I go to a bar and there are only stairs, it sucks. When people pat me on the head instead of shaking my hand, it sucks. When people look at me and think I can't have sex, even though I can, yeah, that sucks too.

But if I'm honest, not a single thought ever comes into my head about what life would be like if I could walk, nor do I get jealous of people who can. And that answer shocks most people, because everyone assumes I wish I could walk. But I don't. I really don't care about the things that I miss out on, because of all the things that I gain being who I am.

My disability has provided me with opportunities, and I don't shy away from that fact. If I'd been born without a disability, would I be a three-time gold medallist, six-time Grand Slam champion and be living the incredibly fun life that I now live? I don't think so.

I'm not ashamed of my difference, in fact, it's something I'm proud of. Because, after all, everybody wants to be different. Everyone has a different car, a different hairstyle, different clothes, different everything. So what better way to be different than to have a disability? The trick is to embrace it and go out there and kill it in your own life.

But I know for a fact that a lot of people don't feel the same way. Because of their difference, they're discriminated against, and that breaks my heart. And I'd be lying if I said there aren't some parts of my life that still get me down, which at times make it tough. I have no idea what it's like to walk along the beach and feel the sand between my toes, nor will I ever get the opportunity. One day, I want to have a kid, and I'm going to have to ask Zack to teach them how to kick a football, because I can't do it. I'd be lying if I said that didn't upset me. But for every one thing I can't do, there are 10,000 things that I can.

People often send me articles about how stem cell research could help paraplegics regain the ability to walk, and I'm often asked if I'd ever try it. My answer is always the same, that there's not enough money in the whole world you could pay me to do it. The reason is simple. I love my life just how it is, wheelchair and all. I used to say that the Dylan who walks and the Dylan in the wheelchair would be the same Dylan, but that's not true. Because the Dylan in the wheelchair is a much better version of any other Dylan who could have lived. And I'm easily the luckiest guy in the world to be living this life, and I wouldn't change that for the world.

Sure, at times, my life has been tough. I'm not going to sugarcoat it. From when I was first born, I was lucky to even make it out of that hospital bed. Some incredible doctors saved my life, and I owe them everything for that. Then, at one point I was so embarrassed about who I was, I let life pass me by while I sat in my bedroom, depressed and not sure if I'd ever get over it. And if you'd told that kid that one day he would be a world champion, Paralympic champion, radio host and, most importantly, happy, he would have told you to get stuffed.

But I'm so glad I was able to get through that, and it was because of all the incredible people I've met throughout my life. I firmly believe you're the product of the people you hang around with, and I've been able to become the person that I am today for no other reason than all the incredible people who helped me along the way. I am so glad they pushed me to get over my insecurities, to better myself and to strive to achieve what I wanted to achieve.

I sit here today really proud of what I've been able to achieve, a person who is true to who he is, proud of who he is, and still hungry to take on the world.

There are a lot of things I want to do in my life and I'm not even close to getting them done. And no doubt, things I never even dreamt of will pop up, and I'll have a crack at them too. After all, life's too short to not grab every opportunity by the horns, so I'm not going to stop now.

# achievements

## WHEELCHAIR BASKETBALL

2008  Beijing Paralympics gold medallist with the Rollers

2010  World Championships title at Birmingham, UK, with the Rollers

2012  London Paralympics silver medallist with the Rollers

## WHEELCHAIR TENNIS

### Quad Singles

2015  Australian Open winner

2015  US Open winner

2016  Australian Open winner

2016  Rio Paralympics gold medallist

2017  Australian Open winner

2018  Australian Open winner

2018  US Open winner

### Quad Doubles

2014  Australian Open runner-up with Lucas Sithole (RSA)

2015  Australian Open runner-up with Lucas Sithole (RSA)

2015  US Open runner-up with Gauri Sharma (INDIA)

2016  Australian Open runner-up with Andy Lapthorne (UK)

2016  Rio Paralympics gold medallist with Heath Davidson (AUS)

2017  Australian Open runner-up with Heath Davidson (AUS)

2017  US Open runner-up with Bryan Barten (USA)

2018  Australian Open winner with Heath Davidson (AUS)

2018  US Open runner-up with Bryan Barten (USA)

## RECOGNITION

2009  Order of Australia recipient

2015  Tennis Australia Newcombe Medal nominee

2015  Tennis Australia Most Outstanding Athlete with
a Disability

2015  Victorian Institute of Sport Award of Excellence

2016  Governor's Award for Victorian Sportsperson of the Year

2016  Finalist for 'The Don Award' Sport Australia Hall of
Fame awards

2016  Australian Paralympian of the Year and Australian Male
Paralympian of the Year

2016  Tennis Australia Awards – Newcombe Medal; and
shared the Most Outstanding Athlete with a Disability
with doubles partner Heath Davidson

2016  Victorian Institute of Sport Elite Athlete with a Disability
Award

2017  Australian Patron for International Day of People with
Disability

# acknowledgements

THANKS TO EVERYONE WHO contributed to making this book possible.

To Jude, Barbara, Maddy and the team at ABC Books, who were always patient with me.

To Grantlee Kieza, who gave me the framework and direction on how to write a book.

To my manager, Mark Jones, who is one of the greatest men to ever live and was the reason this dream became a reality.

To Georgie Saggers, who helped organise my life so I could get this done.

To my beautiful mum, Resie, my dad, Martin, brother, Zack, best mate, Tim Biggin, and first ever coach Greg Warnecke, for giving up their time and helping me remember the best and worst parts of my life.

And to everyone mentioned in this book, and the people who weren't but have had a big influence on my life, thanks for always providing the laughs and smiles that get me out of bed every day. I'm lucky to have you!

And the biggest thanks of all to you for reading my story.

x

# about the dylan alcott foundation

THE DYLAN ALCOTT FOUNDATION is a charitable organisation with the core purpose of helping young Australians with disabilities gain confidence, fulfill their potential and achieve their dreams.

Our mission is to enrich the lives of young people with disabilities by eliminating barriers and empowering them to achieve their vocational, personal, professional and sporting goals through mentoring, grants and scholarships.

For more information visit: dylanalcottfoundation.com.au
Or email us at: info@dylanalcottfoundation.com.au

# *about get skilled access*

GET SKILLED ACCESS IS the intersection between business and people with disability. We work closely with corporates and government to provide real-life, tangible, emotional experiences that drive positive culture change, inclusion, productivity and profitability.

Our purpose is to achieve generational social change by decoding the myths of disability.

For more information visit: getskilledaccess.com.au
Or email us at: info@getskilledaccess.com.au

DOBE | Disability-Owned Business Enterprise

# useful organisations

### Australian Paralympic Committee
paralympic.org.au
Tel: 61 2 9704 0500

### Disability Sports Australia
sports.org.au
Email: info@sports.org.au
Tel: 61 2 8736 1221

### Head Space
headspace.org.au

### Life Line
lifeline.org.au
Tel: 13 11 14

### Reach Foundation
reach.org.au
Email: info@reach.org.au
Tel NSW: 61 2 8218 9200
Tel Vic: 61 3 9412 0900

### Starlight Children's Foundation
starlight.org.au
Tel: 1300 727 827

### Variety Australia

variety.org.au

National and NSW tel: 61 2 9819 1000

NT tel: 61 8 8981 2544

Qld tel: 61 7 3907 9300

SA tel: 61 8 8293 8744

Tas tel: 61 3 6248 4888

Vic tel: 61 3 8698 3900

WA tel: 61 8 9355 3655

### Wheelchair Sports NSW

wsnsw.org.au

Tel: 61 2 9809 5260

### Disabled Sports Association NT

darwin.nt.gov.au/node/6908

disabledsportnt@bigpond.com

Tel: 61 8 8945 4800

### Sporting Wheelies and Disabled Association Qld

sportingwheelies.org.au

Brisbane email: mailbox@sportingwheelies.org.au

Brisbane tel: 61 7 3253 3333

Mackay email: mackay@sportingwheelies.org.au

Mackay tel: 61 7 4953 1991

Townsville email: townsville@sportingwheelies.org.au

Townsville tel: 61 7 4721 4881

**ParaQuad Tasmania**
paraquadtas.org.au
Email: manager@paraquadtas.org.au
Tel: 61 3 6272 8816

**Disability, Sport and Recreation Victoria**
dsr.org.au
info@dsr.org.au
Tel: 1800 BE IN IT (1800 234 648)

**Rebound Western Australia**
reboundwa.com
Email: admin@reboundwa.com
Tel: 61 8 6143 5800